LIVING UNDER TENSION

Other Books

by

HARRY EMERSON FOSDICK

o

o

Living
Under Tension

Sermons on Christianity Today

by

HARRY EMERSON FOSDICK

PUBLISHERS
HARPER & BROTHERS
NEW YORK AND LONDON

Contents

[v]

CONTENTS

Introduction

SELECTING sermons for publication in a time of swift
change like this is obviously difficult. Whatever the situation may be when this volume reaches the reader, it
is bound to differ, and it may differ radically, from the
scene in which the sermons first were preached.

I have tried to meet this problem in part by selecting sermons in which the abiding truth is likely to remain constant
and clear despite shifting circumstances. In doing this, however, I have not elided contemporary references or expressions of conviction concerning immediate issues, which were
interwoven with the message when it was first delivered, but
have let them stand for what they may be worth, trusting the
reader to do his own interpreting.

Needless to say, during these tense months I have made
other statements dealing more specifically with immediate
problems in the national and international situation. As always happens, the more the temporal outweighs the eternal
in any statement, especially in a sermon, the less permanence
its message has, and in such a volume as this detailed discus-
sions of issues likely to be outmoded before publication would
have no useful place.

Behind these sermons lies the conviction that in an epoch
like ours the Church of Christ has a special function, that it
ought to be more than the voice of any government or the
echo of any popular opinion and passion. What war does to
economics, business, politics, to youth and age, to families and
nations, is often discussed, but what war does to the Church
is quite as tragic. The Church in wartime easily becomes the
mere echo of the warring masses, with every distinctive quality of Christ's teaching well-nigh forgotten; it is tempted to

lose its international, interracial, ecumenical nature, and to become only one more agency for hallowing and waging war; it is lured to accept a theology of escape, by which the ethical teachings of Christ are interpreted as inapplicable and unlivable; and in the end it too commonly divests itself of any function that differentiates it from a world gone mad with mutual hatred and suicidal strife.

Against these powerful temptations many in the Church, both pacifist and non-pacifist, are on guard, deeply concerned that Christ's distinctive message should not be submerged in an oblivion worse than any theoretical atheism's denial. If these sermons, even a little, help anyone thus to maintain the integrity of the Church's message in the midst of this catastrophic era, I shall be happy. Certainly, they are sent to the publisher with sincere humility, so difficult is it in these days to be wise, so impossible to escape disproportion, so incredible that anyone, however hard he tries, should succeed in telling the truth, the whole truth, and nothing but the truth.

HARRY EMERSON FOSDICK

June 15, 1941

Acknowledgments

The author wishes to express his appreciation to the following authors and publishers for permission to quote from their copyrighted works:

Pilgrim Press. Stanza beginning "Thou Life with my life" by Eliza Scudder, from the Pilgrim Hymnal.

Lothrop, Lee & Shepard Company. "Two Gods" from Songs of the Average Man by Sam Walter Foss.

Harry Kemp. "The Conquerors."

Living Under Tension

THE mystery of a ship at sea keeping its course day and night through all weathers lies in the fact that it moves in two worlds. On the one side is the ship itself, the sea it rides upon, the storms that beat upon it, the fogs that encompass it, and all the seen universe that surrounds it. But another world is there, invisible, intangible, playing with unseen magnetic fingers on the ship's compass. That is so strange a realm that for ages man did not dream that it was there at all, but now the ship keeps its course by means of it, an unseen magnetic world that guides the mariner even through night and fog and storm.

Human life is like that. We live in two worlds. Sometimes we call this bifurcation "body" and "spirit"—the one material, physical, visible, the other immaterial, invisible, intangible. Like some animals of the sea, whales and seals, that, though their habitat is the water, have another need, and must from time to time come up to breathe the air, so are we. Immersed in the flesh, yet we cannot live by flesh alone but must rise into this other realm of spirit, with its faiths, its ideals, its visions of beauty and right. Here is the mystery of human nature, as of a ship, that it lives in two worlds.

Even in ordinary times the profoundest problems of our lives center in this fact, but in days like these how tragic are the tensions between these two realms! Here in this immediate, factual world we see such catastrophe and brutality as will make our generation rememberable for its horror many a century from now. And yet we inhabit as well a spiritual world, with intellectual insights, with ideals of beauty and loveliness, with faiths and friendships, and with aspirations that lay hold on God and goodness. If we could only live all in one world or all in the other, we might have peace, but what tension is involved in having to live in both!

This was the problem, you recall, in Stevenson's story of *Dr. Jekyll and Mr. Hyde.* Henry Jekyll could not endure the tug of war between his lower and his higher self, and he dreamed of a solution. If only some of the time he could live altogether in his lower world as Mr. Hyde, with no disturbing intimations of a higher life, and if the rest of the time he could live altogether in his higher realm as Dr. Jekyll, with no solicitations from the lower self, then he might have peace. So he discovered the drug that thus would separate his two selves. Recall his own words: "If each, I told myself, could but be housed in separate identities, life would be relieved of all that was unbearable; the unjust might go his way, delivered from the aspirations and remorse of his more upright twin; and the just could walk steadfastly and securely on his upward path . . . no longer exposed to disgrace and penitence." Who here does not understand Henry Jekyll's problem? But no subtle drug can thus avail to separate us into our component parts. We are doomed to the tension of living in two worlds at once.

In particular, we Christians must feel this today. This present world, war-torn and terrible, denies everything that Christ taught and stood for. Cruel and brutal, so that we can hardly credit, though we see it, its insane iniquity, it is, as it were, an incarnate anti-Christ; and in this world, part and parcel of its grim necessities, we must live. Yet we are Christians, too. Not altogether in vain did Jesus teach in Galilee and die on Calvary. We have seen in him and in some who have resembled him visions of a way of life—lovely, elevating, challenging—that found in us response, so that the best in us has risen up to follow him. If we could only live in one world or the other, all anti-Christian or all Christian, then the tension would cease, but doomed to live in both worlds at once, no wonder we are bewildered and confused.

One book in the New Testament from beginning to end is concerned with this problem—the Epistle to the Hebrews. It is a difficult book to the modern reader, couched in the terms of its own time and puzzling to decode, but when one gets behind its ancient idiom to its pith of meaning it is as modern as the inner strain that each of us feels today. For it is all about two worlds, and how men of faith succeeded in living victoriously in both—two worlds, the actual and the possible, the visible and the invisible, the temporal and the eternal, the shaken and the unshakable. Here on the one side is the actual world where Abraham lived, in Ur of the Chaldees, but here is the possible world too, his Promised Land, made real by faith until it became real indeed. Here is the visible world with all its evil, like the Egypt where Moses saw the slavery of his people, but, we read, he "endured, as seeing him who is invisible," until that world unseen proved true. Here is the temporal world, where in the end change alters everything, but here is the eternal world also, where Jesus Christ is "the same, yesterday, to-day, and for ever." Here is the shaken world of turmoil and ruin, but here too is the world secure and inviolable, as we read, "the removing of those things that are shaken, . . . that those things which are not shaken may remain." Scholars say that this Epistle to the Hebrews goes back to Greek influence, to Plato's great vision of the two realms of matter and spirit. Yes, but it goes farther back than that, back to the deeps of the human heart, and to the inevitable problem that each of us faces today: How shall we manage this daily task of living in two worlds?

Let us say, first of all, that we cannot succeed at this task by denying the reality of that higher world. In days like these how tempted we are to try that swift and cheap solution! It is as though the world came to us in two aspects, saying, In which will you believe? On the one side is this hideous war with the inhuman horror of all its accompanying circumstance; and on the other side is the loveliness of life, its music and friendship, its family love, its dedicated search for truth, its elevated character, humane service, and hopes of universal brotherhood. What a mad world that can present itself to us in two such contradictory aspects at the same time! And always this question rises: Which of the two aspects will you take for your criterion of truth, your test of reality, the central object of your faith? Who does not know the subtle temptation in these days to relieve the tension between these two by sinking to the lower level, saying, The immediate, obsessing facts of this present world are real; nothing matters now except these; and all that higher world of faith, and hope, and love that once seemed real can wait? But that is too easy and cheap a way to escape the tension.

Today is not the first time in history when mankind has faced a crisis such as this, and we have reason to be grateful for souls who in other dark eras kept alive in their devotion, despite the strain it cost, that higher world to which man could come back again when the mad days were over

In a commencement address delivered by Douglas Freeman, author of the great life of Robert E. Lee, he described what some people had done amid the horror of their days to keep the light of beauty and of goodness burning for the souls of men to return to. When did Wordsworth write some of his greatest poetry? When Napoleon was collecting at Boulogne the armada for his planned assault upon the English coast at Dover. When did Beethoven write the *Fifth Symphony?* The first year of the Peninsular War, with Napoleon's shadow dark over Europe. When did Beethoven finish that glorious *Seventh Symphony?* When Napoleon was assembling his army on the line of the Niemen River for his assault on Russia. Everybody knows John Keats' immortal sonnet, "On First Looking Into Chapman's Homer":

> Then felt I like some watcher of the skies
> When a new planet swims into his ken.

When did Keats write that? The summer that Waterloo was fought.

What am I pleading for—an ivory tower to escape to from the appalling facts? No! Such souls as these never found in this life an ivory tower of escape, but tension—terrific tension—between the brutal and the beautiful, the evil and the good, the actual and the possible, the temporal and the eternal; and they refused to escape that tension by surrendering the higher realm. They believed in that and kept it despite the strain it cost. And now, in retrospect, Napoleon is dead and gone, an irrelevant episode in history, he has been called, but Wordsworth and Beethoven and Keats are living still.

We need to take this to ourselves today. The temptation is powerful to become so obsessed with the urgent, brutal facts of the immediate world, that faith in Christ and his way of living becomes like a lovely, inefficacious dream. But remember how that lovely dream itself started in the first place—in a world mastered by military empire and filled with the thundering tramp of Caesar's legions. There a little group of people, believing in a spiritual message, accepted the tension of living in two violently antagonistic worlds, Rome's and Christ's, and lo! it was they who in the end survived. Recall the phrase that Winston Churchill used about the Royal Air Force. Once in a while out of a war comes a perfect phrase, and that was one. Said Winston Churchill about the British airmen: "Never in the field of human conflict was so much owed by so many to so few." Lift that phrase out of the dreadful setting of the war and apply it to the early Christians. They were very few, keeping faith in their spiritual gospel in a world that seemed utterly to deny it. Strange, how it looks now in retrospect—"Never in the field of human conflict was so much owed by so many to so few."

Let us go further now to say that not only is it important for us amid these present tensions to keep the higher realm of the Christian faith and spirit intact and luminous for the world to come back to when these mad days are over, it is important that we keep it strong, steady, and operative now while these mad days are on. We need Christ now to pass judgment on our ways and to give guidance to our course.

How obsessing a war is! Nothing else seems to matter except its progress, its appalling incidents, and who wins it. It fills a man's whole horizon, until anything so ideal as the Sermon on the Mount seems an ethereal irrelevance. It is as though in a storm at sea the winds and billows were so turbulent that one could think of nothing else, so that the quiet, intangible world of magnetic powers that plays invisibly upon the compass needle appears feeble and negligible. But it is precisely in a great storm at sea that we most need to keep that compass needle true, that we may know whither we are going, and where we are coming out. Great tempests make that higher world of invisible power not less necessary, but more.

During the last World War, when we just had entered the fray, I spoke to a friend of mine in Washington of my concern about a League of Nations, a federation of the world as the only possible substitute for war, organized goodwill as the only ultimate alternative to organized ill will. I recall his answer: "Well," he said, "here in Washington we are not thinking now about anything except how to win this war." So! that was the trouble! For we did win that war and then what?

Many people today say that this war is different, that we must go far back in history to find its counterpart, as, for example, when the Persians attacked Greece. Yet consider that comparison. In the dreadful days when the Persians assailed Greece, not simply two armies met then, but two ways of living, two philosophies of life. It would have been appalling if oriental despotism had swamped that most hopeful culture of the ancient world. But it did not. The Persians did not conquer Greece. Greece won the war, and then what? Then, that higher life of Greece, which played with invisible fingers on the compass needles of its finer souls, was neglected and forgotten, and Greeks fought Greeks in fratricidal strife. It was not Persia that ruined Greece; it was Greece that ruined Greece.

Alas, the wars that have been fought and won with illimitable courage and sacrifice, only to issue in disillusionment and futility! And unless now we keep vivid in our faith the spiritual verities, seeing clearly that Christ still is right, that the ethic of the Sermon on the Mount is unshaken, that only goodwill—organized goodwill—can ever cure ill will, another catastrophe awaits us, whoever wins this war. It makes little difference who wins the war unless Christ wins the peace. Is it not the special function of the Christian church in days like these to keep clear in our devotion this higher world that war obscures? It is not the function of the church of Christ to help win a war. The church that becomes an adjunct of a War Department denies its ministry. The function of the church of Christ is to keep alive and alight this realm of spiritual judgment and guidance, so that even amid the storm of war we may not lose those faiths and values on which man's hope at last depends.

When we think of Christ today in this warring world, where do we picture him? I cannot picture him in uniform on either side. That does not mean that I am neutral. Most certainly I am not. Sometimes I live more in Britain than at home, so keen my sympathies, so deep my apprehensions, so desperate my hopes. But when I think of Christ I see him on a judgment seat, sitting in sorrowful and stern condemnation on this whole warring world—aggressors, defenders, neutrals—who all together by joint guilt and refusal of his ways have involved themselves in a way of life that denies everything he stood for. The major business of a Christian minister is to keep clear the vision of Christ upon that judgment seat, above our strife, standing for a kind of life that

[7]

we all have denied but to which we must come back if man is to have any hope.

My deep respect goes out to my fellows in the ministry of the British churches. Amid the strain under which they live many of them, pacifists and non-pacifists, are steadfastly keeping Christ upon that judgment seat above the struggle. Here is a statement by a group of British Anglicans, Methodists, Presbyterians, Congregationalists, Baptists, and Friends, and introduced to us by the Archbishop of York himself:

God reigns. That is the fundamental truth. From heaven He reigns—creator and upholder of the world. From the Cross He reigns—making defeat itself the stuff of His triumph. From the heart of His people He reigns—extending His rule by the energy of His love constraining them.

Accordingly:—

(i) We recognize in the troubles and anxieties of this time a just doom—the consequence, according to God's laws, of our neglect of His command and defiance of His will.

(ii) We acknowledge Christ as absolute Lord of Life and Saviour from the sin which brings these evils upon the world. We pledge ourselves and call our fellows to penitence for the past and to new loyalty for the future. Especially we confess our acquiescence in social injustice and national jealousies; and we dedicate ourselves to the establishment of economic and international justice and fellowship.

(iii) We declare that in this allegiance to Jesus Christ we are united to all others who acknowledge Him, in a fellowship which is unbroken by any earthly divisions and persists beneath even the wraths of war. In this unity in Christ we have both the hope of peace in this world and the foretaste of eternal life in fellowship with God.

Think of the situation out of which those high, humble, and Christian words have come! That is no ivory tower! Such men have accepted the tension between a war-torn world on one side, and Christ upon the other, and are trying to keep him there upon his judgment seat, arbiter of their ways, chastener of their pride, guide to their courses.

Upon the other side, one of my friends in the American ministry has said that he was glad about his militaristic attitude because he could throw himself into it 100 per cent with no sense of tension. What a dreadful thing to be said of a Christian now—no tension, only one pole in life, this immediate emergency. As for me, I must accept the tension—a world at war on one side, and Christ on the judgment seat upon the other, and I must keep him there, the condemner of our joint guilt, the chastener of our unrepentant pride, the guide to our only hope.

Finally, we need this higher world of abiding spiritual power and truth that Christ revealed, for our own personal sustenance and strength. Remember what the Epistle to the Hebrews says about Moses. "He endured, as seeing him who is invisible." Well, granite is needed in our characters today. No softness can see this through. We must endure. But how can a man endure if all he sees is this visible, tangible, immediate, shaken, brutal world?

Scholars say that this Epistle to the Hebrews was addressed to the Christians in Rome itself between 80 and 90 A.D. Already the persecutions had begun. When the writer spoke of Moses enduring, "as seeing him who is invisible," he was thinking not so much of Moses as of himself and of the struggling church in Rome. Everywhere in the Epistle one hears the echo of catastrophe and trial. Out of no lotus land, no ivory tower, did this strong letter come. And this was the strength of those first Christians, that they lived not in one world only, but in two, and found in consequence not tension alone, but power, the vision of a world unshaken and unshakable, and so a hope that the author of the letter calls "an anchor of the soul, . . . both sure and stedfast." They could endure.

Certainly, we may be grateful that we do not live now in

this immediate world alone, for then the deadly whisper would inevitably rise, What's the use? Rather, as I see it, this is one of the great ages of man's history. Terrible it is but still it is one of the great eras of all time. Generations from now our children's children will look back on what we do today. The world that once was broken into separate units, far apart, has now been woven together so that what happens anywhere happens everywhere. There is no isolation. We still are trying to carry over into this new world the method of war that man used in the old world. It is not possible; that way is literally a dead end street. Not less but more the Christian ethic towers up, not only as true but as indispensable. We are "members one of another." If we are to be saved at all, we must be saved together. And behind that necessity stands a power greater than man—the very nature of this universe and its Eternal God. Tension there is in that two-world view, but strength also to endure.

Some of us have been in Smyrna in Asia Minor and have visited the amphitheater whose ruins still are there. There Polycarp was martyred, a greatly loved Christian leader who himself knew some of the disciples who had known Jesus. They killed him in the amphitheater, and shortly afterwards the church in Smyrna wrote an account of it in which they dated the martyrdom of Polycarp thus: "Statius Quadratus being proconsul, but Jesus Christ being King for ever." So they lived in two worlds. Fill in the names today as you may choose, but still the truth is there: Statius Quadratus proconsul, Jesus Christ King forever!

Don't Lose Faith in Human Possibilities

ONE powerful influence in the life of all of us is the
fact that our generation has lived through a long
series of major disappointments. To go no farther
back than the Great War, we plunged into that hoping to
make the world safe for democracy, only to recognize later
that the outcome was futile. Then to plans of organized peace
in the World Court and the League of Nations many of us
turned with high hopes, but we have lived to see the great
buildings on Lake Geneva empty shells, while millions march
to war. Then a day of economic affluence seemed to dawn,
filled with hope of the abundant life for all the people, only
to fade into widespread penury that no help has reached.
Even so, we did not believe that the nations would madly add
to all this another world conflict, but today Europe and Asia
are aflame. We have lived through a generation of succes-
sive and colossal disappointments, one frustrated hope piled
on another.

Now in ordinary individual life there are enough
disappointments for most men to handle, but when these personal discouragements that inhere in daily living are set in
a generation where one towering frustration after another
shadows the whole world, a mood is created that none of us
altogether escapes. It impinges like a climate on every one
of us—call it by what special name you will—sadness, hopelessness, cynicism, disillusionment, moral apathy, lost faith in
human possibilities.

It should be worth our while to think of that today, and
you may be sure I am speaking not simply to you but to
myself.

For one thing, any mood that spoils faith in human possibilities strikes at the very core of a man's own personality. An inherent characteristic of personal living is the capacity to look ahead, as an irrigation engineer sees fertility in a desert, or a sculptor sees the statue in the unhewn stone, and creatively brings out the possibilities. Wordsworth is right that personal life involves

> Effort, and expectation, and desire,
> And something evermore about to be.

When, therefore, any generation piles a long series of major frustrations upon those minor ones that commonly discourage us, so that our faith in human possibilities is diminished and our hope is spoiled, that strikes at the very core of personality.

This creative factor of foresight and expectancy is illustriously clear in great persons. In any realm the rememberable figures are pioneering men and women who have faith in what yet may be. As was said of John C. Frémont, the western frontiersman: "From the ashes of his campfires have sprung cities." Indeed, if you wish a text from the New Testament, remember the title that in Moffatt's translation Peter, in his sermon in Jerusalem after the crucifixion, gave to Jesus: "You killed the pioneer of Life." He was that supremely, "the pioneer of Life," blazing trails and everlastingly believing in human possibilities, personal and social. None of us is really a person unless he shares that quality, and this generation is making difficult such sustained faith in the future.

When one stops to think of it, we human beings ought not to be surprised at disappointment. This inherent and ennobling capacity of ours to hope, to plan, to see possibilities, to entertain prophetic insights, necessarily involves the companion capacity to be disappointed. Rocks and trees cannot be disappointed; only human beings can. The farther down in the scale of existence we go, the less disappointment is possible; the farther up we rise, the more disappointment is probable. Disappointment is the obverse side of one of the noblest attributes of human nature.

Here begins our suspicion about the validity of this contemporary mood. Granted that a burned child dreads the fire, and that we who have hoped so much and whose hopes have been so thwarted, dread to start hoping again, and so to face another possible crash of expectancy! Granted, the cynical temptation in the face of this dismaying spectacle of humankind to cry, Blessed is he that expecteth nothing, for he shall not be disappointed! But that is like saying, Blessed is he that never loves, for he shall escape love's hurt; or, Blessed is he that never thinks, for he cannot think falsely. That is not the solution. We ought not to dehumanize ourselves because we happen to live in a disappointing generation. We ought with increased intelligence to look again at this inherent attribute of great personality—faith in human possibility—and see more deeply into it. Who here does not feel beneath this prevalent mood a conviction, that will not down, that the pioneers of life will yet prove right, and from the ashes of their campfires will rise cities?

Another suspicion concerning the validity of this prevalent mood emerges when one considers its emotional sources. This loss of faith in human possibilities is not the hard-headed, realistic judgment it purports to be. It is emotionally engendered by contemporary circumstances. I am not belittling those circumstances. They are terrific. 1914 was bad enough, but then we had rather expected a war, and we had no clear picture of what modern war would be like. This war comes after a long generation full of high hopes of, and serious endeavors after, peace, and it comes in the face of dreadful information about what modern war means. Of course we are disillusioned. Nevertheless, one remembers: In 1848 Lord Shaftesbury said: "Nothing can save the British Empire from shipwreck." In 1849 Disraeli said: "In industry, commerce and agriculture there is no hope." In 1852 the dying Duke of Wellington said: "I thank God I shall be spared from seeing the consummation of ruin that is gathering about us." In 1801 Wilberforce said: "I dare not marry—the future is so unsettled." In 1806 William Pitt said: "There is scarcely anything round us but ruin and despair."

Since those days many worth-while achievements have been wrought, and from the ashes of many campfires have sprung cities. We need not bring theology in here and say what obviously is true—that if a man believes in God, of course there are possibilities. Let us leave theology out for a moment and look at world history in a wide perspective. If we reduce the existence of this planet to a fifty-year span, it took forty-nine of them before the first primitive agricultural stage was reached. In that span of fifty years writing began six months ago, art and literature three months ago, Christianity two months ago, printing two weeks ago, electricity twenty-four hours ago, organized efforts after world-wide peace a few minutes ago, and the creative factors of man's spiritual life that hold the promise of his future are in their merest infancy.

This strange adventure upon this wandering planet in the sky, in which we human beings find ourselves, far from being ended, has just begun. The discouraged mood of a disappointed generation is not an adequate criterion.

Still another suspicion concerning the validity of this prevalent mood emerges when we stop to think what we mean by the word "possibility." Even in ordinary, peaceful days a common picture occupies popular imagination: Here are the facts—the hard, existent facts—and here man stands amid these facts with imagined possibilities in his head, envisioning what he wishes might come true, and, so runs the picture, these facts are real, but the imagined possibilities are dreams.

When that idea of the relationship between the actual and the possible, as a contrast between facts and dreams, is carried over into a day like this, the consequence is disastrous. For the actualities today are tragic, and if the possibilities are only stuff that dreams are made of, then our loss of faith is justified. Is it true that in any situation the possibilities are dreams? Upon the contrary, there is nothing more solidly factual in the world than the possibilities in any given situation. When an Arizona desert has been recovered by irrigation to fertility, the possibilities of that never had been merely dreams. They were facts that had been there for centuries. Even if nobody ever had irrigated that desert, the possibilities would have been there.

So it is that the pioneers of life have always looked at humankind. They were not dreamers, envisioning merely what they wished might be; they were seers, perceiving the potentialities actually there. When Jesus looked at Peter and said, "Come ye after me, and I will make you . . ." he was not dreaming; he was seeing the potentialities in that man. And when in a war-ridden world he lifted the standard of human brotherhood, he was seeing the potentialities in the human situation.

Alas, for one who in these days falls into the common habit of calling that visionary! Is science visionary? Is it not the hardest-headed intellectual discipline we know? How, then, does science look at this universe? Always as a bundle of possibilities. Habitually the scientist looks at this universe and every area in it as a bundle of possibilities, with no telling what might come if we fulfilled the conditions. Thomas Edison was no dreamer. He was a seer. The possibilities that he brought out were factually there. They were there before he saw them. They would have been there if he never had seen them. Always the possibilities are part of the actualities in any given situation.

Today there are few deeper needs in the world than for men and women who will maintain this undiscourageable insight. The factual bases of a federated peaceful world are here. Let men long deny them, they still are here. No more stubborn fact confronts mankind than the potentiality of a world as free from the fear of war as New York State is free from the dread of conflict with Massachusetts. To be sure, as Longfellow said about the lighthouse:

> The startled waves leap over it; the storm
> Smites it with all the scourges of the rain,
> And steadily against its solid form
> Press the great shoulders of the hurricane.

Still, the towering fact remains: A federated peaceful world is possible.

Let us take a deeper look into this prevalent mood. Sometime since, reading a book by Professor Hocking of Harvard I ran on this arresting sentence: "In a question of possibility, negative experience counts for nothing if there is but a single positive success." I was startled. Can it be that when we are considering the possibilities in any situation, if we have one single positive success, that proves the thing is possible, and after that no negative evidence counts for anything? Then I remembered the time when Thomas Edison had seen one thing indicating that an important achievement was possible, and he experimented with it repeatedly, so the story goes, by methods all of which failed. His assistant tried to sympathize with him by saying, "It's too bad to do all that work with no result." "But," said Edison, "we have a lot of results. We now know 700 things that won't work." That is the way the pioneers of life have seen the world. They saw one thing that proved the existence of a possibility. After that no negative evidence could dissuade their conviction or discourage their endeavor. God give us men and women like that today!

From the beginning of Christianity Jesus has meant this to Christians. There is a mass of negative evidence about what can be done with human nature. This sordid spectacle of humankind could easily persuade us that little or nothing can be done, but there Jesus stands, he and some others who have caught his spirit—not dreams, but facts, lives actually lived! That kind of thing has happened. It can happen. It is possible.

Robinson Crusoe lived for a long time on his solitary island, and all the evidence with reference to any human companionship was absolutely negative. Then one day he saw a solitary footprint on the sand. After that, all the negative evidence counted for nothing. That one footprint proved something that no massing of negative testimony, no matter how long accumulated, could disprove. One of the best definitions of faith I can think of would run like this: Faith is believing in the positive evidence of a single footprint, against all the negative evidence that would deny the possibility

Faith is believing, on the basis of a few lovely homes, in the possibility of lovely homes, against the vast mass of negative evidence. Faith is believing, on the basis of a few examples of honest and efficient municipal government, that that is possible, against the vast mass of negative evidence. Faith is believing, on the basis of some victorious spirit, that a man can by God's grace rise triumphant over adverse circumstance and carry off an inner victory, against the vast mass of negative evidence. Indeed, in 270 B.C., Aristarchus of Samos saw, as it were, a footprint on the sands—an intimation that the earth might go around the sun—and he believed it, against all the negative evidence. Centuries afterward, Copernicus read Aristarchus and discovered more footprints and believed them, against the long-accumulated negative evidence, though he dared not publish his book till on his deathbed, and then with a groveling preface. Then came Kepler. Recall the closing sentences of his introduction to his book: "Here I cast the die, and write a book to be read whether by contemporaries or by posterity, I care not. I can wait for readers thousands of years, seeing that God waited six thousand years for someone to contemplate his work." That is faith—century after century believing the positive evidence of the footprints, against the vast mass of negative evidence that would deny the possibilities!

If ever there was a day when men and women with that kind of faith are needed, it is now. In 1860 a man in Maryland said this: "I am firstly a citizen of Hartford County, secondly a citizen of Maryland, thirdly a citizen of the United States." How incredible that is to us. We have now 130,000,000 citizens in this country. Could you find one who would not instinctively reverse the order? That expansion of loyalty to take in a larger group and put it first has happened. It can happen. It is possible. Some day it will happen internationally. Men will put mankind first, and nationalism second. To be sure, in implementing that we will find 700 things that will not work, but in the realm of possibilities such negative evidence counts for nothing. The potentiality is here. More than one footprint is on that sand.

If the church of Christ cannot today supply men and women of such faith, then it fails indeed.

Finally, as we look at the world today in the glare of this lurid catastrophe, our faith in Christ's way of life, and what it yet may do for humankind, may well grow not weak but strong. There are two ways in which a man can face this situation. He may say, Christ's way of life has failed; it is the gentle vision of kindly folk, too soft for this brutal world; Nietzsche is truer than Christ. Or a man may say, Everything else has failed except Christ's way of life. If even after the Great War the principles of Christ had been taken seriously by the nations, we would not be where we are now. This disaster does not advertise the failure of Christian principles; it advertises the penalty that falls upon the world when it refuses Christian principles. This disaster is the judgment of the eternal moral order on a Christless paganism. It cries aloud not that the Sermon on the Mount is false but that the Sermon on the Mount is so everlastingly true that unless we build our social life upon it, we will fall thus from one perdition to another. This catastrophe is not the refutation of Jesus' basic ethical concepts but their confirmation.

Suppose that an epidemic of preventable disease should sweep this country; would we say, Scientific medicine has failed? Were we sensible we would say, We have failed scientific medicine, shirked its support, neglected its admonitions; let us return to it with new intelligence and new loyalty, for it alone can save us. So today, Christ's principles have not failed, but we have failed Christ's principles. And in a world where every substitute is leading us to bloody and murderous ruin, we should with kindled faith and new intelligence return to see what possibilities in human life Christ's way of living can open up to mankind.

At any rate, even amid the horrors of this furious war, let the Christian pulpit strike no fearful and despondent note! The glare of this lurid catastrophe lights up one central and everlasting truth: Christ and his way of living, Christ, and he alone, is the pioneer of life.

Winning the War of Nerves

REGARDLESS of our participation in the outward war, one aspect of the world conflict we all are in and cannot get out of—the war of nerves. Concerning one tight place in Paul's career, when the strain was heavy, he wrote in his Second Letter to the Corinthians, as Dr. Goodspeed translates it: "My poor human nature could get no relief—there was trouble at every turn; fighting without, and fear within." That surely applies to us today—to practically every one of us sitting here so calmly praising God. Behind our outward placidity the war of nerves is on. In one of the most precarious epochs in human history we feel the whole world shaken, and see millions of people feeling like Milton's Satan in Hell when he said:

> And, in the lowest deep, a lower deep
> Still threatening to devour me opens wide,
> To which the Hell I suffer seems a Heaven.

So our poor human nature does get no relief—there is trouble at every turn—"Fighting without, and fear within."

Now the war of nerves has always gone on in human experience, and obviously a man who does not win that, cannot win anything else. Today, however, not only are all our private tensions and strains still here, but the newspapers and the radio storm our minds with the perils and afflictions of all mankind, and our own country is divided in mind, precarious in situation, and full of fear.

In such a nervous time a man's religion ought to count if it is any good. For if a man's Christian faith, and the quality of character it has produced, cannot help in winning this war of nerves, it must be a shallow and conventional affair. Consider, then, some of the strong and saving reactions to these days of strain that we as Christians ought to expect of ourselves.

For one thing, to suppose that a dangerous situation must issue in fearfulness, self-pity, and panic, is to misread human nature. Peril can be a great stimulant. Put one man into a perilous situation, and he is scared stiff. Put another man into the same situation, and he is aroused by its stimulus. Peril pulls the trigger, but what it explodes depends on what a man is loaded with. One man responds with nervous collapse, consternation, and frightened weakness. Another man responds with released energies and stimulated mind.

I am a Quaker in my convictions about war, but that does not prevent appreciation of Winston Churchill's splendid sentence when last summer England faced one of the most disastrous hours in her history and the danger was imminent and terrible. Said Churchill to his people: "Let us therefore brace ourselves to our duty and so bear ourselves that if the British Commonwealth and Empire lasts for a thousand years, men will still say, 'This was their finest hour.'" So in every dangerous situation that we face a choice is possible as to the issue. Peril may mean paralysis or incentive, panic or stimulus.

In dealing with our war of nerves, then, let us start by getting over the idea that a dangerous situation is necessarily lamentable. It is not. Peril is one of the major stimulants in human history, and out of dangerous situations the finest things in life have come. Scientific medicine has been born of fear. From pneumonia to cancer and back again, we face dangerous enemies that we are rightly fearful of, and that fact has proved to be one of the strongest stimulants that has ever moved the human mind to great achievement. If someone says that if he had created the cosmos, he would not have made a world where it takes fearful dangers to wake men up, arouse their powers, and marshal their devotions, one can only say that whoever did make the cosmos obviously thought otherwise. For here we are in a world where, across long evolutionary ages, man has been surrounded by gigantic perils, and where the hope and progress of the race have depended on those who have won the war of nerves, and in danger have found not paralysis and panic but positive stimulus and incentive.

Indeed, here is a strange fact about human nature, commonly forgotten, that if danger is not thrust upon men they go out looking for it. Think of climbing Mount Everest, discovering the North Pole, mapping the Antarctic Plateau, developing aviation, competing in long-distance ski jumps or for automobile racing records, and countless other enterprises, from risky sports to explorations of deadly danger. No man ever had to do a single one of these things. Whoever does them goes out to look for them and chooses to do them. Shall we say, then, that man does them despite the fact that they are dangerous? That utterly misinterprets man's psychology. Man does them because they are dangerous. He craves the stimulus of risk and peril, which is one of the most exciting experiences in life. So Professor Graham Wallas, in his famous book, *The Great Society,* discussing the motives behind the explorations of Columbus, Magellan, and the rest, says: "Perhaps, indeed, it is this desire for Fear rather than the impulse of Curiosity which has been the most important single cause."

This, then, is the first item in dealing with our war of nerves. We are in a dangerous situation, and always in such a case two elements await our choice. Fright, chronic anxiety, consternation—we can find that in the situation; or incentive, stimulus, fresh devotion to values that are threatened, a new centrality of purpose, a new experience of spiritual resource —we can find that. Remember in *Pilgrim's Progress* the day when the foul fiend Apollyon straddled, says Bunyan, "straddled quite over the whole breadth of the way," and cried, "prepare thy self to die, for I swear by my Infernal Den, that thou shalt go no further, here will I spill thy soul." Well, once more Apollyon straddles the road, and what he wants above all else is to spill our souls. The hope of the world is in people who answer, No! Not that! You have tried that many a time in history. You tried that on the great Isaiah and his fellows in the days of the Jewish exile in Babylon, and because you could not spill their souls they found even in the exile a stimulus, and made of it the most spiritually creative epoch in their people's history. You tried that in the Garden of Gethsemane, where a man sweat blood in agony, desiring to escape the cross, but because you could not spill his soul the cross became the symbol of the world's salvation. Many a time you have straddled the road in desperate generations, as you do now, but even this so fearful epoch can be to us the most stimulating experience of our lives, calling out powers and devotions that else we had never known. Let us, therefore, brace ourselves, and so bear ourselves that years from now men will still be saying, This was their finest hour.

If, however, we are thus to discover in danger a stimulus and incentive, we must find some way of cleansing our spirits from the hectic and bitter emotions of our time. This is the second necessity if we are to win the war of nerves. Men talk about war as hard-headed, realistic, and all that, but war really lives, moves, and has its being in a welter of emotionalism, feverish and hysterical. War is about the least rational and the most emotional enterprise of man. Who was it said of his friend: "When that man thinks he is thinking, he is not really thinking, he is only rearranging his prejudices"? That is commonly true in wartime. There are many sad sights in the world today, and our eyes are on the ends of the earth when we think of them, but remember that some of the sad sights are here in this congregation—emotions upset, harassed, embittered, distorted by the strains and tensions of the war.

This essentially hysterical nature of war is most clearly seen when in retrospect we listen to its screaming, as from a madhouse, out of a conflict long gone by. Listen to this quotation: They are "as villainous as the worst pirates who ever infested the sea"; "look at the horde of ruffians, and say what jail has been robbed to bring together these hireling assassins"; "they combine all the vices of savages with the intelligence of the civilized man"; they are "brutal fanatics . . . a nation of criminals." That is a typical Southern utterance about Northerners during the Civil War. And now listen to this quotation: "The cruel and incredible barbarities of the rebels every day accumulate in horror. . . . Dishonor and infamy of every kind; ferocity which Feejees could not emulate; superstition, ignorance, and bestiality." That is a typical Northern utterance about Southerners. What a cross men like Abraham Lincoln and Robert E. Lee, on both sides of the lines, had to bear, trying to keep at least a semblance of reason, some basis of thought and feeling that could make possible a just and decent peace, "With malice toward none, with charity for all."

To that end consider in these days a high use of prayer. Surely nothing is more necessary, more chastening, broadening, Christianizing, than prayer in wartime. To be sure, it must be real prayer and not its burlesque—as though out of the terrific obsessions of the immediate, one climbed a high hill where, for a time, one saw things in broad perspective, with wide horizons, and came down again calmer in soul, more sure of one's direction, less bitter, less turbulent, less deafened with the stridency of contemporary voices, more confident, as Emerson said, of what "the centuries say, against the hours." Who can measure the need today for such a resource whereby our souls are restored?

Winning the war of nerves is not merely a matter of overcoming blue funk and fear. What this present war psychosis does to us emotionally goes deeper and reaches farther than that. One of its first results, for example, is an utterly irrational pride. Against the obvious facts of history, which we know well with our minds, we nevertheless feel that our enemies are all to blame for this mad catastrophe, that we are the innocent and afflicted victims of aggressive evil, rightly boiling with holy indignation; and then with this proud and turbulent soul of mine I move up through prayer into the presence of Eternal God, and try to see what he is seeing. And, standing there, the words of the Pharisee, "God, I thank thee, that I am not as the rest of men," die on my lips. I cannot say them. Joint guilt—all of us stained with the same sin—joint guilt has brought this consequence. And with a humility and penitence that intellectually I know are wisdom, I come back to face the immediate again.

Moreover, along with pride, all wars, of course, roil up the muddy depths of bitterness. Not since the last war have there been so many people in America who cannot talk without screaming. It is as though civilized and humane attitudes were a thin veneer upon our souls, and as though war, cracking the surface, released the black depths of rancor in us. Then my roiled spirit, with its personal prejudices and national self-interests, moves up through prayer into the presence of the Eternal God of all mankind, and tries to see what he is seeing. My soul, how the malignity of wartime makes one forget some things that were everlastingly true before this war, and will be everlastingly true after this war! Ill will never built anything—that is one of them—rancor never created anything. The creative forces in human life always spring from one source, intelligent goodwill. Far back in the evolutionary struggle goodwill began as a small, tentative, experimental venture in an angry, violent, and bitter world, and all we have that is decent in human life has come from the extension and deepening of that. So, coming down from that high hill of prayer, my soul is saying, We must not put that into cold storage just because war is here. The more war and the more madness, the more need of people who keep their heads level, their souls unembittered, their spirits clear of rancor, to whom still the New Testament has meaning: "Be not overcome of evil, but overcome evil with good."

Well, in that regard may God help us to win the war of nerves!

Further than this, however, we must go, if successfully we are to discover the stimulus in danger and keep our emotions wise, steady, and unembittered. We must do something utterly practical—*act,* stop sitting around letting radio commentators and newspaper headlines feed our imaginations, and go out and do something. Says Dr. William Burnham, the psychologist: "The most drastic and usually the most effective remedy for fear is direct action." Of course it is.

Paul believed the two things that we have said so far. The stimulus in danger—he knew that; perils splendidly aroused his powers. The heights of prayer he knew, ascending which, amid the bitterness of his world and the hostility that attacked him, he could write: "If I speak with the tongues of men and of angels, but have not love, . . . I am nothing." But Paul himself could not have won his war of nerves— "Fighting without, and fear within"—if he had not been as well a man of action. He was always doing something about it. He was too busy to sit down and stew in the juice of his own fearful imaginations.

Fear was intended by nature to be an emergency emotion. A quick peril, a quick fear, a quick action and escape—that is the indispensable equipment that nature intended to give us, and from the animal in the forest to a man amid the motor cars of New York's streets, life could not go on without it. But then see what we human beings do! We develop imagination, and that involves the capacity to go about all day filling our minds with fearful pictures, helped by the newspapers, the magazines, and the radio, so that multitudes are all shot to pieces nervously, because from morning till night they live in a world of fear-ridden imaginings, concerning which they do nothing practical. So fear, which was intended to be a healthy emergency emotion, swiftly rising and soon over, becomes instead a miserable state of chronic anxiety and dread.

We Christians ought to do better than that. To say that this is a fearful time is simply another way of saying that it is a needy time, calling, therefore, not alone for anxiety but for practical action. Have you ever been in a train wreck? Have you ever found yourself amid the ruins of derailed and battered cars, surrounded by broken bodies, dreadful deaths, and human agony crying for help? That is a fearful experience. But if you yourself have two legs and two arms that still work, and you plunge in to help, do something, translate the situation into a call for action, you so forget yourself that you do not collapse. That young woman driving a bus through London's streets while the bombs are falling is more poised, steady, and serene than multitudes of jittery Americans, for the simple reason that she is doing something.

And yet, my friends, there is plenty for us to do. There are refugee committees needing help, agencies for the relief of want in Britain, Greece, France, China, and, if the way can be opened as heaven grant it may be, in the under-nourished conquered democracies. There are avenues through which anyone in this congregation, differing as we do about American policy, can express himself in helping to shape our national course in this trying time. And behind all this, there are the innumerable means of social service to our own America, which is now, and we pray may continue to be, the best hope of preserving one standing place for undevastated democracy to keep its footing and prove its worth. Whether or not Apollyon is going to spill our souls depends in many of us on this basic matter. Granted that this is a perilous time, then what? Shall that mean brooding, morbid, chronic anxiety, or shall it mean a practical vision of human need that calls us out into active service where we forget ourselves?

Finally, we may well be thankful we do not have to live through days like these without an undergirding faith that God is not dead. To discover stimulus in danger, to climb spiritual heights where one's emotions are clarified and calmed, to achieve healthy-mindedness through action, all that is important for us, as it was for Paul. But underneath this, the ultimate meaning of life for us, as for him, and the ultimate source of steadiness amid strain, lies not in anything we can do, but in something that everlastingly is. I believe in the living God.

What this can mean in difficult personal experience, Chesterton put into his lines:

> Though giant rains put out the sun,
>   Here stand I for a sign.
> Though Earth be filled with waters dark,
>   My cup is filled with wine.
> Tell to the trembling priests that here
>   Under the deluge rod,
> One nameless, tattered, broken man
>   Stood up and drank to God.

Granted that such confidence is not easy! In dreadful days of war like these, faith in God is a great venture. Recall what Walt Whitman said about war! He did not use conventional pulpit language but he told the truth. Said Whitman: "They are hellish business, wars—all wars: Sherman said, War is hell: so it is: any honest man says so—hates war, fighting, bloodletting: I was in the midst of it all—saw war where war is worst—not on the battlefields, no—in the hospitals: there war is worst: there I mixed with it: and now I say, God damn the wars—all wars: God damn every war: God damn 'em! God damn 'em!" That is not cursing; that is prayer. Nevertheless, I will not hold even war so close to my eyes that it shuts out all the wide horizons and becomes the single determining element in my philosophy of life. The course of human history is like a great river. It has broadened its banks and deepened its currents. Moreover, its smooth and comfortable stretches have not been its most decisive. It was when the rapids, the cataracts, and the whirlpools came that the river made its major changes in direction. That mighty river has not ceased its flowing now, and the God who is stronger than its roaring floods is not dead.

Sometime since I read a single sentence that started my pulses going at a faster clip. It concerned the history of the ninth century, A.D., and it said this: "Under Alfred the inhabitants of England for the first time learned to think of England as a whole." So, for the first time in history, England was not thought of simply as Wessex or Sussex or Northumberland, but as England. To be sure, they did not take in Wales or Scotland. It would have seemed impossible that those foreign lands ever could belong, but they could think of England as a whole. Granted that centuries of strife would come and go before the fact of England's wholeness was realized, but a prophetic event had taken place—England had been thought of as a whole. Today multitudes, as never before in history, are thinking of humanity as a whole. Granted that it is an idea and not a realized fact, and that it may take centuries before the fact comes true, but it is one of the most prophetic events in human history.

This is not simply a dreadful era; it is also a great era, one of the most decisive, and in the end, it well may be, creative, man has known. Behind the welter of conflicting influences that have plunged us into this catastrophe, stands a towering fact: We must now think of ourselves as one world. We may resist that fact, fight it, cast ourselves, like the fools we are, against it, but a hand is on us that no power of man can in the end withstand—some day mankind is going to be one world. The God of ongoing history is not dead.

Christian Faith—Fantasy or Truth?

FOR many reasons these are difficult days in which to hold the Christian faith. The major events of our time are so essentially anti-Christian that against their terrific background Christian faith seems to many to be mere wishful thinking, a pleasant fairyland. Indeed, its very desirableness is used as an argument against it. Granted, men say, that the Christian faith is comforting, sustaining, bringing solace and encouragement to men in trouble. But, they add, that is precisely the reason why the Christian faith has developed—not because it is objectively true but because it is subjectively comfortable. So in one book after another we are told that Christian faith is a lovely fantasy, creating a world of make-believe where men and women, up against cruel facts, find encouragement by fooling themselves. As one of Galsworthy's characters put it: "There *is* something about a Church . . . there's beauty in it, it's a pleasant drug."

No preacher today can plead for Christian faith because it is desirable without knowing that some in his congregation are thinking, To be sure it is; it is comforting and encouraging; that is why people are religious; the stark facts of this cruel universe and the dreadful ills of human life are insupportable for most of us unless we conceal them, dress them up, decorate them in some comforting faith. Did not one poor woman in Robert Lynd's *Middletown* exclaim, "Land sakes! I don't see how people live at all who don't cheer themselves up by thinkin' of God and Heaven"? That is the origin of religion, men say; it is an illusion that cries, Cheerio! in our disappointed hours; it is spoofing on a grand scale. As one youth put it: "Religion is nothing but a chloroform mask into which the weak and unhappy stick their faces!"

Augustus Caesar was barely five feet seven inches tall, pale and delicate, with a weak throat and poor circulation, who all his life had to live on a strict diet and constantly struggle against bodily frailty. Yet see what Augustus Caesar did! One element in his amazing career is undoubtedly the fact that in youth he visited Theogenes, a famous astrologer, to have his horoscope cast, and when Theogenes saw the young man's horoscope, so runs the story, he was so impressed with the marvel of it that he fell on his face and worshiped him. You and I do not believe in astrology, but you see Augustus did. It was a superstition, but, being believed, it worked. All his later life through difficulty, peril, burden-bearing, and inner struggle for self-conquest, he kept an undiscourageable faith in his destiny, which the stars had foretold. Such, men say, is Christian faith; it is a psychological shot in the arm, not objectively true but subjectively stimulating.

Over against this prevalent view we put today the testimony of the New Testament. The Fourth Gospel was written about 100 A.D., when the Christian church had had time to take the measure of Christ's meaning and to see his gospel against the background of one of the most difficult periods in human history. And at the heart of the Fourth Gospel, again and again repeated, is the conviction expressed in the words attributed to Jesus. Jesus said, "I am . . . the truth." Not a stimulating ideal merely, not a consoling faith, not a happy stroke of wishful thinking, but the realistic truth! Pretty much everything in our Christianity today depends on the issue we thus are faced with: What is our Christian faith—comforting fantasy, or reality?

All we can hope to do in dealing with so vast a subject here is to block out a few areas where the evidence lies that the Christianity of Christ is not a pleasant spiritual drug but is true.

In the first place, we may well ask, Since when has great religion been primarily pleasant and comfortable anyway? This whole picture of religion as mainly a search for comfort contradicts obvious facts. Look even at orthodox Christianity! Is it comfortable? Was Calvinism comfortable? Predestination, the damnation of non-elect infants, the eternal torture chamber of hell—there was small comfort in that, and some of us in our boyhood were driven by it nearly to hysteria. That is why Henry Ward Beecher had to challenge the orthodox religion of his day with its terrific doctrine of God, insisting, as he put it, that God is not a thunderstorm that has to be approached under an umbrella.

Of course, Christian faith can be caricatured. It is often perverted into a religion for comfort only, but the main tradition of Christian thought and life never has been primarily comfortable. The religion of Christ was not chiefly comfort. Without the cross we cannot understand him at all; in the cross his life and teaching centered. He had no light-hearted view of life that let him stay, pleasantly drugged, in Nazareth, but a heavy-handed, serious view of life that caused him to walk at last the dark road to Golgotha, saying to his disciples: "If any man would come after me, let him deny himself, and take up his cross, and follow me."

What does one mean by talking, then, of religion's being a pleasant drug? Listen to Gandhi, one of the most serious religious spirits of our time, as he says of God: "He is the most exacting personage in the world and the world to come." Gandhi could have lived countless times over an easier, more peaceful life had he not believed so deeply in God and his purpose for India and the world. God has not so much saved Gandhi from trouble; God has got Gandhi into trouble. Everybody here who has ever had any serious dealings with faith in

God knows what Gandhi means by calling him an "exacting personage."

To be sure, there is another side to Christian faith, represented in Whittier's lines:

> Drop thy still dews of quietness,
> Till all our strivings cease;
> Take from our souls the strain and stress,
> And let our ordered lives confess
> The beauty of thy peace.

Nevertheless, even Whittier's religion is not half expressed there. Whittier was first of all a social reformer. In his elder years, when he was a famous poet, he wrote this: "I set a higher value on my name as appended to the Anti-Slavery Declaration of 1833 than on the title-page of any book." Many think of Whittier in mystical seclusion writing pious and consoling verse. We should think of him also in Concord, New Hampshire, going to speak at an anti-slavery meeting, facing a crowd on the way that pelted him with rotten eggs until his black Quaker coat ran yellow with the stains. We should remember him bitterly hated, and lampooned for years in the press of the United States as a traitor. No, when we find a man who has deeply entered into the Christian faith, we find a man who has discovered not fallacious comfort but a deep, demanding seriousness in life. Great religion has always been not first of all a search for comfort, but a search for righteousness and truth.

In the second place, let us now go further and see that Christian faith at its best, far from being fantasy, meets one of the basic tests of reality. If in any realm we fulfill conditions and get results, if when we meet the law-abiding requirements the universe responds, we know that we are handling reality.

Behind this whole idea that Christian faith in God, and in the creative power of the Spirit, is nothing but elaborate spoofing and wishful thinking, lies the presupposition that only the materialistic aspects of the universe are real. Men take for granted the physical cosmos and then say, Well, the spiritual is a mysterious something that we make up to comfort ourselves with. But, my friends, the physical aspects of the universe are just as mysterious as the spiritual. This whole physical structure is incredibly made up of negative and positive poles of invisible electricity, arranged in patterns of mathematical equations. How can any man take it for granted? As Balfour says, "We now know too much about matter to be materialists."

Nevertheless, we are sure that in dealing with the physical aspects of the universe we are dealing with reality, and for this reason: When in that realm we fulfill the law-abiding conditions, the universe responds. Something real is there. When Archimedes leaped from his bath and ran about the streets crying "Eureka," why the excitement? He was having one of the most thrilling experiences in human life. He had tried an experiment; the universe had responded to him, and he knew that he was dealing with reality. When Newton discerned that the movements of the heavenly bodies could be subsumed under one law and that his figures were working out correctly, he fell into an agitation so intense, we read, that he could not go on with the computations and "was obliged to desire a friend to finish them." His emotion was justified. He was trying an experiment; the universe was responding to him, and he knew that he was dealing with reality.

Well, throughout the ages, in all great religion, men have fulfilled conditions in the spiritual world and the spiritual world has given response—creative, transforming, powerful response. To be sure, religious ideas have changed, just as scientific ideas have hanged, but in both realms great spirits have fulfilled conditions and the universe has responded to them. In both realms the cosmos has answered, saying, Something real is here. Indeed, out of that experience in the spiritual life have come the most towering characters in history, so that Benjamin Kidd, in his classic work on society, says that that kind of religion has been the most powerful element in the social progress of mankind. To laugh all that experience out of court as fantasy and spoofing is incredible.

Are not ideas real? Nobody ever saw them. They are not physical. An idea is as invisible as God and yet we can discern what happens when the conditions are fulfilled in that unseen realm. As John Eglinton put it: "Without an idea man is frivolous, anarchic, dissatisfied, despicable. With an idea, the long-hoarded initiatives of his nature are liberated, he strains forward to new consummations." To explain away the world of ideas as our delusion, imagined to make this materialistic cosmos more meaningful, will not do. Whenever in any realm we fulfill conditions and the cosmos responds, we are dealing with reality.

Listen to Paul, praying that "ye may be strengthened with power through his Spirit in the inward man; that Christ may dwell in your hearts through faith; to the end that ye, being rooted and grounded in love, may be strong to apprehend with all the saints what is the breadth and length and height and depth, and to know the love of Christ which passeth knowledge, that ye may be filled unto all the fulness of God." That does not sound like spoofing. That does not sound like a weak and unhappy man sticking his face in a chloroform mask. That sounds like a great character fulfilling conditions in the spiritual world, to whom the spiritual world has made response. Innumerable souls across the ages, experiencing such response, have heard Christ saying clearly, "I am . . . the truth."

Let us go further now into a third area of evidence. Whenever in any realm we run across powerful personality—not now ideas in the abstract any longer, but personality itself, potent, creative, smiting the world with rememberable impact, one can have a fairly impressive confidence that he is handling the real.

I would not say that every idea my father had corresponded with the real. My father would not have said that himself. But my father was real, and were anyone to argue that the essential factors producing that potent character were fantasy, self-deceit, and make-believe, that kind of argument would run into this insuperable difficulty: It must take more than fantasy, self-deceit, and make-believe to produce anything as real as that. To believe that so much reality can come from unreality calls for a credulity I cannot attain.

This attack on Christianity, therefore, as a chloroform mask, confronts its insuperable difficulty in Christ himself, and in people who have shared his spirit, his quality of character, his kind of life. It must take more than a chloroform mask to produce anything as real as that. The trouble with this new attack on the Christian faith is that it proves too much. It explains away as the result of self-deceit, not simply the great religious characters, but the great spiritual characters in every realm. For if this universe were basically materialistic, and all our spiritual life were but our endeavor to conceal, dress up, and decorate for our consolation the cruel facts, then that would be true not simply about religion but about art. That is what Joseph Krutch, one of the most honest atheists of our time, frankly says in his book on *Experience and Art*. So *that* is another chloroform mask into which the weak and unhappy stick their faces; and music is another, and poetry another, and love another. If once you let this argument get started, it does not stop with religion. It takes in art, music, poetry, love, the deepest faiths undergirding human personality, and the ultimate hopes of society. They are all engulfed in the same abysmal explanation, as nothing but our comfortable way of making an intolerable world more livable. It would make even the supreme creative characters of history, the Platos, Beethovens, Michelangelos, great saints, great prophets, great lovers, great seers, and Christ over all, the greatest fools of all, most beguiled by fantasy, most misled by deceptive and consoling imaginations.

Well, any theory that makes the greatest characters the most deluded of the fools has something the matter with it. *Ex nihilo nihil fit*—"Out of nothing, nothing comes." That the noblest aspects of human life are mere creations of fantasy is an incredible creed. I have seen too many people who, coming under the influence of Christ and discovering through him not only ideals of character but resources of power, have been transformed, as Paul said, from character to character, ever to believe that creed. One who lives beside the ocean and sees the tide come in to fill bays and inlets as they never could fill themselves, cannot be persuaded that nothing real and deep is needed to explain that. What is happening in this little bay cannot be explained without the whole ocean and the gravitational pull of the skies upon it. Something real and eternal is evidenced in that rising tide. No more can we explain great character as due to mere delusion. There, at least, I hear Christ clearly say, "I am . . . the truth."

To one more area of evidence I ask your thought. Strangely enough, it is this present world itself—this terrible, upset, catastrophic world, trying to manage its affairs on anti-Christian principles. Many people, who would not have been concerned with philosophic arguments that the Christian faith and way of life are delusive, are thinking today that Christianity is delusive because this present hideous and diabolical world scene shows Christianity up as utterly impractical. To which I answer: The Christian way of life impractical? Do you think, then, that what is going on in the world today is practical? This demonic regime of anti-Christianity—would you call it practical—economically practical? in terms of human happiness—practical? in terms of hope for the kind of world our children will have to live in—practical? Do you call this essence of all evil, war, practical? Rather, this world disaster with all the voices of its need cries out that unless we can achieve the hard-headed realism of the Christian ethic and put it into practice, we are personally and socially sunk.

Granted that religion can be the opiate of the people! As one of Warwick Deeping's characters says: "Anything to escape, to colour the spectacles." So some turn to drink and color the spectacles that way; some turn to drugs and sleep it off; some in daydreaming build an unreal world and live in it; some do turn to a religion of fantasy where wishful thinking takes possession of their lives. Their religion is a chloroform mask where, weak and unhappy, they stick their faces.

But it is a cheap and superficial habit to estimate great matters by their burlesques. We do not judge architecture by filling stations and wayside huts; we judge it by its great exhibitions. We do not judge music by its cheap and tawdry expressions; we judge it by its classic and abiding forms. What business have we to throw religion out of the window because of its caricatures? Great religion has been the source of the most creative ideas in human history. And today the Christian faith and ethic with its central principles—the sacredness of personality, the inescapable membership of all mankind in one body, the absolute necessity, therefore, of goodwill not as an ideal but as a working principle, the need of individual regeneration if we are to have a regenerate society, the call to seek first the Kingdom of God on earth, that is, the welfare of all, if there is to be any welfare for each, and the reality of God himself, above all nations, races, and classes, calling for one human family—this religion is no fantasy, no opiate. Rather, look at the mad world today, trying to live on the opposite principles, and see if the closing words of Jesus in the Sermon on the Mount, as Dr. Moffatt translates them, do not ring true: "Everyone who listens to these words of mine and acts upon them will be like a sensible man, who built his house on rock."

In the New Testament the very words "ideal" and "idealism" are not to be found. They are not there. But the word "truth" is there again and again. The Christian gospel was not idealism but realism, not a message, first of all, about what ought to be, but about what is. God *is*, Christ *is* his revealer, man *is* the child of the Eternal Spirit, there *is* an eternal purpose which he purposed in Christ, all men *are* inextricably members of one body, love *is* the law of life—such are the basic realities.

Surely some of us need to take this to ourselves. We are growing older. Forty years old, fifty years old, sixty years old—the decades pass, and with the years, by an inevitable drift, we are thinking about life one way or another. Happy the man who with the passing years is more and more persuaded that what Christ stands for is the truth!

Winning the War of Ideas

THERE is, I take it, no serious question as to what the revolutionary idea of human society is that one finds in the New Testament. That radical Christian philosophy has two elements. It starts with individual personality as the unit of supreme value. Persons, one by one, are children of God, each with eternal issues in his life, and what happens to persons, and what becomes of them, is of supreme concern. And then, because persons, one by one, are thus supremely valuable, racial, national, and class lines that divide persons are of secondary importance. A person is a person, whatever his race or class or on whichever side of a national line he happens to have been born. So in the New Testament individualism moves inevitably out into universalism. The New Testament begins by saying: "It is not the will of your Father who is in heaven, that one of these little ones should perish," and it ends by saying: Therefore, neither male nor female, Jew nor Greek, Scythian, barbarian, bond nor free, but one man in Christ.

One cannot fully understand the radical revolution Jesus wrought in human thinking without approaching him this way. He began with a kind of individualism that inevitably goes on to universalism. Christ died "for every man," says the New Testament. That is individualism. It lifts persons up one by one into supreme importance, but it inevitably involves universalism. Christ died for every man, of every race, every class, every nation. As Dr. Goodspeed translates that text in the Epistle to the Hebrews: He tasted "the bitterness of death on behalf of every human being."

This Christian philosophy, far from being merely historic or abstract, is in the very thick of this present world conflict.

Indeed, I wish we of the democracies were as clear sighted about this matter as are the Nazis themselves. One of the Nazi leaders recently made a statement in which he said that this world revolution is at bottom a struggle between two philosophies, the "racial-national" on one side, the "individualist-universalist" on the other. Those hyphenated polysyllables are his Teutonic way of putting it, but what they mean is clear. This is not simply a war of arms, he says, but a war of ideas, and from the Nazi's point of view here are the two major philosophies involved: On the one side, the racial-national idea—that is, the supremacy of the racial state as the one pre-eminent object of devotion, to which all persons must be subjugated; and on the other, the individualist-universalist idea—that is, the supremacy of persons, one by one, as the object of pre-eminent concern, and, therefore, a universalism that, overriding national and racial lines, sees all humanity in terms of God's fatherhood and man's brotherhood.

Here, indeed, two irreconcilable philosophies confront each other. On the one side, the supremacy of the nationalistic state is conceived as so absolute that the Fascists even sum up the whole duty of man in three words—"Believe, Obey, Fight!" That is to say, Believe in the state, obey the state, fight for the state—that is the whole duty of man. But the Christian gospel sees national lines as negligible in comparison with the great reality that persons, one by one, are infinitely valuable, and that, therefore, all mankind is by right one universal family regardless of nation, race, or class. Today this Christian philosophy is no abstract affair. The world in the end must choose, not theoretically alone, but practically, which road it will travel—the racial-national, or the individualist-universalist. That is the profoundest decision confronting mankind today.

We are tempted to think of Germany, Italy, Japan, as all on one side of this question, and of ourselves, the democracies, as all on the other. To be sure, the Nazi and Fascist

leaders are self-consciously and outspokenly on one side of
the question. That is true. But even one look at ourselves
should convince us that the struggle between these two philosophies is not simply outside us, between nations, but inside
us, inside every one of us sitting here. Indeed, listen to this
letter from a German Christian, written to his English friend
after this war started: "With these lines I have to say farewell to you. We have to expect to be called for military service in Germany. What this means for men like ourselves, who
were blessed in these years of friendship and trust, by fellowship and love of Christians all over the world, that cannot
now be expressed in words. . . . Now we have to go the
way into darkness. . . . And if the day comes when the light
of God and His mercy will shine again upon our peoples and
Churches, then do remember, my dear friend, if I am still
alive, that there is a friend of yours in whose heart all the
spiritual heritage of thirteen years, does not fade away, and
who will be ready for all the work of God after this time of
great temptation."

There is a German Christian within whom the struggle is
going on between these two philosophies. The racial-national
state lays its hand upon him, and for patriotism's sake he
obeys, but deep within him also the individualist-universalist
way of thought and life is, in his highest hours, most real to
him, and to it his soul belongs. We cannot thrust this war of
ideas off, as though it were only a matter of conflict between
Germany and Britain. Inside men and women on both sides
of the battle lines, and inside every one of us here, this war
of ideas is being waged. Two irreconcilable philosophies of
life clamor for our allegiance. How shall we resolve that conflict? What can we do about it? What would you have that
German Christian do? The nationalistic state does have claims
upon us. The question is not simple. Who of us does not face
this issue now?

As we try to help ourselves in this matter, let us say first that we can at least make up our minds to which of these two philosophies we personally are committed as the hope of the future.

If someone says, That is easy—I am all against this Nazi theory of the absolute national state, I beg of you do not say that too lightly. For nationalism has been the dominant doctrine of our whole era, just as feudalism was of a preceding epoch, and we all have been, and still are, under its powerful influence. Granted that when Hitler says, "We do not want any other God than Germany," he states the matter in an extreme form that shocks us! Nevertheless, the creed of nationalism has been the creed of all the world for a century and more, and we all have shared it: each nation a sovereign unit, acknowledging no control save its own independent will; each nation within its own borders exercising an almost absolute control over its citizens, especially in wartime, conscripting life, property, food, business, opinion, and conscience; each nation bolstering up this tremendous claim to supremacy with emotional patriotism that transfers to the national unit the old absolutism of the divine right of kings. This doctrine of nationalism has been the whole world's dogma. Every nation has illustrated it, more or less believed in it and lived by it, and the Nazis and Fascists today are simply exemplifying it in its extreme form and logical conclusion.

And now to recognize that the day for this doctrine of nationalism is done, that in the light of contemporary facts it is as obsolete as feudalism, that its continuance can only mean an ever deeper hell on earth, that a new era is on us in which not nationalism but internationalism is indispensable, calls for a quality and courage of thinking that many Americans are not measuring up to.

We all fear the continuance of this war, but I also fear the ending of it. Wars whip up nationalism in its worst form. Only the other day Mussolini pleaded with his people for hate, "that cold, conscious, implacable hate, hate in every home, which is indispensable for victory." War always works that consequence, so that whichever side wins a war, and whatever problems may be temporarily solved thereby, the total effect of war is almost certain to be more and worse nationalism than before. Whichever side wins, the whole world in the end loses, for the hatreds roused in war make nationalism go from bad to worse. The worst thing about war is what comes when it stops. A man once fell from the roof of his house, and when asked if the fall hurt him, answered, "No, the fall did not hurt me. It was the stopping that nearly killed me." So, the greatest curse of war is not its process, terrible as that is, but its aftermath. The racial-national philosophy in worse forms than before is the most likely winner of all world wars, and the racial-national philosophy, my friends, is Christianity's major enemy today, a more explicit denial of everything Christ stands for than any theoretical atheism could ever be.

See! Hitler is out to unify the world. That is a great idea. The world desperately needs unifying. One way of achieving it is imaginable—a master race strong enough to take the world in hand and whip it into shape. If we say, as we do, that we cannot and will not stand for that, then what is the alternative, since one way or another the world must be unified? Surely, it is not national isolation. I am a non-interventionist so far as belligerency in this war is concerned, but I do not see how any man intelligent in his thinking or Christian in his philosophy can be an isolationist in his planning for the future. Isolationism means keeping the *status quo*. It means the indefinite continuance of the nationalistic structure and theory. No! If in the realm of ideas we are going to defeat Hitler's method of unifying the world, we must do it not by isolation but by another way of unifying the world. That is the only wave of the future I can see.

We have seen strange things in these days—Britain, for example, offering a common citizenship to France. Think of the history of France and Britain, and who could have imagined that that would come, not as an ideal but as a realistic proposal by hard-headed men facing stubborn facts? In our own country *Union Now* with all the other democracies is being proposed and backed by able and patriotic men and women. I am not a sponsor of that proposal in any form so far presented, but the fact that it is proposed is prophetic. A new era has dawned, it says, in which not the old nationalism but internationalism must come to unify the world, for the world must be unified one way or another. One of our public leaders once said about the Socialists, in their endeavors to improve economic conditions, that the only way to beat the Socialists was to beat them to it. I say that about Hitler. The only way to beat his idea of unifying the world is to beat him to it with a better idea.

No one is wise enough to furnish a blueprint of the new internationalism that must come, but the philosophy that must underlie it, if human life is to have any decent hopes, is clear. Not the racial-national idea—only slavery and despair lie ahead of that—but the individualist-universalist idea: persons, free persons the units of supreme value, and, therefore, national and racial lines secondary, subservient, and at last negligible, in the endeavor to make life worth-while for all persons. Well, it would help some if increasing millions of people clearly saw that they must be personally committed to that philosophy as the hope of the future.

This first step alone, however, does not carry us out of our difficulty. We still, like that German Christian, have nationalism on our hands, and not only can we not get rid of it, but we do not want to. There are real values in it. So we must now face the fact that the way out into the internationalism we desire, based on a fundamentally Christian philosophy, lies not in eliminating nationalism but in redeeming it.

Nationalism is not all loss. It is like an eggshell. An eggshell does protect the growing life within it up to a certain stage. Then, to be sure, the shell must be broken if the life is to survive and go on, but despite that, we must not under-estimate the importance of that shell's function. So nationalism has had and still has a great part to play in human life.

For example, every great nation represents within itself some of the finest meanings of internationalism. Were you not brought up, as I was, on books like *The Scottish Chiefs*, and *The Days of Bruce?* How Scotland and England hated each other! What bloody wars they waged against each other! But then nationalism came and included them in one patriotism, eliminating a whole area of war. We constantly think of nationalism as saying, Get your guns! We forget the wide and once violent areas within every great nation, where nationalism has said, Put up your guns!

Consider our own land. In 1760 an Englishman visited this country and wrote this about it: "Fire and water are not more heterogeneous than the different colonies in North America. Nothing can exceed the jealousy which they possess in regard to each other. The inhabitants of Pennsylvania and New York have an inexhaustible source of animosity in their jealousy for the trade of the Jerseys. Massachusetts Bay and Rhode Island are not less interested in that of Connecticut. Even the limits and boundaries of each colony are a constant source of litigation. In short, such is the difference of character, of manners, of religion, of interest in the different colonies, that I think, if I am not wholly ignorant of the human mind, were they left to themselves, there would soon be a civil war from one end of the continent to the other; while the Indians and Negroes would, with better reason, impatiently watch the opportunity of exterminating them altogether." So that is what we once were like here; and then nationalism put us together and across a vast continent said to millions of men, concerning old animosities, Put up your guns! Thus nationalism has blazed the trail out toward internationalism, and in a country like this has shown, over a vast area, how through federation we can get both unity and liberty.

Moreover, the national state today is of incalculable importance in the realm of social service. In our new world of interrelated living, the old negative idea of government—that government is best which governs least—has necessarily been overpassed, and a positive idea of government has risen, so that no one can be concerned about wide areas of social service without caring about the nation. Public health, social insurance, unemployment, labor conditions, monopoly conditions, conservation of natural resources, housing, hospitals, educational institutions—no one can care about such areas of personal and social need without caring about the nation. Nationalism done for? Not if it is redeemed. It can be a trail blazer into a new era for liberated personality.

The place to begin working out the individualist-universalist philosophy of life is within the nation. The defense of democracy must start within democracy. It is much easier to damn the Nazis because they outspokenly deny the individualist-universalist philosophy than it is to practice it ourselves. We have barely begun to do that here. One million, eight hundred thousand sharecroppers in a desperate plight —that is no application of the individualist-universalist philosophy. One of our nurses working in the destitute portions of this city used a phrase the other day—"the dangerous poor." So! The poor so poor that they are the breeding places of physical and moral ills contagious to the whole community; the poor so poor that they are tinder for the flame of violent resentment and revolt—that is not the individualist-universalist philosophy. Or racial hatred—anti-Semitism that turns up little Hitlers even in this city—that is the racial-national philosophy at work in America. The last presidential election was important, was it not? Americans were stirred to vote that time, were they not? Well, in one state in this Union 5.2% of the people voted. In three other states 10.0%,

10.3%, 10.4% respectively voted. Why? Because of discriminatory laws deliberately passed to shut out from the suffrage certain races and classes. One of the best definitions of democracy I know is that it is the individualist-universalist philosophy put into practice. But if that is so, we are not yet a democracy.

Lord Milner, a great Englishman, on one occasion said: "The last thing which the thought of the Empire inspires in me is a desire to boast—to wave a flag, or to shout 'Rule Britannia.' When I think of it, I am much more inclined to go into a corner by myself and pray." So when I think of America today, neither flag waving, nor singing "The Star-Spangled Banner" expresses my patriotism. I want to go away by myself and pray that in this country we may succeed in redeeming nationalism until we become here a real democracy, an incarnate argument for the individualist-universalist gospel.

Finally and logically, then, this leads us to face our own personal lives. For if this Christian philosophy is ever going to be the basis of a new internationalism, and, as precedent to that, of a redeemed nationalism, it must, precedent to that, be believed and lived by persons above the average and ahead of the time. All the major changes for the better in human history have started in individual consciences. The other day I ran upon this sentence: "Smith College began in the conscience of a New England woman." All worth-while things thus begin in people convinced of a new idea, captured by a new vision of what might be, who, as a creative minority, begin living on the basis of that new vision long before its public acceptance seems possible. Today the victory of the Christian idea of life over the racial-national idea depends ultimately on that.

Indeed, how many of us, honestly searching our own consciences now, can find areas where we ourselves are living on the racial-national basis?

All racial prejudice involves that. It is not merely our personal whim and fancy that we do not like Japanese, Jews, Italians, Negroes, or what you will. All such lumping of masses of God's children in one group, and cherishing prejudice and dislike against them, is our share in the most powerful enemy that Christianity faces today—the racial-national philosophy. Let us, at least, get ourselves out from under the support of that anti-Christ! It is easier by far to shout in general for the defense of America against the Nazis than it is to be sure that we ourselves are not entertaining some of the worst attitudes that naziism stands for, and racial prejudice is one of these.

Or again, all subjection of the individual conscience to the nation, so that the nation becomes, as it were, God, and we give up our honest convictions even when we are persuaded that the nation is wrong, is the racial-national philosophy. We honor Niemoeller because in the face of that philosophy, grown dominant and arrogant, he refused to surrender his primary allegiance to the one God of all mankind. In forms less dramatic there is plenty of call now among us for that incorrigible refusal to surrender conscience to the state. That refusal is basically involved in being a Christian, and happily it is involved as well in being an American. Listen to this from a decision by Chief Justice Hughes: "In the forum of conscience duty to a moral power higher than the State has always been maintained. . . . The essence of religion is belief in a relation to God involving duties superior to those arising from any human relation." Every Sunday in the Navy the white flag of religion is flown above the stars and stripes. It is the only flag that ever is flown above the stars and stripes. It is the symbol of a whole theory of life, the essence of our liberty, and the evidence of our protest against the racial-national philosophy. The state is not God.

Any way we look at it this war of ideas is going on within us all. We commonly call it dictatorship against democracy, but that suggests today an outward battle between some nations and others. True enough! Desperately true! But the conflict runs deeper than that. It is a war between profoundly diverse ideas, and that war must be ultimately won within ourselves. Outer battles will not settle it. Alas, in the very process of trying to win a modern totalitarian war, the democracies themselves inevitably swing over toward the dictatorial philosophy. This deeper war, that was here before the outer battle started and will be here afterwards, must be won in the minds and spirits of men, and the whole Christian cause is involved in it. Christ died "for every man." So long as that faith stands, and even a few believe it, the individualist-universalist gospel, which is the hope of the world, will not perish from the earth.

What Keeps Religion Going?

THE Book of Job is one of the great dramas of the ancient world. It is not easy to translate, and the best endeavors are not the standard versions but the freer renderings of independent scholars. So Dr. McFadyen, in the fifteenth chapter, translates the accusation that Job's false friends, speaking through Eliphaz, hurl at Job because he doubts the current theology: "See!" they cry, "thou art destroying religion." More than 2000 years ago men were saying that. On a man like Job, who doubted the contemporary creed, they brought down the stunning charge: "Thou art destroying religion." Nevertheless, while the old creed that Job doubted has long since perished, religion still is here. Men like the friends of Job have thought they saw religion being destroyed innumerable times, but it persists. What keeps religion going?

This fact is clear, that religion is one of the little group of fundamental interests in human life that everlastingly change, and yet everlastingly persist. Are not these two characteristics, persistence and change, the marks of the most important elements in human experience? Some things we cannot get rid of—they persist; but at the same time, we cannot keep them static—they change. Whenever we find those two qualities, persistence and change, in the same field, we may be sure that we are dealing with something important.

Some things mankind can finish and be done with, but not music, that persists, and changes from tom-toms to Beethoven and beyond; not architecture, that persists, and changes from mud huts to Chartres Cathedral and beyond; not agriculture, that persists, and changes from Ruth's sickle to McCormick Harvesters, soil chemistry and beyond; not science, that persists, and changes from ancient Chaldeans studying the stars to a new telescope with a 200-inch reflector and beyond; not religion, that persists, and changes from old credulities and world views to new thoughts of God and larger apprehensions of his meaning. Religion is like language. Languages have perished, but language goes on.

Now this is not only a historical matter of great import, it is a personal matter too. Who of us has not had some cherished theological idea smashed to pieces, seen some old religious world view disintegrate, until we too cried, Thou art destroying religion? Everyone here has used these words of the friends of Job. Today we consider the fact that men have said that from the beginning, and still religion goes on. What keeps it going?

In handling so large a subject, all one can hope to do here is to suggest certain deep sources from which religion perennially rises in man's experience, so that not only can mankind as a whole not escape it, but you and I personally are inevitably bound to deal with it one way or another.

One such profound source is obviously the need of spiritual meaning in our life in this mysterious universe. Ages ago a wandering star passed too near the sun, and drew out from it by its gravitational pull this planet that ever since has swung around its solar center, has gradually cooled off, given birth to life, and become the habitat of our strange human race. What does it all mean? Macbeth calls life

> . . . a tale
> Told by an idiot, full of sound and fury,
> Signifying nothing.

Is that the answer? That would be strange, for we here live in two worlds, one material, physical, tangible, visible, the other spiritual, intangible, invisible, the one made up of things we can weigh and measure, the other made up of ideas, ideals, of intellect, conscience, creative genius, of faith, hope, love.

In that latter world, invisible, we really live, and not by bread alone. In Santayana's phrase, man's oddity is "that interest of his in things not edible." What does it mean?

If only increase of scientific knowledge cleared up the mystery the case would be simpler, but it does not. The more we know about this universe, the more mysterious it is. The old world that Job knew was marvelous enough, and his description of its wonders is among the noblest poetry of the race, but today the new science has opened to our eyes vistas of mystery that transcend in their inexplicable marvel anything the ancients ever dreamed. What does life in such a world mean?

Now meaning is spiritual. If this cosmos is an accident of electrons and protons going it blind, then there is no ultimate meaning. But if God is real, if his purpose runs through all creation, if we are spirit, the children of Eternal Spirit, and so can be fellow workers with God for an end unseen and unimaginable, but worth everything that its achievement costs, then this universe and our lives within it are packed with meaning. That is the profound issue involved in religion, an issue persistent, tenacious, inescapable, outlasting the rise and fall of all special theologies. Demolish religion's theories a thousand times, and it will still lift its head in men, crying, Life does have eternal meaning!

Here is the explanation of an experience familiar in our time. Many people have given up Christianity, supposing that they were merely surrendering faith in religion, only to discover that what they really had surrendered was faith in life itself. They thought religion was a mere parenthesis in the sentence of life. They supposed they could drop the parenthesis and not miss it. But now, having dropped the parenthesis, they find they still have the main sentence on their hands, with the insistent question rising, What does it mean? And it begins to dawn on them that Christian faith is all about that. Christian faith is no parenthesis. It concerns the meaning of the whole sentence of life.

As a Christian minister, I should not particularly mind people losing faith in religion if that were all there were to it. Plenty of things go under the name of religion that a man had better lose faith in. One does care, however, about the shattering experience coming to countless people who have lost faith in life itself. When a fine-natured, socially useful atheist of our time comes to his life's end, saying, "The outstanding fact that cannot be dodged by thoughtful men is the futility of it all," one does care about that. When one of our fine dramatists, whose plays we all have enjoyed, says in his autobiography, "There is no reason for life and life has no meaning," one does care about that. Such men have not simply dropped a religious parenthesis; they have lost meaning out of the whole sentence.

Many a time in my life I have heard the cry, Thou art destroying religion! This or that creedal or customary appurtenance of religion became incredible, and men thought the Christian faith was done for. No, my friends, the deep fountains of Christian faith are not so easily dried up. Forever it rises in man's soul, crying, There is a basic, ultimate, eternal, spiritual meaning in this universe, and in our lives! That keeps religion going, because that keeps life going. One man has just written a brief biography of his friend. His friend was a success in business, and died worth over $40,000,000. But at seventy years of age his verdict on life was "Vanity of vanities; all is vanity." "He died," writes his friend, "in the midst of luxurious surroundings with a handful of ashes in his grasp." So a man can stand almost any adversity if he keeps a strong faith that there is ultimate meaning in life; but if he loses that faith, then though he gain the whole world he has lost his soul.

Another perennial source of religion that will never be exhausted is the presence in our lives of profound personal experiences that no materialism ever can adequately account for. Every one of us has them. Life is shallow enough, but not so shallow that any one of us escapes the deep hours when we stand face to face with some spiritual reality that no materialism can adequately explain.

The evidence for this lies in the very fact that when we sing, for example, "Dear Lord and Father of Mankind," we know what Whittier means. That experience of inner spiritual companionship is not alien to us. When Helen Keller was a little girl they brought Phillips Brooks to her to teach her something about God, and with the sign language he did his best to describe the inner presence of the unseen Spirit, until suddenly her face lighted up and she signaled back that she had always known there was a God, but had not before known his name. There is revealed one of the profoundest truths about the human soul.

It is a strange thing that when the supreme seers of the race describe their profoundest insights, something deep within us understands. When Elijah, after the earthquake, wind, and fire, heard the "still small voice," we know what that means. When Jesus says: "Go into your room and shut the door, pray to your Father who is in secret," we may not do it, but we understand it. When Wordsworth says,

> . . . I have felt
> A presence that disturbs me with the joy
> Of elevated thoughts,

we have felt that presence too. And deep in man is an unconquerable conviction that in such experiences there is something that materialism cannot account for.

In how many different ways men have tried to explain the persistence of religion! Some have said it was the work of priestcraft. That now is recognized as nonsense. Some have said it was man's desire for a comfortable opiate, but that explains only the perversions of religion. The basic reasons for religion's perpetuity lie deep in man himself, in those experiences of the spiritual life of which materialism can give no adequate account.

We all have hours when beauty plays upon our souls like winds on an aeolian harp. We all know hours of love—deep, true, and tender, asking nothing, willing to give everything, like parents with a little child. We have hours of intellectual illumination, when our minds are quickened and a new idea reorients our lives. We have hours when the sense of honor is regnant, and to our consciences, commanding a hard duty, we give a strong affirmative reply. We have hours when a power greater than our own is mysteriously at our disposal, and Paul's words, "Strengthened with might by his Spirit in the inner man," are real. And then materialism tries to explain these, and other experiences like these, saying, as one modern atheist has just written: "The realm of spirit" is "a sort of invisible vegetation flourishing in some of the stars." My word! Raphael's sense of beauty, Einstein's intellect, Christ's spirit, a sort of invisible vegetation that flourishes on some of the stars? No! Demolish religion endless times and it still will come back, crying, That explanation explains nothing! These experiences of men's souls are too real, too deep, too universal, too significant, too transforming to be so cheaply disposed of.

See what was troubling those false friends of Job! They had a theological theory that God must immediately bless all good men with prosperity and curse all bad men with misfortune, and that, therefore, all prosperous people were thereby proved to be good, and all unfortunate people were thereby proved to be bad. That was the current theology. And Job did not believe it; he saw through it into its shallowness and falsity, and he vehemently denied it. It was because of that Eliphaz said: "Thou art destroying religion!" And now history, looking back, calls those friends fools, and blind. That theology of theirs and countless others like it have gone, but deep beneath them all, persistent, fundamental, inescapable, are the great experiences of the human soul in its supreme hours, which no materialism can adequately account for. In the old days when Phillips Brooks held consultation hours at Harvard University, one student came to his office and said with an anxious air: "Dr. Brooks, I would like to talk over some of my doubts; but I don't want to disturb your faith." And Brooks broke out into uncontrollable laughter. Disturb his faith, he who knew the deep experiences of the soul that only God can adequately explain!

A third source from which religious faith forever rises in the life of man is found in human history. Though religion were destroyed countless times, it would still come back, sure that hands stronger than ours are on the reins of mankind's life. Man did not make himself; he was made. It was not man who brought the organic out of the inorganic, and created life. It was not man, the animal, who deliberately set out to climb the ascending road toward Christ; he was set upon that road by a power greater than his own. Man is not the original creator of goodness, truth, and beauty; he discovers them. Something greater than man has been making man and dealing with man.

Now this general truth out of which religion perennially springs is made vivid in one special experience repeated again and again in human history, namely, where right defeated turns out to be stronger than wrong triumphant. That is a strange, recurrent fact. The defeats of righteousness are stronger than the victories of evil. How far can evil go? It can go a long way, even far enough to crucify Christ. But it has its limits. For lo! even though it goes so far, yet that defeat on Calvary turns out to be a victory, as though evil contained within itself the seeds of its own destruction, so that Caiaphas and Pilate, who thought themselves the winners, are the losers, and Christ's day, far from being over, is yet to come. What is it, in a merely materialistic world, that could make that kind of event possible?

Professor Charles A. Beard, one of the leading historians of our time, was asked sometime since what major lessons he had learned from history, and he answered that he had learned four. Here they are: "First, whom the gods would destroy they first make mad with power. Second, the mills of God grind slowly, yet they grind exceeding small. Third, the bee fertilizes the flower it robs. Fourth, when it is dark enough you can see the stars." So! That is what secular history teaches.

This self-defeating quality of evil that Professor Beard sees everywhere in history will, I suspect, be exhibited, soon or late, in great affairs now afoot. In *Mein Kampf*, for example, Hitler wrote this: "By means of shrewd lies, unremittingly repeated, it is possible to make people believe that heaven is hell—and hell, heaven. . . . The greater the lie, the more readily will it be believed." Skillful and audacious mendacity can be a powerful element in public policy. That is true. But Hitler should have remembered the old German saying: "Lies have short legs." So the old Germans said. Lies can go a little way, but then they reach their limit and their nemesis. First, your enemies will not believe you; then the onlookers will not believe you; then your allies will not believe you; then even your friends will not trust you. There is in mendacity itself, whether it be Hitler's or our own, a self-defeating quality. Lies have short legs.

If this world and ourselves within it were but the chance by-product of mindless dust going it blind, why should lies have short legs? Why should crucifixions turn out to be supreme triumphs? Why should Nero from his golden house put Paul to death upon the Appian Way, and centuries after, Nero be a by-word and derision while Paul's insights sway the minds of multitudes? Why should not only a poet sing

> Though the cause of Evil prosper, yet 't is
> Truth alone is strong,

but a hard-headed historian say that history teaches that "whom the gods would destroy they first make mad with power"; that though "the mills of God grind slowly, yet they grind exceeding small"; that "the bee fertilizes the flower it robs"; and that "when it is dark enough you can see the stars"? Some power greater than man has hold upon man. All our pictures of him are but children's drawings. All our imaginations of him are but fable and parable. But though our theologies about him change and our theories perish, still religion will rise forever in the mind and spirit of man, saying, The Lord God omnipotent reigneth!

From at least one more deep source religion perennially rises in the soul of man—from the fact of great personality. For personality at its best is a momentous fact. Amid the horror of the world and the shame of man's degraded life, one thing cannot be taken from us—we have seen in great souls what personality can mean. The modern mind balks at miracles, but after all, how miraculous a supreme person is, a comprehensive intellect, a luminous character, a creative genius, a sacrificial spirit! How ever did anything like that come to pass on this wandering island in the sky? Einstein may explain the cosmos, but if he does, who, then, can explain Einstein? Bach may account for the deep secrets of great music, but if he does, who, then, can account for Bach? Christ may elucidate the mystery of spiritual life, but who, then, will elucidate the mystery of Christ himself?

There are only two things that ultimately can be believed about great personality in this world. Either it is an accident, or else it is a revelation, one or the other. Either it is mere chance, like a spark luckily struck off by falling stones, or else it is the unveiling of an eternal quality at the heart of all things.

Now materialists have to see great personality as an accident. Stones and stars are to them revelations; atoms and electrons tell us something everlastingly true about the universe, says materialism, but intellect, character, spirit, are accidents; there is nothing like intellect, character, and spirit, eternally at the heart of the cosmos. Over against that, religion stands, and will not have it so. Great personality is not an accident, it cries, but a revelation! Whenever goodness, truth, or beauty shine in human life, they are rays of an eternal sun. As Professor Montague, of Barnard College, says: "What is highest in spirit is also deepest in nature." On that conviction religion takes its stand. Destroy its theologies endless times, it will come back, crying, Great personality cannot be an accident! It is a revelation, the light of the knowledge of the glory of God in the face of Jesus Christ. So to many of us in dark days when theories break down and abstract arguments fail, some strong, inspiring person comes, a soul that matter cannot explain, nor yet explain away, and lo! our faith comes back again, as in the New Testament, crying, "I know him whom I have believed."

> Our little systems have their day;
>   They have their day and cease to be;
>   They are but broken lights of thee,
> And thou, O Lord, art more than they.

All through this congregation now are folk who have been tempted and are being tempted to surrender Christian faith. I beg of you, take the measure of what you would be surrendering. That human life has in it basic spiritual meaning; that the deepest experiences of our souls represent reality and can be explained only as the impact of an Eternal Spirit; that human history is under a sovereignty greater than man's; that supreme personality, Christ above all, is not an accident but a revelation—against that religion even the gates of hell shall not prevail.

The Inescapable Judgment

OUR forefathers' view of life differed from our own in
at least one particular. We moderns characteristically
think of ourselves as the arbiters and umpires of life,
passing intellectual and moral judgment on it. We see ourselves as the judges. Our forefathers saw themselves standing in the presence of an Eternal Arbiter, who judged them.

To be sure, this contrast can be overstated, but it is real.
Some of the most characteristic factors in our modern world,
the development of science, the popular trust in intelligence,
the spread of education, the exaltation of the free and sovereign individual, all the elements of humanism, issue in this
result—that we see ourselves as the judges of life, the umpires of its rights and wrongs, its truths and falsehoods. Is
not that what our critical faculties and our consciences are
for? Who will pass discriminating sentence on life if we do
not? This modern attitude we all must recognize in ourselves.
But our forefathers saw themselves not sitting on, but standing before a judgment seat that was infinitely greater than
themselves, and listening to sentence passed on them.

Today I raise the question whether in that contrast the
truth is all on one side, and especially whether we moderns
have not forgotten something. Pilate, for example, was a
typical modern at the trial of Jesus. Was he not there to
judge the case? Was it not his duty to use such critical intelligence as he had to decide the contentious issue? He was
the arbiter and umpire. But now, in retrospect, one sees what
was really happening. Jesus, though he said not a word, was
sitting in judgment on Pilate. Pilate was not so much judging as he was being judged.

One reason for the fading from our modern religious

thought of this idea that we are under judgment is that our forefathers pictured the matter in terms incredible to us. They dramatized it as a cosmic courtroom with an anthropomorphic God upon the judgment seat, and they postponed it, making it a post-mortem assize, where some day we all would stand before the judgment seat of God. Alas, how religion suffers from its symbolism! It takes an eternal truth and pictures it in the figures of speech of a generation that understands them. Then centuries pass, and a whole new set of mental categories and cosmic outlooks occupy the minds of men, so that the old pictures are meaningless and incredible. Then out goes the baby with the bath. Men throw away the living truth because the frameworks of thought in which it has been set are no longer at ease in their imaginations. So the abiding fact that we face judgment from an Arbiter infinitely greater than ourselves has largely vanished from our modern Christian message.

Today I confront myself and you with an idea of the divine judgment that seems to me inescapable. John stated the matter in the third chapter of his Gospel, the nineteenth verse: "This is the judgment, that the light is come into the world, and men loved the darkness rather than the light; for their works were evil." So! Who can escape that?

This picture of judgment as light, showing up what cannot stand the light, should appeal to us moderns, if only because it was deliberate modernism when John first wrote it. John's Gospel was addressed to the Greeks. They did not like, any more than we do, the old Hebrew picture of a dramatized, post-mortem, cosmic courtroom and an anthropomorphic judge. They had Plato behind them, and neo-Platonism running through their thought. They needed a new picture of the divine judgment if it was to be real to them, and John, knowing that it is the truth that matters, not the transient frameworks of imagination it is set in, gave it to them. "This is the

[62]

judgment, that the light is come into the world, and men loved the darkness rather than the light."

At once that begins to hit home on our lives. If a man should say that the earth is flat, or that it was made in six days, or that insanity is caused by devils, what would be his judge? Light has come into the world. When a generation chooses ugliness in music, as though there were nothing better than jungle discords for modern orchestras to imitate, what is its condemnation? That light has come into the world. When homes are rancorous and children mistreated, when vindictiveness consumes a man as though the end of existence were to get even with another, when nations plunge into war, what is the condemnation? That light has come into the world, and men love darkness rather than light.

This inescapable judgment confronts us all. When light comes anywhere it shows things up. Even when we are physically soiled and disheveled, we stick to the shadows if we can. Beautiful, light may be, but it is also a discriminating test. It is always a judge. What got by in the dark, now that the light has come, can get by no longer. Moreover, light has come into the world in one realm after another, so that every one of us is under an inevitable judgment, not outwardly dramatic, as though we stood in a cosmic courtroom, not postmortem, as though we merely feared a future sentence, but as John pictured it to the Greeks, real, inherent, essential, present, and continuous—light showing up things in us and in the world that cannot stand the light. My soul! this is the judgment!

As we endeavor to discover the range and meaning of this truth, consider first that here lies the real significance of sin. There is no sin until light comes, and then there is. When men had only tom-toms it was not reprehensible in them to love that monotonous cacophony best of all, but now that Bach and Mozart and Beethoven and Brahms have come, it is artistic sin.

All sin, in a real sense, is thus belatedness, being behind the times, clinging to ancient darkness after the light has come. Once cannibalism was not wrong. It existed among our forefathers in northern Europe and Britain down to the fourth century A.D., and there was no guilt about it. But then the light came. After that it was sin. Once polygamy was not sin. Our early Old Testament is full of it. But then light came. The loveliest family relationship possible to man rose like dawn over the horizon—one man and one woman loving each other so much that they did not care to love anyone else in the same way at all, and so threw around their children the affection and security of an abiding home. After that anything less was wrong. Always light makes the darkness visible.

This is the whole idea of sin in John's Gospel. All sin is the refusal of light. Jesus says in the fifteenth chapter: "If I had not come and spoken unto them, they had not had sin: but now they have no excuse for their sin." Just so! Christ by his coming created a whole new list of sins. They had not been sins before. They would not have been sins if he had not come, but now they were sins.

We constantly picture Christ as beautiful. He was beautiful, as light is, and there lies a difficulty—light shows things up.

Is it wrong, for example, to take vengeance on a personal enemy? Once it was not. Cicero was a good and conscientious man, but an enemy of his was killed in battle and a year and a half later Cicero was still dating his letters: "The 560th day after Bovillae." But not long after Cicero another kind of person came into the world who said: "Love your enemies," and in his life and death exemplified boundless, undiscourageable goodwill. And ever since, some men, at least, standing in the light of that life, have felt their vindictiveness condemned, until magnanimity has risen to great heights in some, saying even in the midst of a bitter war: "With malice toward none, with charity for all." Judgment is not so much being sentenced to punishment; judgment is being shown up by light. We sing "Walk in the Light," as though that were a glorious experience, but it is one of the most searching that any man can know. Ah Christ, in spite of yourself, just by being what you are, inevitably you are our judge!

The old story runs that a social worker, having tried in vain to persuade a slatternly family to clean up their home, brought to them the loveliest potted plant she could find and put it in their living room. There it sat in judgment on its slovenly surroundings. First they tidied up the living room to make it a fitter place for the new gift, and then the living room sat in judgment on the rest of the house, until they cleaned that up too. Beauty had come into the home and had condemned their slatternly ways. That was the judgment.

Whenever light comes anywhere, we at once begin being judged by the way we treat it. Tennyson sings:

> We needs must love the highest when we see it,
> Not Lancelot, nor another.

Alas, if that were only true! But it is not true. We need not love the highest when we see it. We can refuse to love it. So there it stands, judging us. Where is that happening in our lives today?

Consider, in the second place, that this truth reveals the deeper meaning of faith in Christ. The typical modern question about him is, What do we think about Christ? That is to say, we sit in judgment on him. We try to get all the historic data there is, to use our critical faculties as intelligently as we can, and so to make up our minds what we think about Christ. But whenever we come upon deeply Christian souls, always a profounder inquiry is present: not alone, What do I think about Christ? but, What does Christ think about me?

Forbes-Robertson, the actor, in his autobiography says that

[65]

in his London club there was a rather vehement atheist named Crow, who constantly voiced his disbelief in Christ until he was stopped by a quatrain, written by one of the members, that soon became the common property of all the club.

> We've heard in language highly spiced,
> That Crow does not believe in Christ,
> But what we're more concerned to know,
> Is whether Christ believes in Crow.

We are not denying the importance of that first question, What think ye of Christ? but all profound faith in him involves the second also, and a great transformation could take place in some lives here were they to pass over that line. See how we sit upon our little judgment seats, passing sentence on what you will, and saying even that we think so-and-so about Christ. But what does he think about us?

A few weeks ago Dr. Zinsser, one of the finest-spirited scientists of our time, fell on sleep. During his last years, as he faced death, he wrote his autobiography in the third person, as though it were about another man. He was an agnostic. He had no clear idea of God, or faith in him. Yet at the end he wrote this about himself: "He became more firm in his determination to see things out consistently along his own lines of resignation to agnostic uncertainty—as his father had done before him. Moving further away, therefore, from faith in any comprehensible conception of God, he yet grew closer in conviction of the wisdom and guiding integrity of the compassionate philosophy of Christ." So even the agnostic acknowledges the light that came in him, as though to say that the test of life would be to know what he thinks of us.

Once war was not sin. The light had not come. Even today on all sides of the battle line multitudes of men and women would say, I believe in Christ. But what if all of us together, out of every tribe, tongue, people, and nation, ruining with our insensate brutality the hopes of generations yet unborn, could genuinely face that higher judgment seat and ask, What does Christ think of us?

As for more private matters, somewhere in this congregation some individual needs this truth.

Let us now go further, to face a strange new aspect of our truth, namely, that when one thus thinks of Christ in terms of light, it is difficult to separate his activity as a judge from his activity as a savior. Light condemns, we have said; but light also saves; it is the source of every lovely and redeeming thing we know. So John says, on one side, as Dr. Moffatt translates him: "This is the sentence of condemnation, that the Light has entered the world," but on the other side, he says: "In him was life; and the life was the light of men." Here is a mystery, that condemnation of sin and salvation from it should come commingled together.

The trouble with all lesser ideas of judgment is that they are negative, unredeeming, crushing. They are like some unskilled psychiatrists who can take you all apart and tell you what is wrong with you, but cannot put you together again. The Eternal Arbiter on his judgment seat, concerning whom Jonathan Edwards preached his awful sermon on "Sinners in the Hands of an Angry God" until women fainted and strong men clung to the pillars of the church in agony—what redeeming thing can he do for me? That idea of judgment blasts the soul with terror and dismay.

Has someone here been thinking that the entire concept of judgment anyway is an outgrown superstition? No, my friend, we cannot get away with that, not in the new scientific world of the reign of law—immutable, irrefragable, cause and consequence linked in an enforced companionship that is never broken. A momentous doctrine of judgment is at the center of the whole scientific view of the world, so that while ministers have dropped it from their preaching, scientists everywhere have been taking it up, physicians, economists, sociologists, physicists all saying, If you do this, you will get that; "Whatsoever a man soweth, that shall he also reap." How terrific even our modern scientific ideas of judgment can be!

Then this New Testament idea appears, saying to us, Light comes into the world; it does show our evil up, make our darkness visible, leave us without excuse, but light is also life-giving. It shines not alone upon our sins, but upon our possibilities; it makes luminous not only the shadowed selves we are, but the finer selves we might grow to be; it convicts us not simply of our evil, but of our potentialities; it reveals the winter of our sin, but it makes possible our spring, for, being light, warmth comes with it. The very light that judges us, saves us—that is a great gospel.

These are dark days in which we are living now. But how do we know that they are dark? Because light has come. That is something. Until 5000 years ago, says Dr. Breasted, there was no such thing as social conscience at all, no light to make even the darkness visible. But now there is. There are Christian souls in whom Christ's way of living has been gloriously exemplified. There are Christian families where the beauty of boundless goodwill has made a heaven on earth. There are Christian friendships and communities where, being members one of another, we have proved that we never find our lives until we lose them in the larger life of the fellowship. Light has come that today both shows up this hideous madness of our fratricidal strife for the brutality and insanity it is, and, being thus our judgment, is the hope of our salvation too.

For mark this: When light once comes it stays. Recall in John's Gospel the verse as the King James version gives it: "And the light shineth in darkness; and the darkness comprehended it not." No, that is not what the Greek means. Listen to Moffatt: "Amid the darkness the Light shone, but the darkness did not master it." Listen to Goodspeed: "The light is still shining in the darkness, for the darkness has never put it out." That is what it means. There is a magnificent phrase in an old prayer which addresses God as the "true sun of the world, evermore rising, and never going down!" See the historic truth in that! Christ came, and they crucified him, but he was light, and you cannot stop that with a cross. Bach was forgotten for a hundred years after his death, but he was light, and that cannot be stopped by a century of neglect. Even a feeble light like the dawning idea that the earth may be round, at first only a pinprick of illumination, can at last conquer a world of darkness. How small a candle Columbus had when he first sailed west, so that President Lowell of Harvard used to say: "When Columbus set out he did not know where he was going; when he arrived he did not know where he was; when he returned he did not know where he had been, but all the same he discovered America." One of the most impressive aspects of the story of evolution is the gradual emergence of friendship, for example. How timid its dawn, hardly a thread of radiance on the horizon! How slow its spread—Ruth and Naomi, David and Jonathan, Damon and Pythias—a strange new radiant idea of what human fellowship might be, until Greece came to her glory, that ancient illuminator of the race, and Aristotle in his great work on "Ethics" devoted two books to friendship, which, as he said, "holds mankind together." It is amazing to see that wherever light comes it stays—long neglected, yet it stays, shrouded in eras of gloom, but it grows, alike condemning and saving, judging men's evil and widening the area of radiance amid the dark.

This fact of commingled condemnation and salvation in Christ, the light of the world, is the explanation of a strange contradiction in the Gospel of John. For one can put over against each other two sets of texts from that Gospel that seem to cancel each other out. On the one side are sayings like this: "I came not to judge the world, but to save the world," and again: "God sent not the Son into the world to judge the world; but that the world should be saved through him." So Christ does not judge the world. But then come sayings like this: "For judgment came I into this world"; "If I judge, my judgment is true"; "The Father . . . hath given all judgment unto the Son." So he does judge the world. There is a head-on collision! Yet the explanation is as plain as day. Christ is light. He cannot help judging the world. Being what he is, he condemns it. But that is not what his coming was all about. His mission is not negative—positive! not condemnatory—redeeming! He is the physician who can show you what is the matter with you in order to cure it. He came not to judge, but to save.

Do not get one side of him without the other! If you let him, he can be the most discouraging figure in all history. Who can go into his presence and not be condemned? But he is not a judge sitting on the bench; he is not a mere exemplar of the inexorable reign of law. To each of us here he can mean what he meant to Peter. For when Peter first faced him he felt and said the inevitable thing: "Depart from me; for I am a sinful man, O Lord." There he stood, judged. And Jesus answered: "Come ye after me, and I will make you—I will make you—fishers of men." So Pompilia, in Browning's "Ring and the Book," said of her friend:

> . . . Through such souls alone
> God stooping shows sufficient of His light
> For us i' the dark to rise by.

When Prayer Means Power

THERE are three ways in which men get what they
want—thinking, working, praying. Concerning the first
two no one has any doubt; if we are to fulfill our desires, of course we must think and work. But concerning the
third, doubts are plentiful. In many minds such baffling questions rise concerning prayer that that whole area of experience is nullified.

In part, this difference is due to the fact that thought and
work have not been ritualized. We are supposed to think
wherever we happen to be, to work wherever our tasks carry
us. These two ways of getting what we want run through the
common hours of every day. They are not centered in a
special building with a steeple on it, and we do not cast ourselves into a special posture, like kneeling, when we engage
in them. But prayer has been ritualized; it is associated with
sacred places, sacred practices, special moods, and special
postures. So for many people prayer seems a formal, conventional, technically religious performance that they do not
understand, and so they are left with only two ways of fulfilling their life's desires—they think and work.

Yet even casual consideration suggests that from such
lives something has been left out whose omission is a personal tragedy. Powerful personality is never created simply
by thought and work. Powerful personality has deep interior
resources of inspiration and intake. Call it what we will, we
find in every great soul something that goes beyond thinking
and working—inner receptivity, sensitiveness, and hospitality
to a world of truth and power higher than the self. Great
living is not all output in creative thought and work; it is

[71]

also intake, the openness of the soul to the Over-Soul, the quietness that can hear a still small voice, an inflow, as though, in William James' figure, we were bays open to a great deep where the tides rise. Everybody here knows that this third area of experience is real, not simply religiously, but psychologically, factually real.

One of the major tasks of the church today is to help people to recover and to make effective in their lives this third realm of experience, which is the realm of prayer. After all, that area of experience is no more intellectually mysterious than thinking and working are. There are philosophical problems involved in the process of thinking that never have been solved; there are theoretical questions about the operation of free initiative in working to which no one knows the answer; and there are profound mysteries in this inner enrichment and empowerment of life when the tides of the Over-Soul flow in. But all these three are factually real, and it takes all three to make a strong life.

Especially in these days we need them all. In this tremendous generation, of course we must think and work, but who of us does not feel that the more strenuous our thought and work become, the more we need that third realm of experience? Paul, in his letter to the Ephesians, called it being "strengthened with power through his Spirit in the inward man," or, as Dr. Moffatt translates that verse, "a mighty increase of strength by his Spirit in the inner man."

At the start, it may help some of us if we clear away certain common misunderstandings of prayer. Almost all of us as children start praying by asking for things. Prayer then is begging, and just as we use our fathers and mothers as means for obtaining what we want, so we try to use God, saying, Give me this or that. But when we grow up—if, indeed, we do grow up—that early, egocentric universe of childhood dissolves and we find ourselves in this vast cosmos whose God

is no errand boy of ours. So one boy who grew up in the last
generation described his experience:

> As wider skies broke on his view,
>   God greatened in his growing mind;
> Each year he dreamed his God anew,
>   And left his older God behind.
>
> He saw the boundless scheme dilate,
>   In star and blossom, sky and clod;
> And as the universe grew great,
>   He dreamed for it a greater God.

That greater God can no longer be an errand boy, prayer to
whom means saying, Bring me this or that.

In consequence, many modern people swing over to the opposite extreme. Prayer, they think, is merely autosuggestion.
It is purely subjective, a kind of psychological dumbbell ex-
ercise by which one raises one's own spiritual muscle. God
thus is left altogether out of prayer, and a man alone with
himself gives to himself, as it were, a spiritual massage. But,
my friends, that does not account for the facts. Ages ago
Isaiah described a fact when he said: "They that wait upon
the Lord shall renew their strength." And a few weeks ago
Dr. Alexis Carrel, one of our foremost scientists, described it
again: "Prayer is . . . the most powerful form of energy
that one can generate." All the way from Isaiah to Alexis
Carrel, ask anyone who ever entered into this experience
what its nature is, and he will say that it is not simply a man
alone tinkering with himself; it is more like a man gone spiritually dry within, who far down in his soul clears away the
clutter of impeding obstacles until the cool water of a rising
spring, whose sources are far beyond himself, wells up to
refresh and reinvigorate his life. To use a modern figure,
prayer is plugging in on a current whose sources are cosmic
and not simply individual, a current that brings light and

power. That is the way Professor Wieman of the University of Chicago put it: Prayer is completing the circuit.

This then, in general, is what we mean by the third realm of experience necessary to great living. It is not begging God, as though he were our errand boy; it is not self-isolated auto-suggestion. It is an inner openness to the Spirit from whom comes, in Paul's words, "a mighty increase of strength." What, then, are some of the elements that enter into this experience?

For one thing, if we are to get it we must deeply feel the need of it. In all great matters the sense of need must precede the discovery of the experience. Of what possible use to some of us is the higher mathematics? Most of us can go on month after month and never think of the higher mathematics. But were we bridge builders, trying to throw a great span across some river like the Hudson, then we would have to have the higher mathematics.

So some kinds of persons feel no need of prayer. They can think a little and work a little, and get by. That is all they want of life. But they are not the persons who most have elevated and dignified the human race. Out of that group who feel no need of this third realm of experience, we never get our great musicians, saying with Handel about the "Hallelujah Chorus": "I did think I did see all Heaven before me, and the great GOD Himself"; we never get great prophets, saying with Ralph Waldo Emerson: "When I watch that flowing river, which, out of regions I see not, pours for a season its streams into me, I see that I am a pensioner"; we never get anybody remotely like Christ, saying: "I am not alone, but I and the Father." Such creative souls did think and work, but the deeper secret of their greatness was that far within themselves they knew how to complete the circuit and become the media of liberated power.

In ordinary life two experiences call out the conscious need of this deep kind of prayer—being up against something too much for us, and undertaking something too hard for us. If someone here is not up against something too much for him, or is not undertaking something too hard for him, the chances are that he will not know what we are talking about and will not care. What, to him, is all this higher mathematics? But can it be that in these days that is true of anybody here?

The question is often asked whether there is now afoot in this country a return to religion. No general answer seems possible, but here is a typical individual whom I meet more and more frequently. He has been conventionally a Christian, believing in God, thinking the church a good thing to belong to, valuing his Christian heritage, and it may be hard at work on many Christian tasks after the fashion of those women whom Jonathan Swift once described, who, "out of zeal for religion, have hardly time to say their prayers." But today such merely outward and expressive Christianity is to this individual not enough. He is up against something in this terrific world and in himself, and to meet it he must be something that he now is not. He faces, as never before, the need of inward resources of strength for daily life. He is thinking and working as hard as he can, but such thought and work are life's branches, the expression and output of one's self, while rootage is his need—not more branches but rootage—by which life strikes deep into the solid earth and draws vitality and strength from unfailing sources. I have seen some remarkable transformations of life in this congregation recently, in people who for the first time have discovered what that kind of experience can mean: "A mighty increase of strength by his Spirit in the inner man." They needed it.

For another thing, if we are to gain this kind of experience, we must not only need it, but clearly see that it cannot be achieved merely by trying hard. The common property of thinking and working is to try hard. We put our wills into our thought and work. But now try your will out in this deeper realm, where the profound issues of your soul's life

[75]

are concerned. Will to have resources of inner spiritual power that make you adequate for life! Will to have what Wordsworth called

> . . . central peace, subsisting at the heart
> Of endless agitation!

Concentrate on the matter, and, focusing your volition, will to have a mighty increase of spiritual strength! Where will such futile straining of volition get you? For here is a basic psychological fact about every one of us—we cannot will such experiences of inner enrichment and power. They do not come by trying, but by another method altogether: "Spirit of God, descend upon my heart."

To be sure, we may have to put our wills into it in order to get to Carnegie Hall on time. We may have to think hard and work fast to make the schedule click. But when now we are in Carnegie Hall, and a glorious symphony is being played, if all we can do then is to try hard, we might just as well not have come. That occasion, like all supreme occasions, calls for another realm of experience—receptivity, spiritual hospitality, the sensitive and understanding openness of the soul to the Over-Soul, the capacity to let the tides flow in when the sky calls to the deep. And if someone says, That is easy; being receptive and responsive is a simple matter, I say, No! It is a thousand times easier to be the kind of person who can hustle, put his back into it, and get the things that trying hard can get, than to be the kind of person who also can complete the circuit until he becomes a medium for liberated power.

What mature person can escape facing this problem sometime or other as the most practical issue in his life? Soon or late, life confronts every one of us with situations that cannot be handled well merely by trying hard. In a crushing grief, an irretrievable bereavement, is there nothing one can do except try hard? In an overwhelming temptation, when the emotional floods are too strong for our volitional resistance, is there nothing to do except try hard? In a day of world-wide catastrophe on a shaken earth, where no one can see a week ahead, is there no source of steadiness, no fountain of fortitude and courage, except trying hard? The phrase "practical Christianity" has generally been associated with activity, doing something useful and serviceable. I agree. That is practical Christianity. But there is another aspect of Christianity that for ages our fathers and mothers have called prayer, from which at their best they have gained interior resources of spiritual power that enabled them to carry on when carrying on was hard, and that in days like these is practical, if anything is. It is not begging God for things; it is not a man's tinkering with his own soul; it is inwardly establishing contact with a resource of power whose endless supply comes from a great deep. "The water that I shall give him," said Jesus, "shall become in him a well of water springing up." My soul! That is practical.

Consider still another element in this experience. If it is to be real, we must apprehend the fact that when we are alone we are not alone. This is one of the most profound and mysterious facts in human life—the consciousness that, being alone, we are not alone. We may well see in the Garden of Gethsemane a picture of a universal human experience. Jesus left the world outside the Garden gate; he left the major group of his disciples at the Garden gate; he left his three closest friends within the Garden gate, and then in solitude he went out under the olive trees—

> Into the woods my Master went,
> Clean forspent, forspent.

But there, alone, he was not alone.

Explain that experience as we will, it cannot be explained away. Elijah amid the loneliness of the desert all the more clearly hearing the still small voice; Socrates ascribing all that was worth-while in his life to the guidance of his inner angel; Epictetus, the Stoic, saying: "When you have shut your doors, and darkened your room, remember never to say that you are alone; for you are not alone, but God is within"; Jesus saying: "Enter into thine inner chamber, and having shut thy door, pray to thy Father . . . who seeth in secret"—there is a fact of human experience, antedating and outside the Christian tradition as well as within it, not to be explained away. And if someone says that this is an ancient matter, that will not do.

> Thou Life within my life, than self more near,
> Thou veiled Presence infinitely clear,
> From all illusive shows of sense I flee,
> To find my center and my rest in thee.

That is modern.

Here, indeed, is the truth that Professor Whitehead of Harvard was dealing with when he said: "Religion is what the individual does with his own solitariness." Well, what do we do with our solitariness? What do we make of this mysterious inner companionship, this sense of presence, this strange effect of solitude that makes a still small voice more audible? Some of us are not making much of it, but possibilities are there to which no man knows the limit. The major gift of science to the world is a mighty increase of power. Did science then create that power? Not a bit of it! Science discovered that power in the universe and set it free. Science found out the conditions, fulfilling which, the endless dynamic forces of the cosmos are liberated. Electricity is none of man's making, but man has learned how to fulfill the conditions that release it. Atomic energy is a force that man did not create, but that some day man may liberate. Man by himself is still a puny animal; a gorilla is much the stronger. Man's significance lies in another realm—he knows how to fulfill conditions so that universal power not his own is set free. The whole universe as man now sees it is essentially a vast system of power waiting to be released.

In the spiritual realm this is what prayer means. Prayer is inwardly fulfilling conditions so that power is released. I do not believe in miracles in the old terms of broken or suspended law, but I have to believe in these scientific miracles, incredible things done by science through the releasing of cosmic power; and I have to believe in personal miracles, incredible things happening in people and to people and for people who have liberated the divine resources. Listen to Dr. Hadfield, one of the leading psychiatrists of England, describing his failure in trying to cure certain nervous patients until he brought to bear on them, he says, "faith in the power of God which is the substance of the Christian's confidence and hope. Then," writes Dr. Hadfield, "the patient has become strong." So he wrote a book entitled *The Psychology of Power*, that might be called a psychiatric sermon on our morning's text. For the old experience at the heart of great religion is going on still in those who discover that when they are alone they are not alone.

To play fair with our subject, however, we must note one more element in this experience. It is not simply comforting, reassuring, enriching, empowering; it is also searching and demanding. Someone here, up to this point, may have resisted the impact of this sermon on himself, saying, After all, what mankind needs today is people who will put their minds to the task and go out and do something for the world. Surely, mankind needs that. But who of us does not know what it means to face a situation where we cannot do much for the world until, first of all, we have done something with ourselves? The longer an orchestra plays, the more it needs to be tuned up. The farther an airplane flies, the more it requires ground service to put it into shape again. There is no evading that law in any realm. When an orchestra or a personality is out of tune, it cannot do anything well for others until it has first done something with itself.

At that point, the profoundest experience of the race has been that there are regenerative forces, not within our power to create, but within our power to appropriate and assimilate. That is true about our bodies. The days come when we cannot physically do anything more for the world until we have done something with ourselves. We are played out and done in. Would any physician say to us then, Think it through and work it out; hard thought and labor are what you need. But it is hard thought and labor that have depleted us. Now we must have intake. Now we must re-establish relationships with sunshine, fresh air, and the open country, and drink in what we never could create, but can appropriate. Why do we try to live as though that universal law, obvious in our bodies, were not true also in our souls?

Nevertheless, when that experience is translated to the spiritual realm, it is not simply comforting and reassuring, but searching and demanding, too. In that deep and inner companionship where we face the still small voice and seek to be made right within, costly and sacrificial things often must be done. Before Niemoeller faced Hitler, we may be sure that Niemoeller faced God. Before he did what he did do for the world, he had to do something with himself—and it was not easy. I am not promising anyone ease and comfort only in this profound experience of prayer. Jesus did something for the world on Calvary, but behind that lies his experience in the Garden, where he sweat blood, praying, "Not my will, but thine, be done!" Whatever form this inner communion takes, this is true: No powerful personality ever brought saving help to the world without this third realm of experience within him. All through this congregation, made up of people who spend their days thinking and working, this problem runs today. We are not going to do what we could do for the world until, far within, we have done something with ourselves.

If that regenerating, re-empowering experience is to be ours, then we must give God a chance. We said at the start that one reason why thought and work seem real and prayer seems unreal is that prayer is ritualized, and thought and work are not. But that is not the whole truth. Any serious thinker does have special times of seclusion and quiet which he gives to thinking. Any serious worker does have special places and methods by means of which his work gains competence. Many of us, however, vaguely and in general agreeing with what we have been saying this morning, never give the inner companionship of the divine Spirit any special time. Less and less frequently we nourish it with worship, deepen it with reading, enrich it with meditation. John Owen lived in the seventeenth century, but one could almost think he had airplanes in mind when he wrote: "When Christ comes . . . upon the soul, he hath no quiet landing-place."

Personally, I should hate to live through days like these without the deep experience of divine companionship, and of available resources greater than my own. I know that the old Hebrew story about the three Israelites cast into a burning fiery furnace and walking through it without so much as the smell of fire upon their garments, is a tale and not actual history, but it is a symbolic tale and a true parable for our times. For this is written of them, that there walked with them through the burning fiery furnace one like unto "the Son of God." Who here does not need that experience? No furnace so fiery hot that there does not walk through it with us a divine companion, from everlasting to everlasting God.

Mankind's Deep Need—the Sense of Community

A SINGLE look at the world reveals how deplorably we are split up into fragmentary and conflicting individuals and groups. We often say that this is a crazy world, and in the literal meaning of that word it is true, for crazy comes from the French, *écrasé*, which means broken and shattered. We human beings ought to be a co-operative community, using the resources of this planet for the common good, and we are not.

In practically every service of public worship in the church we employ the Lord's Prayer, but how many have clearly noted one of its most outstanding characteristics: "When ye pray," say, "Our." "Our Father . . . our daily bread . . . our debts . . . our debtors." If one supposes that that communal emphasis is due to Jesus' intention that the prayer should be used only in public when the disciples were together, recall, upon the contrary, that he just had said to them: "When thou prayest, enter into thy closet, and when thou hast shut thy door, pray to thy Father which is in secret." Even there, where each was alone, each was to say not simply I, and mine, but our.

No more vital problem confronts humanity today than learning to say *that*. Human life is caught now between two contending currents—on the one side, the unifying forces that create proximity; on the other, the disruptive forces that prevent community. Is there any greater tragedy in life, whether in a family or in a world, than thus to have proximity without community? Sometimes on the Maine Coast the stormy wind blows in from the open sea at the same time that the tide flows out from the great tidal rivers that indent

[82]

the shore. Then let the boatmen look to themselves! There is tumult in the waters when those contending forces meet.

So today from one side come the countless agencies that produce proximity. Once Daniel Boone, the Western frontiersman, saw new settlers passing near his isolated cabin, and he asked the travelers where they were living. When the answer came that they were about seventy miles away, Boone turned to his wife and said: "Old woman, we must move; they are crowding us." As for nations, how great the distances once seemed, but now see how inextricably intertangled all peoples are! Proximity confronts the world. While, however, countless forces thus crowd us together, many tear us apart: economic forces, breaking us up into angry and competing groups; specializations, disrupting us into countless fragmentary tasks; racial antipathies, making us hate one another; national hostilities, making us fight one another; and through all these the moral factors, envy, covetousness, prejudice, and all uncharitableness, that prevent community.

In this situation, thrown together by some forces and disrupted by others, one thing is obvious. We cannot unscramble ourselves. We cannot go back to the old days of isolation. When a river has flowed down from the Adirondacks to Poughkeepsie, it cannot flow back again. There is only one way out of the situation—forward, through proximity into community. Moreover, at our best we ought not to want to go back. The most desirable blessings in human life come from fellowship, from beautifully putting things together with a right sense of their community. God cried to hydrogen and oxygen, Say our! and when they learned aright the principle of community, water came, and rain, and dew, and the sea, and the Yosemite. Creation itself, whether in God's nature or in man's art, consists in putting things together in a community. They say that in Wagner's opera *Die Walküre* there are a million notes, but what makes the opera

[83]

great is the way the artist combined these isolated items into a community and cried, Say our! What thus is true in nature and in art is true in human life. The loveliest fellowship man knows is a good home, and there we say not I, and you, but we, and our. From a solar system or an elm tree to a symphony or a stained glass window, or from these to a lovely family or a fraternal world, putting things beautifully together is the essence of creation and the glory of life.

Let us throw the light of this truth upon certain areas in our experience today, and first of all upon the discouraged mood of many who feel that human nature is so essentially selfish that we never can build a communal life. It is natural, they think, for man to say I, and my. Self-preservation is the basic instinct, they say; and to teach men on a large scale to say we, and our, is artificial, like teaching gorillas to eat at table with a knife and fork; you can do that with a few gorillas, but it does not go deep—still, they are gorillas. So man, behind his superficial co-operation, they say, is still an egocentric animal, saying I, and my! To which I answer, Do you really think that that is a complete statement? One need not minimize the power of egocentricity in human nature to think that statement unbalanced. Alongside this deep-seated selfishness in man, just as deep-seated and original is something else—the need of comradeship. A lonely child, wanting companions, said once to his mother: "Mother, I wish that I were two little puppies, so that I could play together." That childish remark is, nonetheless, psychologically profound. Said the old Latin proverb: "One man is no man at all."

What, for example, is the basic element from which, so the anthropologists say, stems out practically every characteristic factor in human life? Language. This it is, they say, which marked evolving man off from the animals and blazed the trail of his ascending life. And what is language? It is man's persistent endeavor to escape from his solitariness, to discover a world of companions, to create a device of communication so that he may have comrades with whom he can think together, speak together, play together, plan together, and build a communal life. That instinct of comradeship is as deep-seated and original in man as is his selfishness.

Indeed, before man, it began among the animals. Listen superficially to the animals, and you might suppose that they were saying, There is barely enough food to go around; what I get you lose; what you get I lose; there is between us an unavoidable antipathy; we are natural enemies. But lift your thought even a little, and it is as though the animals were saying, It may be we were mistaken; it may be that our mutual antagonisms are superficial and our common interests profound; it may be that if you and I were blended into we, we could do more for all of us together than either you or I could do for each of us alone. So bees hive, and ants build colonies, and birds flock, and wolves hunt in packs. The solitary ichthyosaurs, the giants of the primeval slime, have perished, but the birds, the bees, the ants, have survived—the co-operators, who learned to say Our.

Shall we human beings, then, say that we are so selfish we cannot build a communal life? Shall we not rather say that selfishness itself leads us to a communal life? We want physical health for ourselves, but that is no longer an individual matter alone but a communal matter. Epidemics know no boundary lines. We can have health only if the community shares it. Our deepest needs are of that quality. From good drinking water, which is not a matter of our individual wells but of the communal reservoir, to the morals of our children, which are not the fruit of our influence alone but of the whole bent and trend of the community's life, our self-interest and our sense of community involve each other. We want economic prosperity, but this last decade must have shown us that we cannot have it unless it is shared by the whole mass of the consuming community. We want peace; our individual lives are torn by this war, and our children's world is threatened by its impending consequence; but we cannot get that alone as individuals or as nations—that is a matter of building a world community. Let no man say we are too selfish to get a communal life! Let him say, rather, that if our selfishness has any intelligent understanding of the realistic facts, it will lead us to a communal life. We cannot have anything we want most unless we share it. We cannot be saved at all unless we are saved together. We are one body with many members. We had better say Our!

Let us throw the light of this truth upon another area of our experience—our religion. For here is a major shame, of which we Christians ought to repent: Whereas religion ought to help unify men, it divides them instead. An honest preacher would not wish to go further with this subject without facing that fact. Someone, hearing this plea for community against human alienations and estrangements, may well be saying, So! but what the preacher represents—religion—is one of the worst causes of discord in the world. "Physician, heal thyself!" Have not the worst wars been religious wars? India today might be free, if only the Hindus and the Moslems could get together across their embittered religious lines. Remember the Irishman, weary of the long feud between Catholics and Protestants in his country, who cried: "Would that all Irishmen were atheists so that we could live together like Christians." As for America, look at our religious divisions spoiling fraternity. Wanted: a religion that will stop accentuating human alienations, and help the world say Our! "Our Father . . . our daily bread . . . our trespasses"!

How familiar is the kind of person in whom religion instinctively results in his saying I, and my—*my* church, *my* doctrines, *my* prejudices—and then, looking across the boundary to folk of another tradition, he says They—*they* with their mistakes and falsehoods. But once in a while we meet a man whose religion is of another quality and consequence, who, dealing with any human life, Catholic, Protestant, Jew, Hindu, or Moslem, shows an inclusive spirit that says Our.

Commonly when this plea is made for magnanimity, inclusiveness, generosity in religion, some think that it is a plea for a thinned-out faith of surrendered personal convictions. Upon the contrary, it is a plea to get down to the two basic convictions of all great religion. What are they?

First, one God! Sometimes I think I will stop preaching about everything except monotheism. It is basic. Everybody says he believes it, and practically nobody does—not really. Most people seem to think that monotheism moves chiefly in the intellectual realm—that it is a philosophy. But that is historically false as to its origin, and morally shallow as to its consequence. Monotheism came up in the Old Testament out of social struggle, racial antipathy, and war. It was the insight of great prophets proclaiming that across all human alienations there was one God, and every son of man his child. "Have we not all one father?" cried the prophet. "Hath not one God created us? why do we deal treacherously every man against his brother?" That is monotheism. Across all lines that men have drawn, it goes, saying first of all and deepest of all: "Have we not all one father?"

The other basic conviction in great religion is the value of every personality. Some kinds of individualism break life up into fragments, but not this kind of individualism, Jesus' kind, which reaches beneath all divisions and lifts up every life, whether Jew or Greek, Scythian, barbarian, bond or free, saying, You are a child of God, a person of infinite value. That breaks down all boundaries and opens the door to a universal humanity. How desperately we need that kind of religion now. Almost every other influence in life makes us think of people in fragmentary groups. The two sexes, old and young, employer and employee, white and black, rich and poor, educated and uneducated—how split up we are! And then, to have a religion that not only accentuates these differences but furnishes a whole new category of sectarianisms and partisanships is tragic. Great religion goes down beneath all these divisions, lifts up every man into the light, saying, You are a son of the one God, and a brother in the one family.

When we plead for that kind of religion, we are not pleading for a thinned-out and washed-down faith of surrendered convictions. We are pleading for a religion that has gotten itself grounded on a firm foundation, sustained by the two pillars that upheld the whole structure of Christ's life—one God, our Father; every man sacred, our brother.

Let us turn the light of this truth upon another area of our experience—democracy. Democracy consists in saying Our. That is what it is. Autocracy says, My government; democracy consists in all the populace saying, Our government. The despot says, My people; democracy says, Our people. Today we are seeing democracy assailed by powerful enemies from without, but still I suspect the graver dangers are within. Our democracy is deplorably broken up into competing and estranged groups—economic, social, racial, industrial, religious. The splintering forces are dominant. One feels the granulation of American life. No attack on American democracy from without can ever wreck it unless within we forget how to say Our!

If within our democracy we are going to save ourselves from this peril, there must be some major shifts of emphasis in our American life in these years ahead.

For one thing, concerning the family. It is in a good home that we human beings first of all learn to say Our. A family does not start with an individual but with a trinity—father, mother, child—each one saying not so much I, and they, but we, and our. We cannot have a nation of communally minded men and women, taking within the compass of their care the needs of others as though they were their own, unless we have a nation of good homes, where that spirit gets its initial start and its vital nurture. I sometimes wonder whether we are not going to see a movement of reaction on the part of womanhood against some of the major trends of this last generation that have carried many women far away from home-making, in one of the most significant migrations in all history. I would not surrender a single gain of all the many that have been won this last century by woman's strike for freedom to enter every realm of human endeavor and prove her mettle. But today the deep necessities of our social life, and the profound, inalienable needs and aptitudes of womanhood itself, suggest a compensating movement of balance and counterpoise. One way or another, we must exalt the home— the most indispensable unit in our society. For everybody who ever has learned really to say Our, learned it in the first place as Jesus did in Nazareth, in the holy family.

If we are to save our democracy from this inner granulation, we must have another shift of emphasis, from a too great content with the motive of private profit, to a more inclusive care for the economic well-being of the whole community. How terribly our financial inequalities split us up into antagonistic groups! Sometimes I think it sheer hypocrisy on Sunday morning to repeat the Lord's Prayer here— "Our daily bread." Every significant economic movement in the world today is dealing, one way or another, with this problem—how to escape the old, out-dated, too-individualistic, *laissez faire* economy, every man for himself and the devil take the hindmost, which splits us up into angry groups —how to find a way to meet our common needs together. Communism is about that, and socialism, and the co-operatives, yes, and corporate capitalism itself, gathering together industry in great units and distributing ownership. One way or another, economic proximity forces on us all the problem of economic community. Just because we hate communism, rightly fear it as a false and perilous solution, let us not forget the towering problem itself. Our democracy never will be safe until it is economic as well as political, until our daily business draws us together around common interests instead of splitting us apart, until all the people can really pray: "Our daily bread."

Whatever we do with our homes and our economics, there is still another area where we need a shift of emphasis. We must exalt at the heart of this nation a unifying spiritual tradition. Democracy can survive powerful centrifugal pulls, if it has the centripetal pull of a unifying spiritual tradition— speaking the same language, loving the same great literature, holding memories of the same past, believing in the same God, cherishing the same scale of moral values. My fellow citizens, look to that, if you wish to keep our democracy together.

When in the last century de Tocqueville, the French aristocrat, visited us, he expected to see democracy a failure, and to his amazement he found it working. He put his finger on this central cause. These Americans, he said in effect, amid all the things that divide and estrange them, have great areas in common—a common spiritual tradition, a common faith, a common scale of moral values—and when they debate their differences, they debate them within the area of an undergirding and inclusive community of ideas and ideals.

When this present war is over and the assault of communism and naziism on democracy from without is spent, still these problems will be left. O America, look to the things you have in common. You can be strong only as you learn how to say Our!

Finally, throw the light of this truth upon our private lives. We as individuals never can deeply help anybody unless we say Our. A mother smitten with blindness, appreciating the goodness of her son, phrased her gratitude thus: "It is not so much that he does things for me, as that he fixes things so that we can do them together." No deep personal need is ever met with less than that.

That is one reason why trouble often leaves a life more useful than it was before, for after facing hardship a man can lay his life alongside another life and say We, and our. A man in great despair came to see me some time since, and as he started on his story I recognized my own great despair, the deepest trouble that I ever met, suffered years ago. So, as he began to tell me how he felt, I said: "Don't you tell me how you feel; let me tell you!" So I drew for him a blueprint of all that was going on in his mind and heart. In amazement he looked at me and said: "My God, how did you know that?" So he and I were on common ground, and I could help him, saying, We, and our. Among your personal relationships are some people whom you so could help. They are on your wave length, friend! *They are on your wave length!* You could say Our, with them, if you would.

Some years ago a young man went down to Panama with a business group, fell into bad habits, drank too much, until his derelictions became too obvious to be winked at and the chief summoned him to an interview. The youth went up trembling. He had a wife and children back home here. He knew he well deserved to be fired. He was frightened. But someone who chanced to hear the conclusion of the conversation says it ran like this: "Son," said the chief, "we are not going to drink any more, are we?" "No sir," said the youth, "we are not." "And each week we are going to send so much money back to the wife and children, aren't we?" "By heaven, sir," said the boy, "we will!"

You can tell how fine a thing is by the qualities that it requires. What does it take in a man to say I, and they? Pride, conceit, vanity, callousness, selfishness—such qualities can say I, and they. What does it take to say Our? Humility, magnanimity, generosity, kindness, humaneness, unselfishness. You never meet a finer thing on earth than a person who thus incarnates the Lord's Prayer: "Our Father . . . our daily bread . . . our debts . . . our debtors . . . lead us not into temptation . . . deliver us from evil."

How to Stand Up and Take It

TWICE in the book called by his name, Ezekiel the prophet says, "The Spirit entered into me, and set me upon my feet." Certainly, Ezekiel needed that experience. He had been a youth in Jerusalem when the Babylonians came down on the city, utterly destroyed it and carried the most important citizens to exile in Babylonia. There he was, an exile amid the oppressive splendor of his conquerors, his own people uprooted, dejected, whipped, and wretched. And something happened to Ezekiel that put his name into history. He became one of the major creators of the new Judaism, helping to make possible at last the return from exile, the rebuilding of Jerusalem, the beginning of a new era in man's spiritual life. "The Spirit entered into me," he said, "and set me upon my feet."

There are two aspects to the relationship between ourselves and the world: one, what we do to the world; the other, what the world does to us. In prosperous times our major emphasis is on the first: we go out happily to do things to the world. But the time comes to all of us, as to Ezekiel, when the situation is reversed: the world takes the initiative and does things to us. Trouble, antagonism, disaster confront us, and the major question in our lives is whether or not we can stand up and take it.

Pretty much everything we care for most depends on stamina, fortitude, morale. Of course this is true about the nations at war. Hitler is right in this regard—the outcome of this war depends on which side cracks first. In America this issue may not confront us in so dramatic a fashion, but in this congregation now how much of our problem as individuals, as families, as citizens, as Christians, centers in the question of stamina! Can we stand up and take it?

Indeed, quite apart from the present crisis this experience is a permanent element in human life. No man escapes situations where all his chances of positive, creative living depend not alone on what he can do, but on what he can stand. Only so did Handel write his *Messiah*. Says his biographer: "His health and his fortunes had reached the lowest ebb. His right side had become paralyzed, and his money was all gone. His creditors seized him and threatened him with imprisonment. For a brief time he was tempted to give up the fight—but then he rebounded again to compose the greatest of his inspirations, the epic *Messiah*." So, whether or not that "Hallelujah Chorus" was going to be written hung in the balance there, teetered on the thin edge of doubt, until, in what looked like a hopeless situation, the Spirit entered into him and set him upon his feet. What he could do depended on what he could stand.

That kind of story has been endlessly repeated, so that Ezekiel is a parable for all of us. All around him his exiled people were lying down and going to pieces. Who could blame them? Shall men be asked to hope when there is no hope, to believe in the unbelievable, to think that out of such disaster any good can come, that folk thus ruined can once more be a power in the earth? So, lost faith, lost hope, lost morale were everywhere, until there arose in the midst of those exiled Jews another kind of character. The Spirit entered into him and set him upon his feet.

This morning we take it for granted that we would like a share in such stamina. Our instinctive admirations go out to it. These are difficult days and we know we need it. What goes on in the life of a man who has it?

For one thing, a man like Ezekiel certainly started by tackling himself. He could never have tackled that difficult situation as he did if he had not first of all tackled himself. That man had sessions with himself.

Long centuries separate him from us, but with regard to the matter we are thinking of now, time makes little difference. We know Ezekiel well. He had every alibi a man can have for cracking up and giving in. What kind of crazy, hopeless situation was that for a young man to face? He had hours of self-pity, when he felt endlessly sorry for himself. He had moods of resentment, when he rebelliously cursed the world and the day he was born into it. He had hours of bewilderment, when he could not see a step ahead, and in his bafflement cried, What is the use? He had moods of discouragement, black melancholy, into which he fell as into an abyss. Who does not know what went on inside Ezekiel? But something else too—ever and again a voice that cried, Nevertheless, you can play the man; stand up and take it!

Such a man we all admire. Human nature can be dreadful; especially in what it does, it is often dreadful. But our admiration is measureless for some people—plain, ordinary, everyday, undistinguished people—when we see what they can stand and still come up smiling. A minister recently asked an eminent surgeon how, in his experience, folk faced suffering and death. A surgeon ought to know. He thought for a moment and then answered: "Most of them act like heroes." Call it sportsmanship if you will; it is one of the things that fine sportsmanship teaches; deep in human nature there is a magnificent capacity to play the game through gallantly.

Here are two philosophies of life. One is determinism, saying that heredity and environment decide everything we are or do, so that we are

> But helpless Pieces of the Game He plays
> Upon this Chequer-board of Nights and Days.

The other philosophy is free will, saying that we can do anything we choose. Either one by itself is false. Determinism is not the whole truth; heredity and environment do not decide everything. And free will in the absolute sense is not true either; we cannot do everything we choose. Those two partial insights must be added together to get the truth. For when heredity and environment have done their utmost to a man, there still remains in every one of us this strange capacity to take what heredity and environment have done, to answer it, to make our individual response to it, to meet it with a distinctive rejoinder of our own, to stand up to it and do something with it. As another put it, we do not slap an alligator on the back and say, Be an alligator, old chap! We know he cannot help being an alligator. But we do slap a friend on the back and say, Be a man, old chap! for we are not sure whether he is going to be a man, and we know that he has it in him to be one if he will.

We may be sure, then, that Ezekiel started by having sessions with himself. Even victorious Babylon and his exiled people could not furnish an alibi for himself. Let us look to ourselves in these days! Many a man blames the world at large for his collapse, when the real trouble is within himself. For the ultimate hope of the world is in individuals who reproduce an old experience: "The Spirit entered into me, and set me upon my feet."

A second thing I am confident happened in Ezekiel. He saw that a difficult situation can positively call out a man's powers, educe from him capacities and faculties that pleasant and prosperous situations never demand, and so never produce. He saw that he could become a real man, not despite the exile but because of the exile. Real men and women are like trees on the Maine Coast—the south wind warms them, the sunshine nourishes them, the northeast gales strengthen them, the winter cold toughens them. All weathers go to make them.

I am concerned about America now in this regard. I belong with those who think that for us to become belligerents

[95]

in this war would be the greatest tragedy in the history of the Republic. From every point of view, realistic or idealistic, I am convinced that such belligerency would be supreme folly. At the end of every road of argument I follow stands a warning to the United States: "Stay Out of This War." But I am concerned about some of those who agree with me in that. I fear that their motive is primarily the hope of ease, of freedom from trouble for themselves, of perpetuating a comfortable *status quo*, a fallacious dream of happy isolation from the vast problems and disasters that confront mankind. That seems to me a fool's paradise. Belligerency or no belligerency, we are inextricably part and parcel of the world, and, soon or late, every evil that afflicts it is our evil, every catastrophe that befalls it is our catastrophe. He who expects ease and comfort is asking for what he has no right to, and what, I suspect, he will not get. One way or another we must take it, and the question is whether within ourselves we are of such quality that the more trouble comes, the more our powers are called out; the more difficulty rises, the more dimensions we discover in our characters; the more life demands stamina, the more stamina rises to meet it. That is good sportsmanship too; the harder the game, the more strength, fortitude, intelligence and skill let it pull out of you!

See then, what Ezekiel must have done within himself! He shifted the center of his life to a place where the difficulties he faced did not unmake him but made him. If a man is primarily after wealth, the world can whip him. If a man is primarily after ease, and comfortable pleasure, the world can beat him. But if above all else a man wants to be a man, then he can capitalize almost anything that happens to him. Remember the words of Sir Thomas Brown, the Christian physician: "Live unto the dignity of thy nature, and leave it not disputable at last whether thou hast been a man." Let any person seriously start with that desire paramount, and the northeast gales can strengthen his roots, the winter cold toughen his fiber. Everything that happens to him will leave him, as all his friends can see, more of a man than he was before, and, like Ezekiel, he will be the admirable person that he is, not alone despite the exile but because of the exile. No wilderness, no Moses! No exile, no Ezekiel! No cross, no Christ! The great souls have had their powers called out by the very troubles that they faced. How can one be a disciple of Christ without that quality? He stood up and took it.

Surely something else, however, went on inside Ezekiel. He saw that when God made him, God had put into him some qualities that were meant for just such difficult occasions, that he was fitted out by nature with certain basic psychological powers, if he only used them well, that could stand him in good stead in that evil hour.

Pugnacity, for example. How terribly we misuse it; to what bloody ends we let it run! Yet how indispensable pugnacity is, and to what high employments it can be put—this inner flare of combativeness that stands up gallantly to life's difficulties, saying, No, I do not propose to be whipped. Like every other basic instinct, pugnacity is an elemental endowment that ill used can ruin the world, or well used can help to save it.

One of the finest things about sportsmanship is that it channels pugnacity into helpful courses. A good game is a good fight. Sportsmanship is in part what William James asked for, a moral equivalent for war, using man's combative instincts, developing them, releasing them, controlling them, and channelling them in socially wholesome courses. Everybody needs pugnacity if in the face of life's difficulties he is to stand up and take it, and if today that iron string could be set vibrating in some discouraged life here, it would be worth-while having met together.

Certainly, no pugnacity, no Ezekiel, no Paul, no Martin Luther! Indeed, no pugnacity, no artists even like Millet.

Millet's *Angelus* is beautiful, we say. But in 1859 when the artist finished it, his situation was not beautiful. That year he wrote: "We have only enough fuel to last us for two or three days, and we don't know how we are going to get any more; for they won't let us have any without money." While Millet was painting *The Angelus*, his mother died, and when he could not raise the carfare to visit her upon her deathbed, he was near despair. While he was painting *The Angelus*, he toyed with the idea of suicide, and resisting it drew a sketch of an artist lying dead at the foot of his easel and a woman crying out, "Suicide marks dishonor!" How often beneath the loveliest creations of art, character, sainthood, and social service one finds this deep-seated, underlying, indispensable, but oft forgotten foundation, the combative instinct that refuses to give up the fight!

We who are pacifists wish some people would stop mixing up the two words "pacifist" and "passive." "Pacifist" comes from two Latin words, *pax* and *facio*, and it means peacemaker. It is a positive word, being true to which involves all the strong, intelligent, morally combative faculties we have. "Passive," however, comes from another Latin word altogether, *patior, passus sum,* meaning to suffer, to submit. These two words have no kinship; they are poles asunder. It was when Ezekiel was whipped that he was passive. But when the Spirit entered into him, and put him upon his feet, he joined the elect company of spiritual combatants concerning whom we sing yet:

> They climbed the steep ascent of heaven
> Through peril, toil, and pain.

Nevertheless, we have not told the whole story when we have said that the prophet tackled himself, saw that trouble could call out his powers, and tapped anew the deep resources of combative courage. Ezekiel believed that whatever happened, God was not dead. As one of the Psalms tells us, his enemies in Babylon cried in scorn, as some cry today, Where is now thy God? but still he did not believe that God was dead.

We have been living through a generation when a cautious skepticism has been cultivated as a virtue. We have wished above all else not to be credulous. But the world has always been saved in a pinch by people who believed in the unbelievable. Recall the days when our forefathers here were trying to build a united nation when it seemed impossible. A little over 150 years ago, in 1787, Nathaniel Gorham, delegate from Massachusetts, rose in the Constitutional Convention and said this: "Can it be supposed that this vast country, including the western territory, will, one hundred and fifty years hence, remain one nation?" Well, could it be supposed? That seemed as impossible to many then as an effective and peaceful federation of the world seems to many now. And then, as always in a pinch, the situation was saved by people who believed in the unbelievable. Moreover, habitually in history, undergirding such men's persistent endeavors, one finds strong faith in God. As Lincoln said about slavery, it will end "as sure as God reigns and school children read."

I feel sorry for people who have no faith in God, not so much theologically as practically sorry. For if there is no God, then some form of materialism is the explanation of the universe, and that means that we came from nothing save the dust, are going nowhither save back to it again, and the whole course of history on this planet is an accident of fortuitous atoms going it blind. Nothing in the end will come of it. That is no philosophy of life to empower man in days like these to stand upon his feet and confidently face difficulty, sure that it is everlastingly worth-while to do so. According to one of George Moore's novels, the Irish peasants, poor and starving, were set to building roads, not because the roads were needed but only to keep the peasants busy, and furnish an excuse for feeding them. So they built roads that ended in dreary bogs and served no useful purpose for anyone, and George Moore says: "The road which leads nowhere is difficult to make, even though starving men are employed upon it; for a man to work well there must be an end in view." That is true about life, and the curse of thoroughgoing irreligion is that it sets men to work on roads that ultimately lead nowhere.

When the Spirit entered into Ezekiel and set him upon his feet, be sure that he had caught a fresh vision of God and of his purpose for Israel. So Ezekiel belonged to something greater than himself. He who could not be strong for his own sake alone could be strong when he forgot himself and thought of Israel and Israel's God. What he could not be and do for himself, he could be and do for his people. God was not dead. His purpose was not finished. His people's tragic situation was not the last word. God builds no roads that lead only to dreary bogs with no outcome. Ah, Ezekiel, if you could see now how right you were, believing in the unbelievable because you believed in God, you would be amazed.

I challenge myself and you, my friends, to such a faith today. The world desperately needs it. The weight of history is on our side, when in the face of these present tragedies we still believe in the unbelievable because we believe in God. Our children's children will yet look back on us, thankful that we did not crack up, give in, and lose our faith, if we let the Spirit enter into us and set us upon our feet.

Nevertheless, one further matter is the climax of this experience which we are studying. Note how Ezekiel puts it: "The Spirit entered into me." This thing that happened to him was not so much something he did, as something that was done to him. He did not get it by willing it alone, by thrusting his volition after it, but by receiving it. The Spirit entered into him. He was played out, done in, all gone, and lo! in an hour of spiritual receptivity he opened his life to a power greater than himself that set him upon his feet.

The danger in a sermon like this is that it should seem to many an appeal simply to their unaided wills. Tackle yourself! it says. Let trouble call out your powers! Awaken the combative instincts that refuse to give up the fight! Believe in God and his purpose, still unconquered and unconquerable! But true as all this is, this is something we do, and for all our effort it can be ineffective unless it comes to its fulfillment in an inner receptivity, an awareness of available resources from beyond ourselves, as though the sea at flood-tide poured in and filled a bay, in a way the bay with all its effort never could fill itself. Ezekiel did not set himself on his feet. He was set on his feet.

At its deepest, this is what religion means to some of us. The basic reason why men and women lie down on life instead of standing up to it is that within themselves they run out of power. The ability to stand up and take it is a power question, and power is not something we get merely by blowing on our hands and willing it, but by opening ourselves inwardly to spiritual resources greater than our own, and appropriating them. The water that I shall give you, said Jesus, shall be in you "a well of water springing up." "Strengthened," said Paul, by God's "Spirit in the inward man."

Life is a difficult game. It is no place for a cry baby. To play it well and play it through takes stamina. And it is inspiriting to look back on history and see how the ostentatious conquerors rise, fall, and are forgotten, how imperial policies that once seemed everything appear nothing now in retrospect, while like mountains, seeming to rise higher the farther we recede from them, stand out the souls who had such inward resources that for mankind's sake they played the game and played it through. The Spirit entered into them and set them upon their feet.

The Means Determine the End

EVERYONE knows how commonly our high determinations peter out. We resolve that we will overcome some unfortunate habit, will have a lovelier family life, will deepen our friendships, will do better work in our vocations, or, thinking as citizens, that, God helping us, we will stay out of war. But such resolutions concern final ends rather than the means to them and our wills cannot deal directly with ends, only with means, so that, making idealistic decisions about ends and letting the means take care of themselves, we wake up to discover that the means have determined the ends.

That this is a live matter now in man's public, if not his private, life, must be evident to anyone who reads the current books. On every side one runs upon this proposition that the means determine the end, stated with urgency, almost as though it were a fresh discovery whose recognition and practical application were critically needed. A novelist, Aldous Huxley, writes a whole book about it. Publicists, like Gerald Heard, proclaim it, and from many diverse sources we are reminded that mankind is out for high ends—peace, security, justice, brotherhood, and what not—but the means used are not pertinent to the ends sought, and the means determine the ends.

When Jesus, beside the well at Sychar, told the woman of Samaria that he would give her living water to drink, she, misunderstanding, said to him: "Sir, thou hast nothing to draw with, and the well is deep." Today that could profitably be said to us. The objects of our dear desire do lie deep—international peace, economic security, social justice, inward spiritual resource, and profound Christian faith and life. To such ideal ends we profess devotion; but the means—there lies the difficulty. Sir, life says to us, thou hast nothing to draw with, and the well is deep.

To make this clear to our imaginations, consider two illustrations, one from public, the other from private, life.

First, Russia. Many Americans do not understand that what the Communist party in Russia started out to get was not an autocratic, dictatorial state, but democracy. The most widely-based industrial and political democracy in the world was communism's aim. Only temporarily would they use ruthless repression as a means, employ violence in the killing or the exile of minorities, and suppress liberty of speech and press! Temporarily, as a means, they would take a short-cut through undemocratic methods to reach a democratic goal. And in consequence look at Russia. Violence grows by what it feeds upon. The more you suppress liberty, the more you have to suppress liberty. The more you use tyranny as a method, the more you get tyranny as a result. So Mr. Chamberlain, twelve years a resident of Russia, thoroughly convinced at first that communism alone could save civilization, now sums up the matter: "I think the overwhelming weight of historical evidence is to the effect that the means determine the end, and that an idealistic goal, pursued by brutal methods, has a tendency to disappear from view."

We Americans need to learn that lesson by heart. We never can get peace by unpeaceful methods, or democracy by undemocratic methods, or liberty by illiberal methods. Always, the means we use must partake of the quality of the goal we seek. It is a towering falsehood that the end justifies the means. The profound truth is that always and everywhere the means determine the end.

Turn now to an illustration from private life, the love that leads two happy and hopeful people into marriage. This is the common property of all marriages, that the goals the lovers have in view are beautiful. No two of them but aim at living out their lives in happiness and fidelity together. But how often these high and eagerly desired ends are missed, not because the aim itself is despised but because the means are mistaken! We cannot get lovely homes by unlovely means or faithful homes by unfaithful methods. In a family the means we use must partake of the quality of the goals we seek. And sometimes the minister, guessing in advance that these two eager and romantic lovers do not understand that, wishes he could successfully warn them. Sir, he would say about abiding marital happiness, you have nothing to draw with, and the well is deep.

Let us then deal with this matter whose ramifications run out to all our public and private living.

In the first place, we start with ourselves in the church. Here is one reason for what Paul called "the foolishness of preaching"—when one makes a public address, desiring to stir the imagination and stimulate the finer emotions, ideals are much more thrilling to speak about than methods, just as a dining room is more kindling to the imagination than is a kitchen. The kitchen is the place of means, methods, techniques; the dining room is the place of ends and consequences. But in the church, too, the means determine the ends, and we should not let the foolishness of preaching blind us to the truth of this similitude in the spiritual realm.

For preaching can be foolish. It can appeal to man's finer emotions about ideals and goals generally agreed on as desirable, and the more eloquent the preacher is the more he is tempted to leave the matter there, satisfied with the momentary emotional effect. Today, for example, I could break into lyric utterance about the loveliness of childhood and mean every word of it. For childhood is lovely and to have children is one of the richest rewards of life. But most parents I know agree with that already. The trouble with most parents is not that they do not love their children, sacrificially wish them well, and desire to draw out from them the best

that's there. The trouble is that many parents do not feel all
that enough to take time and pains to master the means and
methods for carrying it out. The results are often disastrous,
for in the training of children, no matter how fine our intentions are, the means determine the end.

President Neilson, of Smith College, was once taken to
task by some commentators on the ground that in an after-
dinner speech here in New York he called mother love a
failure. I heard that speech, and what he actually said was
critically true. The trouble with mothers and fathers is not
that they do not love their children but that too often they
suppose loving their children will by itself train their children,
and so they mistake the fine-intentioned end for the inter-
mediate mastery of intelligent means. They adore their children but often they would not even join a parents' class in a
church to find out the wisest way to bring them up. As such
parents, full of love but empty of method, stand before the
unguessed possibilities of a new life entrusted to them, one
well could say to them, You have nothing to draw with, and
the well is deep.

To be sure, I feel as much as you do the shallowness of
what someone has called the "how to books," *How to Win
Friends and Influence People,* how to do this and that! Yet
the caricature should not hide the reality. What some of us
need more than anything else, in our private lives, our religious experience, our families, is to face the critical issue of
"how to."

A young minister came to see me some months ago in a
total collapse about his ministry. Now he says that all is
changed since that interview. What, then, did we talk about?
Not his aims and ideals. They could not be improved upon.
But he was like a man, who, setting his heart upon getting
from New York to San Francisco, had got on a train that
was going to Spuyten Duyvil. His methods had no effective

relationship to his ends. How many of us, do you suppose, are in such a case?

You can see where we shall lay our emphasis before this sermon is done. The popular talk about the simplicity of the Christian gospel, as though it were an easy and artless matter, as the old phrase had it, "to come to Jesus," is dangerous falsehood. In times like these to possess powerful spiritual life, "Hid," as the New Testament says, "with Christ in God," able to meet the storms and surmount the temptations of these troubled days, is not easy. That well is deep, and multitudes of people miss its living water not because of wrong ideals but because of mistaken or neglected means. They cry, San Francisco! when they say their prayers, but the daily methods of their living land them at last in Spuyten Duyvil.

In the second place, consider some special kinds of moral and practical peril we run into when we neglect this area of truth. In sharpest contrast with what we are saying stand the folk who say that the end justifies the means. A long and tragic history that idea has had. So Caiaphas doubtless thought that the crucifixion of Jesus was not ideal, but, fearing that Jesus would stir up the populace, and Rome resent it, he judged that "it was expedient that one man should die for the people." So the end, he thought, justified the means, even though they meant Christ's crucifixion. Nothing in the human record has been so abominable that it has not been defended by that formula.

Today we are dangerously tempted to surrender to it in public affairs. We Americans want two things supremely, democracy and peace. Those are desirable aims. Few things more worth serving invite man's public devotion than a just and effective democracy and a secure and honorable peace. Who among us does not want them? Well, then, if peace and democracy are so supremely desirable, is there anything we would not do for their sake? So we travel the old path worn smooth by the emotions of centuries until we say we care so much for democracy and peace that we will fight for them. Now, if by "fight" you mean wage war, I beg of you walk around that formula for a long time before you let it fool you, as it has fooled millions of our predecessors. Is war an effective method for gaining or defending either democracy or peace?

Once before we went into a war to make the world safe for democracy. Let no man impugn our motives. No nation ever had a higher aim in view. We, the people, by millions, were willing to make any sacrifice for that high aim. We started out to save democracy, and we finished in a world enjoying less democracy than there had been for generations. The reason is not difficult to see. War is not a democratic method. Modern wars must be fought under dictatorship. The day war is declared in any country, conscription starts, totalitarianism begins, liberty of speech and press is limited, and regimentation takes possession of the field. That is inevitable in any modern war. A nation that gets on the military train, crying, All aboard for the San Francisco of democracy, ends necessarily in the Spuyten Duyvil of dictatorship. The means determine the end. Were I to paraphrase Daniel Webster's speech, I should pray that when for the last time my eyes behold the sun in heaven, they may not behold it shining on the tragic spectacle of a great democratic nation that took the warpath to save democracy, and ended by itself being no longer a democracy.

Do not suppose that I think the problem easy, or that, because I am a Christian pacifist, I think any neat pacifist formula by itself alone covers the case. May heaven have mercy on all officials in democratic countries today, trying to handle wisely this desperate situation! But let us, the people, keep steadily in mind this law, as deeply imbedded in the moral world as the law of gravitation is in the physical: The means we use must partake of the quality of the ends we seek. We cannot get peace by unpeaceful means, justice by unjust means, democracy by undemocratic means. The means determine the end.

In the third place, let us note that in the recognition of this basic law lies one of the major secrets of strong personal character. Why have some of the world's failures been in the realm of character such great successes that they shine now like stars in the firmament of man's recollection? The almost prosaic reason is that they would not use evil means, that they steadfastly refused to do wrong that good might come. Could not Jesus have been a success—that is, escaped the cross, lived to a ripe old age, preaching impressively within limits of safety, and could he not have argued for that as an end so defensible in terms of long-time service that it would justify the compromise it cost? Jesus' greatness of character hinged on this matter we are talking of. He would not do evil that good might come.

Living is like running for political office. The candidate says to himself that he wants the office for a good end and will use it, when he gets it, for public service. But as a means he puts himself under financial and political obligations to people a public servant has no business to be under obligation to. So when, with all his high aims and fair intentions, he comes at last into the possession of the office he sought, he finds himself caught in the trap of his own methods, the means he used now imperiously deciding the end he serves. In how many lives has that kind of experience proved ruinous! In how many characters here is not that the temptation! It would be worth-while having spoken on this theme if one person were made to see that bad means are like a bad compass on a sea trip. I care not how lovely your intentions concerning the haven that you seek; that compass you are using as a means, day by day, will determine the end.

The mind of man is nowhere more full of self-deceit than here. Could we have talked confidentially with Judas Iscariot and Benedict Arnold the nights before their treacheries, they would have told us of fine ends in view that justified their betrayals. The pith and marrow of great character is that it looks to the quality of its means. Of one thing about us all we may be sure as we look ahead—we are interpreting what we are headed for in fine terms of high ideals and excellent purposes. But the means! Say to yourself what Wordsworth said:

> Him, only him, the shield of Jove defends,
> Whose means are fair and spotless as his ends.

Finally, let us come more closely to grips with this matter in reference to our Christian living. Why is that so unsatisfactory and ineffective? The trouble is that when it comes to genuine Christian living, fine in quality, radiant in influence, steady in difficulty, victorious in temptation, aware of inward resources of spiritual power, we applaud the ideal but we take no pains with the means of reaching it. This is true in every realm of excellence. Stand in an art gallery before some great picture and see the people pass by. How often, watching their wandering, listless, unkindled eyes, one thinks, You have nothing to draw with, and the well is deep.

One hesitates to make explicit the severe attitude toward oneself which this truth involves. Commonly we blame outward circumstance because our lives are not more rich. I am not belittling circumstance. It is tremendously important. It can be crushing. You may be sure that in a city like this there are at least three kinds of people who are not tempted to minimize the effects of circumstances—physicians, social workers, ministers. We see the disastrous result of evil environment too constantly to forget it. Nevertheless, there are multitudes of us whose poverty of spirit, whose thinness and unsatisfactoriness of life are not due to unfortunate circumstance. The main trouble lies within ourselves. We have nothing to draw with, and the well is deep. That is true not only of great books, great music, great art, but of the resources of spiritual power which God has made available in Christ. We cannot possess that merely by believing in it or accepting it as an ideal. We need constantly practiced methods—worship, prayer, quiet hours, directed reading, directed meditation, fellowship in the church, where the social forces of common aspiration come to our help. We must have something to draw with.

Some families here today, if they take this in earnest, will have to alter their manner of living. For when a Christian family comes to New York it faces often a momentous decision. On the one side is a way of living which I hesitate to describe lest I be unjust. What shall we call it? The night-club, cocktail-hour, sensation-seeking, light, superficial method of life, not necessarily bad but not good either, and on the other side is a way of living that really puts the Christian life, the Christian church, and the finest resources and interests of the community at the center of attention. One of the most tragic sights one sees—how often have I seen it! is a family moving to this city, keeping still the Christian name and the Christian ideals, joining the church and never consciously surrendering a single one of the old high aims and purposes, but surrendering to the practical day-by-day method of living that leads down, not up. Always the epitaph of such a family is foreordained: The means determine the end.

This is the reason why the tragic evils of our life are so commonly unintentional. We did not start out for that poor, cheap goal. That aim was not in our minds at all. Of all the men who land in Sing Sing, who ever made Sing Sing his goal? Not the ultimate intention but the means and methods used lead to our Sing Sings. That is why the road to hell is always paved with good intentions, and that is why I am not celebrating high ideals, lofty aims, fine purposes, grand resolutions, but am saying instead that one of the most dangerous things in the world is to accept them and think you believe in them and then neglect the day-by-day means that lead to them. Ah, my soul, look to the road you are walking on! He who picks up one end of a stick picks up the other. He who chooses the beginning of a road chooses the place it leads to. It is the means that determine the end.

The Modern World's Rediscovery of Sin

A TRAGIC fact lies behind the New Testament's understanding of Christ: "Thou shalt call his name JESUS; for it is he that shall save his people from their sins." So, like the Star of Bethlehem seen against the night, the very birth of Jesus is seen against the background of man's sinfulness.

In this regard a clear contrast exists between the Christianity of our fathers and the liberal Christianity to which most of us have become accustomed. To our fathers sin was a horrid reality, a deep-seated depravity in human nature in which from birth we all shared and from which only the grace of God in Christ could save us. The old theology was centered in that conviction, the old hymnology expressed it, and the old pictures of hell made lurid the endless horror of sin's consequence.

Liberal Christianity, however, has on the whole been complacent about human nature. Modernism grew up in an era when progress was in the air, with evolution as the process behind life and education as the means of liberating life. It was the time of fresh discoveries, idealistic hopes, alluring prospects, dominant optimism. So our liberal Christianity has everywhere been characterized by an ideal view of human nature. To be sure, there were failures to be outgrown, inadequacies to be overpassed, ignorance to be illumined, selfishness to be corrected, but no such tragic depravity at the heart of human nature as made Pascal call man "the glory and the scandal of the universe . . . a monster, even beyond apprehension." Now, however, we face a difficult era, with such cruel and depraved things afoot in the world as some of us have never seen before. I do not believe the old theology; I am glad many of the old hymns have been dropped from the hymnal never to return; the old pictures of hell are to me an incredible anathema. But how can one be content with this soft, sentimental, complacent type of liberalism that thinks comfortably of human nature? It is said that a modern teacher wrote an elaborate book on religion's meaning, and when his friends called his attention to the fact that in it he had not even mentioned sin, he said: "Oh well, there ought not to be any such thing." Say what we will about our fathers' incredible ways of stating the matter, they were infinitely more realistic about the facts of human nature than is such superficiality.

Today we and our hopes and all our efforts after goodness are up against a powerful antagonism, something demonic, tragic, terrific in human nature, that turns our loveliest qualities to evil and our finest endeavors into failure. Our fathers called that sin. If you have a better name for it, use it, but recognize the realistic fact.

Certainly, every path that man is traveling today leads to the rediscovery of sin. There is scientific inventiveness, for example. How full of hope for man's abundant life that once seemed! Here were gifts in endless affluence that he could use to build a better earth. But see to what tragic misuses they are put! We have achieved electric lights but they have not lighted the way to justice and brotherhood. We have mastered refrigeration but it has not cooled the angry passions of man's heart. We have built towering skyscrapers but they have brought us no nearer God. We have achieved giant power, but it never has been powerful enough to save a single man from his inner evil. Rather, we invent airplanes and get bombers, invent automobiles and get tanks, explore chemistry and get incendiary bombs, create world-wide intercommunications and use them to produce blockades and famines. We blame our forefathers for even believing in infant damnation, but we, as it were, with our organized starvation and our bombing of cities, have taken over the job ourselves, using for our purposes the very gifts that were to have saved us. There is something demonic in human nature that can use the best for the worst.

Or consider education. A century ago in Boston, Horace Mann believed that crime could be practically eliminated in this country by increase in the size and number of our tax-supported schools. Well, we have built tax-supported schools in size and number beyond anything that Horace Mann dreamed, yet we are not through with crime. Indeed, add up all that we spend in America on education. That is an immense sum. Add to that all we spend for churches. That is another great sum. Add to that all we spend for charity. That is another large sum. Yet when we have added them all together, we are told that crime in this country costs us $500,000,000 more than them all. Moreover, into that crime goes every educated ingenuity from which education was to have saved us. Here again the old proposition proves true that the worst calamities that fall on man come from a combination of high intelligence and low desires.

Or consider man's spiritual qualities: loyalty, responsiveness to great leadership, patriotism, the sense of community and fellowship. In themselves they are beautiful. Man has been saved from egocentric selfishness by his ennobling capacities to care for something other than himself in race and nation. Yet look across the world and see what this incomprehensible monster, man, is doing with them! Recently a Christian Japanese woman called upon me. She was one of the most surprised persons I ever talked with. She had just come from Japan and for the first time was seeing from an outside point of view what Japan is doing in China. She told me what one sees inside Japan—the unifying and adoring loyalty to the Emperor, the kindling consciousness of solidarity and community, the sense of Japan's sacred mission in the Far East, the high crusade to save the Chinese people from their false rulers, the aged and kindly mothers who arise in the early morning, even in winter, to speed with their prayers the brave young fellows going to the front. So all wars are fought, and the most damnable things on earth done, whether in China or here, not by stark evil only but by the finest qualities in us, twisted to unholy uses by this demon that our fathers called sin.

Surely our fathers were not shadow-boxing. We have mastered physical nature in ways they never dreamed, but we are still up against human nature. What to do about that? Physical nature is a realm of necessary law-abidingness, where we can trace cause and consequence and make ourselves masters of the outcome. But human nature presents us with something new and different—freedom, that high and terrible gift of freedom, that can take the holiest and make the worst out of it, and an inner wrongness that, so misusing freedom, brings to futility and grief the fairest hopes of men. I am sure that this view of human nature is the first step to a realistic outlook on what life is, and it can add the dimension of depth to our insights.

In the first place, it adds the dimension of depth to our thought of our social problems. All easy-going trust in social panaceas—as though, if we changed this circumstance a little here, or altered that environment there, or took a short-cut yonder, we would come to a happy social consequence—goes back to a radical failure to see that there is something wrong in human nature itself. If someone will not believe this because it sounds so much like the old theology, will you believe it if it is said to you in other terms by the new psychology? Early theologians called this inner depravity of human nature "original sin," and said we are all born with it. Freud calls it "the id," and he says we are born with it too. If you want to call this fact of primitive, selfish, and often perverted emotion, that makes war on ourselves and the world, "id," instead of "original sin," by all means do so, but recognize the realistic fact: A racial inheritance—Freud is right about that—rolling down from generation to generation, ruining all the fair hopes of men, and in the end the source of these tragic disappointments when our fine schemes of social reformation are wrecked.

How easily some people have supposed that the human problem could be solved! In 1893 Hiram Maxim, speaking of his new and terrible gun, said: "It will make war impossible." That is all he knew about human nature. In 1892 Alfred Nobel, the inventor of dynamite, said that his new dynamite factories might end war sooner than peace congresses. That is all he knew about human nature. This incomprehensible monster, man, has it in him to use for wholesale destruction things a thousand times worse than dynamite and Maxim guns.

Or carry our thought to a higher level. We tender-hearted liberal Christians, brought up in the humane tradition, deeply feeling the ills of the underprivileged, are constantly tempted to suppose that if only everybody were privileged that would solve the human problem. Now, I too hate these inequalities that curse our life. They are the shame of our civilization. I want decent housing for everyone, decent subsistence for all. No man worthy of the name can be content until we have a more equitable distribution of this world's goods. But as we hope to escape one of the most tragic disappointments in human history, let us not suppose that that alone will solve the human problem. It is difficult to be a good Christian if one is underprivileged, but do you think it is necessarily easier to be a good Christian if one has all the world's goods? Does the fact that one can live on Fifth Avenue or Park Avenue or Riverside Drive necessarily mean the solution of those elemental problems of human nature that, like God himself, are no respecters of persons? If you think it does, then you do not know some people on Park Avenue, Fifth Avenue, and Riverside Drive. We are going to run from one social disappointment into another until we see that behind all outward evils there is a need in human nature that only a profound spiritual renewal can meet. That is true not only of blind Bartimæus begging by the roadside but of Zacchæus in his counting house and Dives in his palace. That is true not only of a coarse woman of Samaria coming to draw water from the well; it is true of Nicodemus in his study, needing to be reborn.

Recognition of this tragic fact about human nature, far from being the beginning of discouragement, is the beginning of hope. The man who is afraid to face it shows himself unprepared to confront the realistic facts. But the New Testament, which from beginning to end faces it, far from being discouraged, is the most radiant and triumphant book in the world. For the New Testament started with the tragic fact: "Even when we were dead through our trespasses." That is where it started. And then it saw that a saving power had been released into the world through Christ, which could redeem individuals and move them over until they were no longer part of the problem but part of the answer, and then could take groups of people and move them over until on the whole they were no longer part of the problem but part of the answer. In that the New Testament saw the promise of a redeemed manhood. It started with the night and then it saw the Star and was glad. That is the realistic approach to life. As another put it: "To expect a change in human nature may be an act of faith; but to expect a change in human society without it is an act of lunacy."

In the second place, this truth adds the dimension of depth to our thought of ourselves. No man understands himself until he has seen that he shares this inner wrongness, from which he needs to be saved. Once, runs the old story, there was a religious hermit, so holy that the evil spirits sent to tempt him were discouraged. They could not break him down. They tried the passions of the body and failed, the doubts of the mind and failed again. Then Satan himself came and said to the evil spirits: "Your methods are crude. Permit me one moment." So, going to the holy hermit, Satan said: "Have you heard the good news? Your brother has been made Bishop of Alexandria." That got him. He, a poor hermit, and his brother, Bishop of Alexandria! Jealousy swept over him like a flood. He could stand almost anything except the success of his brother. What we are saying is that no man understands himself until he has faced the presence in himself of some such share in what our fathers called "original sin."

In this regard we often deceive ourselves because sin can take such a high polish. Sometimes sin is gross and terrible. It staggers down the street; it blasphemes with oaths that can be heard; it wallows in vice unmentionable by modest lips. Then prosperity visits sin. It moves to a finer residence; it seeks the suburbs or gets itself domiciled on a college campus. It changes all its clothes. It is no longer indecent and obscene; its speech is mild; its civility is irreproachable. But at heart it is the same old sin, self-indulgent, callous, envious, cruel, unclean. As anybody may easily observe, sin takes on a very high polish.

The tragedy in all of this is that my sin is not simply mine individually but my share in the corporate evil that is destroying the hopes of the world. For selfishness, carnality, cruelty, are not merely individual; they roll from generation to generation, spoiling all man's hopes, and my curse is that I can be part of this major problem of the race instead of part of the answer. Indeed, by nature I am part of the problem unless I am saved from being that by some power of spiritual renewal. All seers have said this. I would almost venture that every major work of literature in the world's history has been centered in this truth. Start with the great tragedies of Greece and think your way down through *Macbeth, Othello, Hamlet, Faust, Les Misérables, Romola, The Scarlet Letter, Anna Karenina,* what you will. The great seers have faced the centrality of sin in human life, and our tragic capacity to be part of the corporate evil that spoils the world.

The recognition that this is true about man, far from being the beginning of discouragement, is the beginning of hope. This is what the New Testament is all about, trying to get man to take a serious view of himself and then seriously seek a cure for his malady. Go through this highly respectable congregation here and who of us does not need this? For some here have sinned secretly and are afraid it will be found out publicly, and their lives are anxious, wondering if and when the ambush may be sprung. And some here have sinned and they cannot forgive themselves, and, like a bell buoy tolled by the restless motion of uneasy waves, remorse is tolled by their tossing consciences. And some here have sinned and sin begins to grow habitual, so that, as one plus one plus one adds up an accumulating sum, sin mounts and mounts in size and in control. And some here have sinned and have tried to keep the consequence to themselves and they cannot; it overflows and hurts their family and friends, as though once more the innocent are nailed to the cross because of them. Every man or woman here understands what I am saying. This is not Greek to anyone. No one understands himself till he sees this. No one understands Christ's central meaning apart from this. It would be making earnest with the gospel indeed were we to take ourselves and his saviorhood thus seriously. As Clement of Alexandria said long ago about Christ: "He hath changed sunset into sunrise."

This leads us, in the third place, to note that our truth adds the dimension of depth not only to our thought of our social problems and ourselves but to our thought of Christianity and of Christ himself. Liberal Christianity in some of its forms has succeeded in reducing religion to little more than a kind of spiritual cosmetic, adding a touch of heightened color to a countenance not radically changed. For if one starts with a complacent view of human nature, religion inevitably becomes an addendum, comforting to some, reassuring to those who need it, but not an indispensable salvation. So men treat it as superfluous. But if what we have said today is true, then Christianity has a dimension of depth to it. It is an indispensable salvation from that inner curse that is wrecking human hopes.

Why should moderns shrink so from the word salvation? What is scientific medicine? It is salvation, and when a man takes the measure of disease and what it does to men, sees it flowing across the generations, bringing its recurrent miseries on humankind, he thanks God for the saving hope of surcease from pain, and cure for malady, that scientific medicine brings. Every major activity of man is concerned with salvation from human tragedy, and the Christian gospel has a specialty as real as scientific medicine. It came to save men from that inner wrongness that curses human life.

I should suppose we would feel the need of that today. The human drama is not playing itself out well and no mere shifting of the scenery will fix the drama up. Something profound must happen to the actors if it is to come out right. We need Christ's radical remedy for our radical disease: one God, high over all, in loyalty to whom we are saved from our ruinous idolatries, one human family of every tribe and nation, in devotion to which we are saved from our destructive nationalisms and racialisms, and within ourselves the gospel of forgiveness and power—those two, forgiveness and power—by which, one by one, men and women are transferred from being part of the problem to being part of the solution.

In these terrific days especially we should not be content with formal religiousness. Saviorhood is the essence of Christ, and to face our deep needs in earnest, to repent sincerely and seek forgiveness and power, to take seriously him who for our sakes suffered, the just for the unjust, that he might bring us to God—that would be entering into the meaning of the gospel.

The God Who Made Us and the Gods We Make

THROUGHOUT the Bible there are two ways of speaking about God that at first sight seem in direct opposition. On the one side is the theological affirmation, God is and he made us. On the other side is the psychological affirmation, We make gods and serve them. "In the beginning God created the heavens and the earth," so the Bible starts, but throughout its course we keep running on another point of view. "Where are thy gods that thou hast made?" says Jeremiah; or again: "Shall a man make unto himself gods?"

If this were only ancient history, we could let it lie, but few things go more deeply into our contemporary situation than this contrast between a theological approach to God—one deity who made us—and a psychological approach to those elements in life which gain our devotion and become our gods. God made us—that is theology. We make gods and worship them—that is psychology.

Much of the unreality of our religious experience springs from our failure to note this difference and face its implications. A friend of mine sometime since visited the Planetarium and came back deeply impressed by that visual exhibition of the universe's unity and order. "Man!" he said, "the word chance doesn't fit it! There's mind behind that!" So, he believes theologically in God. But does that necessarily imply anything about those inward deities that he really serves? Upon the contrary, that man conceivably might make drink his god, or lechery his god, or money his god, or nationalism, or race, his god. We theologically can believe in the God who made us, while all the time psychologically we are controlled and dominated by the gods we make.

Sometime since in a national poll 91 per cent of the ballots registered faith in God. One suspects that that average represents the American population as a whole. Man! they would say about this universe, the word chance doesn't fit it; there's mind behind that. Nevertheless, look at the American population! Do not all the political bosses believe in God? I never met a roaring, American militarist who did not believe in God. Sing Sing is not filled with atheists. Men who cherish bitter, menacing, anti-Semitism, one of the most malign influences in America, earnestly believe in God. And we Protestants would all consent: "I believe in God the Father Almighty, Maker of heaven and earth." This practical unanimity of consent to theological faith in the God that made us does not prevent our lives from being dominated psychologically by the gods that we make. Were Jeremiah to say to us again, "Shall a man make unto himself gods?" we should have to answer, Jeremiah, that is what we are doing all the time; there is no habit more familiar in human life.

This aspect of human nature, which is obscured for us because in our vocabulary the word "God" is restricted to the deity who made us, was very vivid to the early Christians in the Greco-Roman world, when polytheism was in full flower. Bacchus was not simply drunkenness; he was a god. Venus was not simply lust; she was a goddess. Mercury was not simply slick and crafty contrivance; he was a god. And Mars and the deified Caesar were gods, and all those major and dominating factors in life that take possession of men, control them, and call out loyalty, were deities in the Pantheon. The accumulated imagery of a rich mythology made easily vivid to those early Christians the situation we are trying to make plain to ourselves today—on the one side, the God who made men; on the other side, the gods that men make. Every day the early Christians could see gods that men made controlling the personal, religious, political, and international life of their time. The god question was critical with them. They had to choose between gods. Should they serve Bacchus or Venus or Mercury? Should they worship Caesar or become devotees of Mars? When instead they chose the God revealed in Christ, *that* was no mere matter of theology as so often it is with us, but was a profound inward, if you will, psychological matter that penetrated to the pith and marrow of their daily life.

The polytheistic language has now largely gone. Sometimes I think it is a pity. It is the only language that is fitted picturesquely to display what we confront in this modern world. To how many is the nation their real god—and that not alone in Nazidom. Let a man, indeed, look down inside his own life. Who really is God there? Commonly not the theological God, belief in whom we may have inherited or persuaded ourselves to by argument, concerning which the New Testament itself says: "The devils also believe, and tremble." Commonly some psychological god is the real one, claiming the honest-to-goodness allegiance of our lives. Until a man has faced the god question thus, he has not been serious about it.

Let us take a further step, and with greater precision try to describe those elements that constitute, in this deeper sense, a man's real god. Wherever a man discovers anything in life on which he relies, his central dependence and deepest satisfaction, and to which he gives himself, his central loyalty—that is his real god. Those two elements always constitute the essential psychological meaning of one's genuine god: one's central reliance and one's central devotion. "He restoreth my soul"—one way or another, a man soon or late says that of his real god. "Not my will, but thine, be done"—one way or another, a man says that to his real god. That is why we say that a man makes drink his god. It can mean his central reliance and his central devotion. That is why we say that a man makes science, or art, or music, or some humanitarian cause his god. It can become his main dependence and his main devotion. When the god question is thus described in inner and psychological terms, it is no matter simply for church on Sunday; it penetrates into the pith of every day's most common attitudes.

Indeed, let us light up this matter by considering what psychological atheism would mean. Theological atheism we often speak about. That means a materialistic philosophy that reduces the universe to the fortuitous self-arrangement of physical elements. But psychological atheism is much more intimate and penetrating. Psychological atheism means a day-by-day life that, whether its possessor believes in the theological God or not, never has found anything on which centrally it can rely, and to which centrally it can give itself. The psychological atheist has no God-experience within, no deep source from which he lives, no major loyalty for which he lives. That kind of life, where a man finds *nothing* that restores his soul, *nothing* that commands his devotion, is one of which it may be said that the man had better never have been born.

I should hate to be a theological atheist and think the universe a mere matter of chance, but if I had to choose, I had rather be that than a psychological atheist. Indeed, a whole sermon might well be preached about a religion for those people who cannot believe in God. There are such folk. They go to the Planetarium and return unconvinced. Even the order, unity, symmetry, law-abidingness and intelligibility of the cosmos leave them unpersuaded. They do not believe in the theological God. Yet how lovely some such folk are! How much we should hate to lose them from the circle of our families and friends! As one watches them one sees that while they do not have our theological God, in a profound sense they do have a psychological god. They have found in life a deep reliance and a deep devotion—some goodness, truth, or beauty they have found, some art, some science, some humane cause, some inner source of satisfaction from which to live, and some worth-while objective for which to live. I am sorry they do not believe in the Eternal God who made us, but sometimes I would like to show such people to some Christians, and say to the Christians, Look at them! There, at least, as far as it goes, is a genuine God-experience. There, at least, is a deity, such as it is, that really commands a man's life. And as for us Christians, professional believers in God, who have inherited a faith in God or persuaded ourselves of it by argument, see how ineffectual that mere theological God is until he has become what in Christ he always seeks to become, a real, interior God, our inner reliance and our day-by-day devotion.

The practical upshot of all this is that this genuine God-experience is never inherited. It seldom lies at the end of an argument. It comes as a satisfaction meeting a profound personal need. I suspect that few people ever get it who have not needed it in some difficult crisis. I know a man, for example, who was once a confirmed alcoholic. He drank one bottle of gin a day, and then two, and when he started to drink three he was concerned, and thought he would stop. He found he could not stop. That frightened him so that he went to the best medical experts he could find. They hospitalized him, diagnosed him, treated him, and finally came back with the verdict: He was a hopeless alcoholic. All his friends agreed with that; he was a hopeless alcoholic. All the experts agreed. And when he looked inside his own life, he had to agree. Now that man had always been an agnostic. He did not have the theological God. But in his crisis he needed God, some vital God-experience, a new reliance and a new allegiance. So, alone one day with all this converging testimony about his hopeless alcoholism pressing in upon him, he went down on his knees in a desperate endeavor to change gods—from Bacchus to God, from this god he had made, to the God who made him and could remake him.

Explain it as you will, that man has never taken a drink

since. He says he has no desire for one. Were you to meet him you would never suppose that this distinguished-looking gentleman had ever been through anything like that. As for the medical men, like good scientists they confess that they are astonished. And as for his agnosticism, you should hear him talk about God—quietly, with a deep sense of mystery, not supposing that he knows much about theology but absolutely sure that whereas a power greater than himself had hold on him, another power greater than himself got hold on him. Since the God that made him has remade him, his God is real, a reliance, and a devotion.

Our experience need not be dramatic and critical like that, but there is nothing the church of Christ needs more deeply today than men and women who have done more than inherit a theological God. How *real* is your God? "He restoreth my soul"—does he mean that? "Not my will, but thine, be done" —does he mean that? "Be ye transformed by the renewing of your mind"—does he mean that?

Let us now take a further step and note the critical importance of this truth for the large affairs of the world today. Indeed, I suspect that this sermon started from my reading of Hitler's book, *Mein Kampf*. I picked up the unabridged edition of *Mein Kampf* rather casually, but when a man has once started it, how can he lay it down? Here is presented with amazing frankness a man's soul and his philosophy of life. At the very heart of it, beating like a pulse in every paragraph, is this fact: that man has a god. Every time he thinks of that god his soul tingles, and to that god he has given the last ounce of his devotion. *Mein Kampf* is a story of one of the most absorbing god-experiences in our generation. But the god is the Aryan race. The only hope of mankind, Hitler says, lies in the Aryan race. Every possibility of mankind's advancement hangs upon the supremacy and dominance of that race. The supreme crime is the pollution of the purity of that race with alien blood, and the one devotion most worthy of human allegiance is the spread, sovereignty, and power of the Aryan race. The only ultimate test of right and wrong, says Hitler, is whether a thing does or does not assist the ascending glory of that one supreme god. With unabashed frankness he praises organized lying, mendacious propaganda, fitted to the passion, prejudice, and ignorance of the mob, if only it will help that race. With unqualified candor he glories in what can be done with a population by systematic terrorizing, if only it will help that race. Again and again he uses the words "fanatic" and "fanaticism" about himself and about his followers as words of praise, especially when with unbounded rancor he reviles the Jews, because anything is right that helps the Aryan race. That end justifies every means. As for the state, his theory is that it is only the political instrument to make possible in the world the sovereignty and supremacy of that race.

Reading *Mein Kampf* makes one wish, indeed, that polytheistic language were native to our tongue. No other can adequately picture what we are facing in this generation. The gods are in the field. Mankind's central question is the choice of gods. Out of the heart of every other problem rises this problem: Who shall be our god—these deities that we have made, or the one God, who revealed himself in Christ?

Do not, I beg of you, leave that matter stranded overseas with Hitler. Hitler is not the only one who makes race his god. Mussolini is not the only one who makes a nation his god. Stalin is not the only one who makes an economic class his god. A capitalist can do that as thoroughly as a Communist. No city that Paul ever traveled through, filled with temples to the deities of the Pantheon, was ever more replete with altars than is this modern world. And now, as in ancient times, the Christian gospel, when it keeps its purity, comes to this generation, saying, These are the gods that you have made, but there is one God who made you—all races, all nations, all classes, all men. Not Mars or Caesar, but the God of all mankind revealed in Christ, he alone is God.

If we should take that seriously it would be no mere matter of theology. Should we be earnest about that, it would shape and mold our attitudes as individuals and our policies as nations. To the Christian pastors in the Reich prisons and concentration camps today, because, like the Christians of old, they cannot worship Caesar, the god question is very practical. The god question has no business not to be practical. See these gods that rend the world asunder! They cannot save mankind. As a matter of most practical fact, they cannot save mankind. Many people today talk as though the present situation were denying the Christian gospel. Rather, it is confirming the Christian gospel. See these alternative and substitute gods! "By their fruits ye shall know them." They cannot redeem the world. As a realistic fact only one God can save the world: the God of all mankind revealed in Christ.

Finally, let us come back to our own individual lives and contritely confess the superficiality of much of our popular Christianity. You recall Charles Lamb's whimsical remark that his children were to be brought up in their father's religion, if they could discover what it was. It is not difficult to discover a man's formal, conventional, traditional religion. That can be put into theological speech. But how difficult it sometimes is to discover about a so-called Christian what his genuine, inner, if you will, psychological religion is, his real reliance and his real allegiance.

Mr. Julean Arnold, long attached to the United States government service in China, tells the story of a Chinese bandit who was wounded in an encounter with some soldiers and taken to a Methodist missionary hospital. There after some weeks his broken leg mended and he was restored to normal physical condition. He was so grateful that he vowed that never again would he hold up a Methodist. Word of that vow spread through the countryside, so that whenever he did hold up anyone the victim protested that he was a Methodist. So the bandit went back to the hospital to find out how he could distinguish a Methodist when he met one. They told him that a Methodist would always know the Lord's Prayer and the Ten Commandments. The bandit, therefore, memorized them in Chinese, and at the next encounter he exclaimed to the victim: "You recite the Ten Commandments and the Lord's Prayer or Heaven help the spirits of your ancestors!" Such external tests of Christianity are easily translatable into Western life. We know them well. And over against these superficial conformities, these traditional signs and symbols of our faith, how profound an experience it is when a man in some significant hour comes into personal confrontation with the God who made him!

One remembers Hugh Latimer preparing a sermon for the next Sunday to be preached at the Royal Court, and hearing a voice that said: "Be careful what you preach today, because you are going to preach before the King of England." But listening further he heard a voice that said: "Be careful what you preach today, since you are going to preach before the King of kings." That is a real experience, where one rises from facing the god we have made to face the God who made us.

It is impossible that a company like this should come together without some being in a moral and practical crisis involving that kind of choice. So midway in his experience came the turning point of Tolstoi's life. He had believed in the theological God, but now he faced something deep and interior. As he put it: "Five years ago, a strange state of mind-torpor began at times to grow upon me. I had moments of perplexity, of a stoppage, as it were, of life, as if I did not know how I was to live, what I was to do." Who does not know that kind of experience—as though life stopped you in midcourse and confronted you with the inquiry, What now are you going to do with me? There came the turning point in

Tolstoi's life when, from the gods he had made, he faced the God that made and could remake him.

Do not, I beg of you, say that I have said that all the gods we make are evil. They are not. The love of home and friends, great music, great books, great art, the loveliness we find in nature, many a deep satisfaction in the human spirit, many a fine loyalty in human life—they are good. But to the Christian the God who made us includes them all, is the fountain of them all, overarches them all. Every lovely thing is a pathway to him; every lovely thing is a revelation of him. We did not make him. He made us—he "inhabiteth eternity"; his "name is Holy"—that is magnificent theology, but, continues the Scripture—and this is the psychology of it —"I dwell . . . with him also that is of a contrite and humble spirit."

The Free Spirit Confronts the World's Coercion

A COMMON remark today is that we deeply need a renewal of the spiritual life. That kind of remark, however, is so vague and general that usually it slips off us without biting in anywhere. I wish we could put teeth into it today.

Why do so many different kinds of people feel that we need a renewal of the spiritual life? Is not the reason associated with the fact that the essential quality of the spiritual life is its voluntariness? Whatever else the spiritual life is, it must be unforced and free. If a man loves his friends, or loves beauty in nature, or creates beauty in art, he must do that willingly, without compulsion. If a man seeks truth, he must be in that realm uncompelled, freely dedicating himself to his research. If a man loves goodness, or worships God, that too must come spontaneously from within. Coerced love is not love. Coerced science is not science. Coerced conscience is not conscience. Coerced worship is not worship.

The Headmaster at Eton College once stood in his chapel pulpit and said to his students: "It's your duty to be pure in heart. If you are not pure in heart, I'll flog you." But that will not do. Purity of heart cannot be coerced. The essential quality of the spiritual life is unforced willingness, and this voluntary area of man's free spirit is pressed upon today by a rising tide of compulsion and regimentation.

Many, to whose lips phrases like "spiritual life" do not naturally come, are worried. The finest thing in them—their voluntary life, that gives to human beings their dignity and distinction—is threatened. They look out across the world and see great systems of totalitarianism endangering it. They look more closely home and see how precariously this free life of the spirit maintains itself against the antagonistic pressures of our time. Voluntariness, which is the indispensable quality of the spiritual life, faces a world that swings more and more toward coercion.

The central thesis of this sermon is that we cannot escape that menace merely by the negative method of fighting against coercion. This is true in part because coercion has a rightful place in life. When one loves one's friends or worships God, one must be free and uncompelled, but when one drives one's motor car, one cannot be free and uncompelled; one must obey the regulations. As the complexity of modern life increases, such areas of regulation increase also, and man cannot save this inner realm of the voluntary spirit by fighting against *that*.

Moreover, even when coercion is wrong and vicious, when dictatorship attacks democracy, it is a precarious method to deal with that by fighting back. For when we make war against coercion we use coercion, and thus widen the area of coercion, so that the voluntary life of the spirit we are defending is the more imperiled by the methods we employ. This is, of course, the supreme tragedy of war. The greatest evil of war is not the deaths it causes, cruel as they are, for all who die in war would soon or late have died anyway. The supreme evil of war is not the suffering it causes, tragic though that is, for that is only a needless addition to the great mass of human misery everywhere and always present. The supreme evil of war is that it accentuates trust in, and widens the area of, compulsive force, so that in any war, among all combatants, the one inevitable victim is the free life of the voluntary spirit that is the glory of mankind.

The only ultimate way in which the free life of the spirit can be saved from being swamped by force is by enlarging, deepening, and replenishing the voluntary life itself until it is too strong to be swamped. The poet who wrote the Fifty-first Psalm prayed about that. The Fifty-first Psalm is one of the noblest upreaches of spiritual life in the Old Testament, and at the heart of it is this prayer: "Uphold me with a willing spirit." That is to say, Enlarge in me the voluntary life; help me to live powerfully and freely from within. As Dr. Moffatt translates it: "Give me a willing spirit as my strength."

America had better lift that prayer for an inner life that will issue in uncompelled character, uncompelled goodwill, uncoerced public spirit. When men go into war the cry is lifted: Wanted, conscripts; but in this conflict to save the voluntary life of man's free spirit another cry is lifted: Wanted, volunteers!

As we endeavor to see the meaning of this prayer for our contemporary life, consider, in the first place, that whenever coercion increases, as it does today, it means that voluntariness has failed. Whenever, in any realm, the world cannot get enough volunteers, it necessarily turns to conscription. This is obviously true in personal life. Every adolescent youth wishes to be free, independent, to do as he pleases. If he is in a good home the measure of such voluntariness that he can enjoy is largely in his own control. If his voluntary life is fine, if he knows how to handle it, if he can push out the frontiers of his freely chosen living so that his family and friends rejoice to see it, then coercion withdraws before that strong and admirable advance of his uncoerced life. But if that youth's voluntary life is poor, weak, unstable, if his freely chosen courses cannot be trusted, then inevitably coercion closes in.

Here is a truth without seeing which I think we cannot understand the major problem of our social life today. When coercion increases and multiplies its impositions, that is because the voluntary, that is to say the spiritual, life has failed. For life is divided into two parts: the compulsory and the voluntary. They are like the sea and the land; they share the earth between them. The more there is of one, the less there is of the other. We, therefore, have our choice. We can develop in ourselves and in our nation a strong and fruitful spiritual life that creates uncompelled character and public spirit, or, if we fail in that, coercion will come flooding in like an encroaching sea. That is the inexorable alternative. One wishes one could shout it from the housetops. Either we are going to have more free spiritual life or else more legalistic compulsion. Either we are going to have more volunteers or more conscription.

Is not this the central problem of democracy? No other form of social organization depends so much on the willing spirit of the people. Trust in *that*, democracy says, and minimize the need of coercion. All of which is admirable so long as in the people we have a voluntary spirit we can trust. But when that fails, no matter how much we call ourselves a democracy, coercion will come flooding in like the seas in Holland when the dikes have broken down.

As a minister of Christ I do not wish to press this home merely to plead my special cause. I am thinking of some of you here, business and professional men and women, who use phrases like "spiritual life" with a certain shyness and timidity. But this thing we are talking of today is a stubborn and realistic fact. Our fathers at their best had a powerful voluntary life. They even said that government was best that governed least. In this country they widened for us, as never had been done before in history, the realm of self-directed, self-controlled, self-dedicated living. They trusted us to go on with that. But that order of life is not merely a political system, self-perpetuating. The maintenance of that order of life depends upon the maintenance of the free and voluntary spirit in the people, creating uncoerced character and public spirit. Democracy depends upon volunteers. Democracy's essential prayer is: "Uphold me with a willing spirit."

Let us go further and note that the recognition of this fact involves a fresh appreciation of the importance of those voluntary social groups that are the underpinning of a decent social order. One outstanding peril of our day is that our eyes are naturally focused on armies and navies, the major agencies of coercion, as though the future of mankind depended upon them. I maintain, upon the contrary, that the future of mankind depends far more upon homes than upon armies. Now a family in its origin is a voluntary group, and out of it, at its best, has come a quality of voluntary living that is today the strongest underpinning of democracy. For our democracy still has strength in it. There are men and women who do possess a spiritual life that issues in uncompelled character and uncoerced public spirit.

A recent writer on political theory dropped into the midst of his erudite discourse this true and homely statement: "A man should not say, 'I live in a democracy,' but 'I experienced democracy last Tuesday afternoon.'" So! Last Tuesday afternoon I met a man whose voluntary life was so fine that one could count on it. He fulfilled the great saying that "the free man socially minded is the hope of the world." He may have been rich or poor, learned or uneducated, a laborer with his hands or an executive in his office, but as one saw his voluntary living one said, The more of such, the more secure are the foundations of the commonwealth.

Whenever in any man or woman we thus experience democracy, we may be fairly sure that that life came from a good home. Plenty of people today, pressed upon by the gigantic coercions of the world, cry, What can we do? Well, if you are in a family, you are at the center of what most needs to be done. The voluntary life must come out of the voluntary groups.

Whatever we Americans do about this present war, we had better get into another war that in the long run will do more for democracy than any outer war will ever do—the conflict for homes, schools, churches, uncompelled public usefulness, professional codes of honor, and public-spirited business codes freely entered into and loyally maintained—the voluntary agencies, that is, that, like dikes, protect us from the sea of coercion. If compulsion mounts among us it is because those agencies have failed. If they have failed, it is because the people have been too blind to see that therein lies the hope of their freedom.

Indeed, let a special word be said about the churches. We have often miserably broken down, but in this area we have done one thing we need not be ashamed of. Here is one dike that again and again the encroaching sea of coercion has come upon and found it would not give, namely: Men and women who have said what Niemoeller said to Hitler, You dare not coerce conscience! You dare not coerce worship! We must obey God rather than man! Take but a single incident out of contemporary history. Mussolini says this: "The Fascist conception of the State is all-embracing; outside of it no human or spiritual values can exist, much less have value." There arises the dreaded despotism of statehood. Confronting that statement of Mussolini, Karl Barth said, in the name of all good religion: "I maintain that the Evangelical Church ought rather to be thinned down till it be a tiny group and go into the Catacombs rather than make a pact, even covertly, with this doctrine." The more there is of that spirit, the less coercion; the less of that spirit, the more coercion. O America, look to your voluntary groups! We will either have more volunteers, or we will have more regimentation.

Let us turn, now, to look at what probably is the greatest difficulty confronting our truth. When coercion increases, as it does today, that is due not simply to the breakdown of the voluntary spiritual life, but to certain inevitable conditions in our modern world. Dean Wicks, of Princeton, put the matter into a neat picture. Our fathers, he said in effect, went to school in a one-room schoolhouse, and when fire broke out the cry was raised, Everyone for himself! But now we go to school in vast, complicated structures, four or five thousand children in a single building, and when fire breaks out we cannot cry, Everyone for himself! If we are to be saved at all we must be saved together, by drill and regulation. That is a true picture of our modern world. The old individualism that cried, Every man for himself! will not do. If we are to be saved at all we must be saved together.

How better can this major fact be put into a single paragraph than by setting in contrast two words that too often are regarded as synonymous: "collectivism" and "communism." As I see the matter they are very different. Collectivism is a realistic fact. We do go to school collectively in vast complicated structures. Telephone and telegraph systems are collectivisms. Railroad systems are collectivisms. Giant power working its unescapable interdependencies is collectivism. Every year the inventions of science weave more inextricably the web that binds man to man, group to group, nation to nation. Collectivism is a major fact. Communism is a surrender to the idea that it must be handled by despotism. Collectivism is the towering social problem of the modern world. Communism is the false solution.

But we cannot escape that menace merely by fighting against communism. The problem of collectivism still is here, nowhere more in crescendo than in the United States. If we do not want that problem solved by despotism, then it must be positively solved by the free spirit of willing men, socially minded, and co-operative enough voluntarily to make despotism needless. Once more, it is only by enlarging, deepening, and revitalizing the voluntary life that we can hope to keep our liberty.

How many groups represented in this audience face this problem today! You physicians face it. The American people some day are going to have scientific medicine at the disposal of all their families. They are not going on by the millions, as is true today, knowing that there are remedies and treatments that would save the lives of their children, but that they cannot get at. That is an intolerable situation. But you physicians are right in fearing what the solution of that problem by governmental regimentation will do to the scientific standards of your profession. Well, then, if you do not wish that problem solved despotically, it must be solved voluntarily by the free co-operation of your profession and the people, by voluntary systems of insurance, or what you will! There, too, the only way we can successfully withstand coercive regimentation is by voluntary co-operation that will make it needless.

You businessmen face this. You do not like these restrictive regulations imposed upon you. Some of them, I doubt not, are the necessary consequence of the fact that economically we live in complicated structures where the old cry, Everyone for himself! will no longer do. But some of those coercions come from another cause altogether—a moral and spiritual cause—the breakdown of voluntary character, of voluntary co-operation, of uncompelled honesty and public spirit, of a willing care for what happens to all the people. As easily try to brush back the sea with a broom as to try to brush back governmental coercion if one forgets that. For here, too, in business, we will either have more volunteers or we will have more conscripts.

How strangely human life, both personal and social, is thus divided into two areas—the compulsory and the voluntary. In the last war a young French soldier lay white and weak upon a hospital bed. The surgeon who had just amputated his shattered arm looked with sympathy at the drawn face and said: "I am sorry that you had to lose your arm." And the young fellow opened his eyes and said with an accent of protest: "I did not lose it. I gave it." There is a fine quality in that. To face a grievous compulsion and flood it with willingness so that the voluntary is stronger than the necessary—that reveals a fine quality.

Henry D. Thoreau put it into an aphorism: "When a dog runs at you, whistle for him." Well, you can do that—with some dogs. If you must lose an arm, you can lose it graciously. If you must grow old, you can do it beautifully. If you must live alone, you can learn to like it. Some dogs that rush at you, you can whistle for. But some you cannot. There are coercions threatening us today which we have no business to whistle for. They threaten the extinction of the dearest values in human life.

As a minister of Christ thinks of them, how can he forbear feeling the profound importance of the religious life and the gospel for which he stands? For this free spirit of the voluntary man that we have been speaking of springs from the great deeps, from faiths that inspire us, philosophies of life that undergird us, motives that spontaneously rise within us, spiritual resources that replenish us. This free life of the spirit is a man's essential religion. O America, you had better look to that! It is no accident that the writer of the Fifty-first Psalm who prayed: "Uphold me with a willing spirit," prayed also:

> Create in me a clean heart, O God;
> And renew a right spirit within me.

The Real Point of Conflict Between Science and Religion

MOST Christians like ourselves take it for granted that the conflict between science and religion is finished. We thus assume that the two are at peace because we think of the conflict as moving in the intellectual realm, and in that realm we are no longer bothered. Once, we say, religion was associated with primitive world views. When these pre-scientific trellises around which Christian faith had twined itself were destroyed, there was tumult and alarm, but now our faith twines around the new trellises with gratitude and satisfaction. Our science and religion are not at odds, we say; we Christians eagerly welcome every new discovery.

Even one who rejoices in such intellectual peace, however, may still feel a serious conviction that we Christians are fooling ourselves about the conflict between science and religion being finished. The real point of that conflict today is not so much in the intellectual realm, where once consciously we met it, as in the practical realm, where every day unconsciously we confront it. The nub of the matter is that religion has always been a way of getting what people want—"The Lord is my shepherd; I shall not want"—but science also is a way of getting what people want, an amazingly efficient way; and it is in this practical realm that the competition between the two now moves. One could almost phrase the motto of our modern civilization thus: Science is my shepherd; I shall not want.

We need go back only a few centuries to find the great mass of people depending on religion for the satisfaction of practically all their wishes. From rain out of the sky to good health on earth, they sought their desires at the altars of their gods. Whether they wanted large families, good crops, freedom from pestilence, or peace of mind, they conceived themselves as dependent on the favor of heaven. Then science came with its alternative, competitive method of getting what we want. That is science's most important attribute. As an intellectual influence it is powerful enough, but as a practical way of achieving man's desires it is overwhelming.

Egypt, for example, depends for its very life upon the inundations of the Nile. Think of the endless prayers that rose from ancient temples when a low Nile threatened starvation. But no more! Science has met that want. The Assuan Dam makes all such praying needless. Ancient Greece fell, we hear, not so much because of human enemies as because of malaria. Think of the prayers from devout spirits offered before Greek altars against that secret and insidious foe! But now no nation that does what science says need ever fall because of malaria. So in one area after another, where for ages religion has had its methods of meeting human need, science comes with a competitive method that works with overwhelming efficiency. From scientific engineering to preventive medicine, from scientific agriculture to psychiatry, what need of human nature will not science meet? So the nub of the conflict between the two lies not so much in science disproving religion as in science displacing it.

What areas of human need science has met in my lifetime! When I was born, Edison was thirty-one years old; Sigmund Freud was twenty-two; Henry Ford was fifteen; Charles Steinmetz, thirteen; Madame Curie, eleven; Orville Wright, seven; Marconi, four; Einstein, minus one. See the realms of human want that science has entered, within the scope of one lifetime! For every person, therefore, who today gives up religion because intellectually he cannot believe in it, one suspects that there are a hundred persons who give up religion because, in view of what science can do for them, they feel that practically they do not need it. Why should not the motto of our modern world be: Science is my shepherd; I shall not want?

Nevertheless, everywhere today among thoughtful people a grave misgiving sets in about that. There is something the matter with that.

For one thing, a serious suspicion rises concerning the adequacy of science to meet human need, because while science gives us implements to use, science alone does not determine for what ends they will be employed. Radio is an amazing invention. Yet now that it is here, one suspects that Hitler never could have consolidated his totalitarian control over Germany without its use. One never can tell what hands will reach out to lay hold on scientific gifts, or to what employment they will be put. Ever the old barbarian emerges, destructively using the new civilization.

This misuse of scientific gifts is the explanation of a major experience through which we older people have had to live, namely, the most colossal breakdown of optimism in human history. You younger people who have come to social consciousness since 1918 cannot imagine the mood of optimism in which we were reared. We lived in the days of the first telephones, the first express trains, the first uses of electricity, the first internal combustion engine, the first of so many ingenious devices, that our lives stood on tiptoe, wondering what new marvel would appear tomorrow. We were the natural disciples of Herbert Spencer and his gospel of inevitable progress. Were I to talk today as we all felt then, you would think me an arrant sentimentalist. And the explanation is that the high hopes built on these scientific gifts have crashed to the ground, as we have faced the realistic fact that man can be so insane and so corrupt that the more power you give him, the more widely will he destroy himself.

War has illustrated this. Ages ago, war was not so much a conflict between armies as between champions. Even the armies of Israel and of Philistia sat on the side lines and watched David and Goliath decide the issue—that was war. Then war grew until it was fought by professional mercenaries. The very word "soldier" comes from the Latin word *solidus*, meaning a "coin." A soldier was a mercenary, and wars were fought by paid combatants. Then as the centuries passed, citizen armies arose; war reached its hands deeper into a nation's homes and gathered up in its arms more of the nation's youth, as in our American civil conflict. Now we have reached the fourth stage—totalitarian war—which includes everyone and everything, men and women, old and young, capital and labor, industry and agriculture, all agencies of propaganda, the home, the school, the church, fused into a single, collective, regimented agency of organized destruction. We need not one word but four words for war. Champions fighting, mercenaries fighting, citizen armies fighting, totalitarian war—these are four different things, and this appalling development in the nature of war has been made possible because of scientific gifts.

> Science is my shepherd; I shall not want.
> It maketh me to lie down in green pastures;
> It leadeth me beside still waters.
> It restoreth my soul:
> It guideth me in the paths of righteousness—

there is something the matter with that.

If someone says I am decrying science, I answer, Upon the contrary, the scientists have done their work magnificently. That is the trouble. They have forged far ahead. They have outstripped our moral character, our spiritual quality, our religious faith. They have given us amazing means, beyond the utmost dreams of our fathers, but now something deeper than science, which builds in men directive faith, strong character, and collective goodwill, must determine to what use the gifts will be put. For the fact is not, as so many think, that the more science we have, the more religion can be discarded, but rather that the more science we have, the more character-building religion is demanded.

In view of that, one wishes one might address all churches and synagogues. If you only knew it, one would say, you are the crux of the situation. Why do you not behave as though you were? The future of mankind swings now on one hinge— not how can we get more instruments, but how can we get adequate character and ennobling faiths to undergird their use? What, then, are you doing with your conventionalities of creed and ritual, your sectarianisms that have no more pertinence to contemporary life than the boundaries of ancient Indian tribes? The world is well-nigh ruined for the lack of what it is your business to supply—great faith, great character, inclusive goodwill. How like the knell of doom across the centuries come the words of Christ: "Man's life consisteth not in the abundance of the things which he possesseth."

There is something the matter with our endeavor to rewrite the Twenty-third Psalm until it reads: Science is my shepherd; I shall not want. Soon or late we will have to bring God back into that Psalm.

For another reason a grave misgiving arises concerning the adequacy of science to meet human wants, because while science is a marvelous provider for some of our desires, there are depths of need in human nature that no science ever reaches. Granted, that in one field after another religion has been beaten out by science as a practical resource! Think of scientific engineering, scientific agriculture, scientific medicine, and psychiatry! One can understand what an American college professor meant, who, sometime since in a chapel address, said: "God becomes progressively less essential." He meant that the conflict between science and religion is not so much an intellectual, as a practical, affair, and that in those areas where pre-scientific religion has fallen down, science comes with an amazing technique to meet man's needs. He thinks that "God becomes progressively less essential."

To which I answer, Nobody is more grateful for modern science than we Christians are, but do not tell us that it can plumb the depths of human need, or encompass the horizons of its want. We cannot even get all we want out of a sunset by science alone. Thank God for the cosmic setting of the evening's glory, and all the knowledge that gives scope and perspective to the scene! But when with a friend we sit beside the sea and watch the sun go down, it takes more than cosmology or a schedule of counted light waves to meet our need. See how the sun throws up the sky his golden arms,

> And with vermilion-tinted fingers toys
> With the long tresses of the evening star.

We are getting out of the sunset what we want, but it is not science only that helps us. Listen to this: "He who can no longer pause to wonder and stand rapt in awe, is as good as dead: his eyes are closed." Einstein said that. It takes more than science to make a great scientist.

This truth is obvious, and we know it well, and yet so pressing is the practical competition between our new techniques and methods of satisfying our desires, and the profounder levels of our personal lives, that the depths of the spirit and the resources for our inner help are crowded out.

On every road where science starts to walk with us, soon or late we come to the place where science has to stop, but where we have to go on. Science says, for example, This is a law-abiding universe; and we answer, That is one of the great discoveries of the scientific mind. But walking up that road with science, soon or late we come to the place where another question rises: Are all the laws physical? Is not the spiritual world law-abiding, too? We can fulfill law-abiding physical conditions and liberate cosmic power for our help. What if we could fulfill law-abiding spiritual conditions within our souls, release power there, too, and tap resources of divine energy from beyond ourselves for our daily need!

What if that is what prayer means, so that the experience of great souls across the ages has rested on an everlasting fact, that the spiritual world is law-abiding also, that there we can fulfill conditions, and release power, until He restoreth our souls. At that point science has to stop, but we, with the profoundest needs of our lives, must go on.

Or science says, I will tell you how this universe runs—its history, the process of its development, the mechanisms of its procedure; and we answer, That is a great contribution. But walking up that road with science, soon or late we come to the place where another kind of question rises—not so much, How does the universe run, as, Whence did it come? Why any universe? Whither does it tend? Is it merely a physical accident, or at the heart of it is there an eternal meaning, a purpose that binds it into a significant whole? And are we, its offspring, only chance by-products of the unthinking dust, or are we children of the Eternal Spirit? At that point science must stop, but we, with the deepest needs of our lives and hearts, must go on.

Or again, science says, I will tell you about yourself—biologically, psychologically, the truth about yourself; and we answer, That is a great boon. But walking up that road with science, soon or late we come to the place where real trouble faces us. No one would belittle what science may do for us there. Thank heaven for psychiatry! But everybody who has ever been in real trouble knows that there we face profounder personal needs than any science can supply, with a battle on between faith and fear, courage and disillusionment, the need of spiritual companionship and an appalling sense of loneliness, between willingness to live and the desire to die, between the hope that there may be some meaning in life and the awful sense of life's futility. At that point to try to say, Science is my shepherd; I shall not want, will not do. That Psalm came from profounder origins. Remember the remark of Rossini, the composer: "Give me a laundry list, and I will set it to music." How much of life is like that after trouble has come, leaving us with the task of setting a barren, commonplace situation, as it were, to music. I have seen that gloriously done, but never except by persons who had faiths, convictions, resources, loves, and loyalties, which are of the very substance of religion. For when real trouble strikes a life, science soon reaches its limits, but we, with our deepest needs, must still go on.

Once more, science says, I will tell you the truth about the human race—its anthropology, its sociology, and all the rest; and we answer, gratefully, What a boon! But we have not traveled far with science on that road before we say, O science, we need something more out of our human fellows than this; we need love, and friendship, and that is not scientific nor unscientific, but something else. In my young manhood I faced a critical temptation that might well have stopped my career before it was fairly started. What saved me was nothing scientific, nothing unscientific, but something deeper—the imagined face of my mother rose in my mind with such dominant restraint that even yet, across nearly half a century, I can feel its power, so that when Paul says "I live; yet not I, but Christ liveth in me," I think I understand, at least a little, what that experience means. So at the place where we need and find the saving power of God-given personalities, science must stop, but we, with our deepest wants, must go on.

We never will successfully rewrite the Twenty-third Psalm and leave God out, especially if we keep in it the sentence,

. . . though I walk through the valley of the shadow of death,
I will fear no evil; for thou art with me.

At that point science has to stop, but we have to go on.

For a final reason this grave misgiving about the adequacy of science to meet human need arises, especially in more thoughtful lives. We have been talking about science and religion as competitors in satisfying human wants. It is time we confronted the fact that there is much more to life than getting what we want. Long ago in a garden a prayer was offered that the world has never been able to forget: "Not my will, but thine, be done." Jesus was not seeking what he wanted. He was giving his life to his God, not that God might do what *he* wanted, but that *he* might do what God wanted, and that experience, the profoundest and most ennobling human nature knows, *is* religion.

When, therefore, someone says that science is enough, I answer, That will never do, if only because science itself comes from more than science. Science itself does not start merely by trying to get what we want. Science has its high origin in devotion to something greater than itself, the disinterested love of truth, from which, as from an overflowing fountain, come all its practical results; and that disinterested love of truth, which is the origin of science, is itself religious. Every great scientist becomes a great scientist because of the inner self-abnegation with which he stands before truth, saying: "Not my will, but thine, be done." What, then, does a man mean by saying, Science displaces religion, when in this deep sense science itself springs from religion?

Ask us at our best what most we want, and we will not answer with an elaborate list of implements and tools, valuable though they are. At our best what most we want, if life is to be worthy, is something greater than ourselves, in which we can everlastingly believe, worth serving, worth sacrificing for, not for us to use but that will use us, giving to life dignity and meaning because life becomes the servant of a cause eternally worth-while. That, most of all, we want, if we are to be real men and women, and that is not the gift of science —that, verily, is a man's religion.

Do not call this sentimental, for contemporary politics are its most vivid illustration. Naziism has become a religion. Communism has become a religion. Many give themselves to such creeds and causes, sacrifice their comfort, their convenience, life itself, saying, as it were: "Not my will, but thine, be done." The most crucial question in the world today is not, How can we get more implements for us to use? but, What shall be the nature of the religion that will use us?

All the religion that science has displaced ought to have been displaced. Religion as an easy way of getting what we want by petition and ritual—magic religion, treating God as a charity organization from which can be wangled doles for improvident applicants—the more such religion science displaces, the better. But when a great soul stands before the highest, some Christian, before God revealed in Christ and his eternal purpose for the world, saying: "Not my will, but thine, be done," there inhere the noblest attributes that human nature can possess.

The Twenty-third Psalm is personal. Let us make it so! It is true, is it not, that with all the implements we get, the deeper question is, What kind of man will use them? It is true, is it not, that on every road life travels, some of the profoundest problems rise just after science has bidden us good-by. It is true, is it not, that as for life's deepest issues, *those* involve the supreme loyalty to which we give our lives.

The Lord is *my* shepherd; *I* shall not want.

. . . . .

He restoreth *my* soul:
He guideth *me* in the paths of righteousness. . . .

What Does the Divinity of Jesus Mean?

THIS sermon springs from endless inquiries sent me by radio listeners. They want to know what the "divinity" or "deity" of Jesus means. They have heard about it all their lives in the church's creeds, hymns, and sermons. Some believe it but are not quite sure what they are believing. Some disbelieve it but are not sure what they are disbelieving. What does it mean? they ask.

The reply to this question, if it is to be vital, must be personal. What does the divinity of Jesus mean to us in the actual practice of our daily lives? Monogamy, for example, is an abstract word, in discussing which men can lose themselves in labyrinthine arguments until someone breaks through, saying, What is monogamy? It is the kind of home I had, where my father and mother loved each other so deeply that they did not care to love anyone else in the same way at all, and so, across the years, threw around their children the security of a lovely and dependable home. That is monogamy. That is what it means. That is why I believe in it. Similarly, the divinity of Jesus has often been discussed as an abstract theological concept until someone has said, The divinity of Jesus was not at first an abstraction at all; it was a fresh insight into life's significance; it was far more nearly poetry than theology, something to sing about, rejoice in, and live by; it was a new and exhilarating message about God and man.

Let us see it in such terms of daily living if we are to know its meaning.

To help clear the air of some prevalent misconceptions, let us say at the start that the divinity of Jesus certainly does not mean that Jesus was not human. Of course he was human.

The first disciples did not start by thinking of him as divine but by taking him for granted as obviously human. He was to them, as he must be to us, first of all man, and then divine in what sense he can be divine, being unquestionably human.

The Master's body was a normal human body like our own, familiar with weariness, hunger, thirst, pleasure, suffering, and death. The Master's emotional life was normally human like our own—sometimes astonished as at the centurion's excess of faith; sometimes compassionate as when he looked on the unshepherded multitudes; sometimes indignant as when he saw his Father's house made a den of thieves; sometimes rejoicing; and sometimes so cast down that he cried: "My soul is exceeding sorrowful, even unto death."

Moreover, Jesus' mental life was normally human like our own. It developed like any youth's. As Luke says, "Jesus advanced in wisdom and stature." He went to the synagogue school in Nazareth, and, sitting on the floor with his fellow pupils, recited in unison the lessons the rabbi dictated. He learned, as we all do, from what he saw, and his teaching everywhere reflects the recollections of his boyhood's home—the sound of wind down the village street, the cost of sparrows in the market place, putting patches on old garments, the working of leaven in the dough, hens gathering chickens under their wings. As for his major teaching, everywhere one catches the accents of the psalmists and the prophets, on whose writings he had been reared.

More particularly to our purpose is the humanness of Jesus' spiritual life. He prayed, not as though he were God, but as though he were man. Sometimes he prayed in triumph, as on the Transfiguration Mountain, when his face shone; sometimes he prayed in grief, as in Gethsemane, when it is written: "Being in an agony he prayed more earnestly." All his life he lived in such humble, filial dependence on God, and when fulsomely praised he retorted: "Why callest thou me good?

none is good, save one, even God." So his life was lived, his work done, his sorrows borne, his temptations faced, in the spirit of simple, childlike dependence on God. Of course he was human, and he must be divine in what sense he can be divine, being assuredly human.

With this clear assertion of the humanity of Jesus in the Gospels, modern Christians are familiar. But many moderns do not know that throughout its early history the church fought some of its most serious theological battles to maintain its hold on this humanness of Jesus. Suppose I should say that Docetism was an early heresy that nearly tore the church asunder and that it concerned who Jesus was. Would you not naturally suppose that the Docetists must have doubted his deity? Upon the contrary, they asserted that he was God but they did not believe that he was man. They said that he only seemed to be born with a body, to possess flesh and blood, to suffer and to die. And the church fought the Docetists tooth and nail and drove them out. Were I to say that a heretic, Apollinaris, convulsed the church with his idea of Jesus' nature, would you not suppose that he must have doubted his deity? Upon the contrary, he asserted that, but he denied that Jesus had a human soul and a human will, and the church withstood him and cast him out. Throughout the early centuries some of the most serious battles in the church were fought in the endeavor to keep a firm hold on the real humanity of the Master.

We start then with this truth, that Jesus was human and that he must be divine in what sense he can be divine, being assuredly human. What, then, does the divinity of Jesus mean?

In the first place, it is an assertion primarily not about Jesus but about God. Everything else, I think, is seen awry unless that is clear. The divinity of Jesus is primarily an affirmation about God. Isaac Newton looked at the falling apple in the orchard until he overpassed looking at it and looked through it into a universal law. The astronomer looks at the star until he overpasses looking at it and looks through it into a cosmic truth. Those first disciples looked at Jesus until they overpassed looking at him and looked through him into a revelation of something eternally true about God. That is the way all universal truth is discovered, by looking at something significant until one looks through it and sees an eternal matter. So the disciples looked at Jesus until, as Paul said, they saw "the light of the knowledge of the glory of God" in his face.

Most of us here believe in God but how diverse the meanings of such faith! This diversity springs from the variety of answers we give to one central question: Where is God—not What, or Who, is God? as so commonly the question is put, but Where is God? That is the crucial inquiry. Where do we look for him?

In response to that question some say we find God in the universe at large. The profoundest cosmic fact that science gets its eyes upon is not matter—if indeed, modern science knows what matter means—but a mathematical equation, and that is mental. God, says Jeans, the physicist, is like a great mathematician. So, in the organizing mind at the heart of the universe, we see God. Well, I agree. But is that all?

Others say we find God in the beauty of the world. More than a mathematician is at work here—an artist too, to whom symmetry, proportion, harmony, balance, color, are so real that, from microscopic creatures, invisible to unaided eyes, to the stars above, there is a beauty in the world where we find God. I agree. But is that all?

Others say they find God in the moral order of the world. This is a spiritually creative universe. It produces personality. It insists on obedience to moral law as the price of personal and social peace. It brings its heavy judgments down on human sin. It says that we must live co-operatively if we are to live well. There, in that moral order of the world, we see God, some say. To that also I agree. But is that all?

To find God in the organization of the cosmos, in the beauty of creation, in the moral order of the world, is good. But as some of us know well, all *that* can leave a man untouched in the personal depths of his life. What happened to the disciples, however, cannot leave a man untouched in the depths of his life. For there swam into their ken the strongest, loveliest personality the world has known, and they looked at him until they began to look through him and to see the most significant thing ever seen in the religious history of man—God there. The best life we know, they said, is supremely the place where we can see God. Not simply in the organization of the cosmos, the beauty of creation, the moral order of the world but here, in the mercy, saviorhood, love, and will of Christ, here—though it be the most daring assertion ever made about deity—is revealed God. What is highest in human life, revealed in Christ, they said, is deeply grounded in the universe; God is like *that*.

If we do not so see Jesus when we look at him, what do we make of him? I am taking it for granted that we recognize in him a transcendent quality. What, then, do we make of this most amazing, potent, spiritual life that has visited the world? In the long run we make of him one of two things: either an accident or a revelation—one or the other. He might be an accident, a fortuity in a materialistic world, the chance product of blind forces that never purposed him and never cared. He might just have happened. Or it might be that those first disciples were on the trail of the everlasting truth when they looked at him until they looked through him and saw in him the revelation of the Eternal. That is the great question about Christ. Is he an accident or a revelation?

In every realm one runs upon that kind of question. When men first picked up magnetized iron, they faced it. What was this extra quality, this strange power which made iron more than iron, iron plus, so that it exercised a potency that ordinary iron did not possess? Was this strange extra an accident, or a revelation of something profound in the constitution of the cosmos? As always happens, it turned out to be a revelation. If we cannot avoid such questions even about magnetized iron, we cannot avoid them about the quality of Christ. To call him an accident in the universe seems to me preposterous. At any rate, I personally must range myself with those first disciples who looked at him until they looked through him and saw in him "the light of the knowledge of the glory of God." They went out into the Roman Empire with this thrilling message to deliver, that God was like Christ.

In the second place, however, while the divinity of Jesus is primarily an assertion about God, it is also an affirmation about Jesus. It does put him in a unique place. Once after an appreciative paper on Shelley's poetry had been read, one member of the group arose in the discussion, saying rather truculently that he could not see anything in Shelley, to which the reader of the paper, replying later, simply remarked: "Mr. So-and-So says that he does not see anything in Shelley. Poor devil!" If a man can see nothing special in Jesus, that, I suspect, is the answer: Poor devil. Most of us, however, do not belong in that class. We can feel the transcendent quality of Jesus' life and understand at least a little the experience the disciples must have had with him.

First, of course, came a recognition of his spiritual superiority. A visitor at one of the services of Frederick Denison Maurice in Cambridge, England, when that preacher was at the height of his power, came out completely subdued and awed, saying, "There was something divine there not of this world." So from the beginning the disciples must have felt about Jesus.

Then, I suppose, came the sense of moral challenge in

his presence. He was not easy to face. You recall what Iago said about Cassio:

> He hath a daily beauty in his life
> That makes me ugly.

With shame and contrition the disciples felt that. The Master was not easy to live with. Peter's first reaction was not comfortable: "Depart from me; for I am a sinful man, O Lord." He had a daily beauty in his life that made them ugly.

Then, I suspect, there grew in them a strange sense of the Master's rightful authority over their lives. He taught them, said Matthew, as one having sovereignty. Make no mistake about this. His authority did not mean regimentation. He never made James like John or John like Peter. His authority, as with all spiritual excellence, issued not in regimentation but in stimulation. Under his sway qualities and powers began coming out in them unguessed before, qualities and powers original, individual, creative, each man becoming more truly himself, the more he became Christ's.

As this kind of experience, which no one can adequately put into words, progressed, see how inevitably the disciples moved up from one stage to another in their thought of him. At first they may have said, God sent him. After a while that sounded too cold, as though God were a bow and Jesus the arrow. That would not do. God did more than send him. So I suspect they went on to say, God is with him. That went deeper. Yet, as their experience with him progressed, it was not adequate. God was more than with him. So at last we catch the reverent accents of a new conviction, God came in him. That was not so much theology at first as poetry. It was an exhilarating insight and its natural expression was a song. God can come into human life! they cried; God has come into human life! Divinity and humanity are not so separate that the visitations of the Eternal are impossible. "God is love; and he that abideth in love abideth in God, and God abideth in him"; "Know ye not that ye are a temple of God, and that the Spirit of God dwelleth in you?" "In the beginning was Mind and the Mind was with God, and the Mind was God. . . . And the Mind became flesh, and dwelt among us (and we beheld his glory, glory as of the only begotten from the Father), full of grace and truth." So they sang it. God can come into human life because God has come into human life.

At its best, that is what the church has always meant by the divinity of Jesus. Do not, I beg of you, tie this great affirmation up with miraculous accompaniments, such as the virgin birth. I am not deeply concerned whether you believe the virgin birth as a historic fact or not, although, as you know, I cannot believe it. But I am concerned that no one should tie up in one bundle the virgin birth and the divinity of Jesus. The divinity of Jesus was not physical. That is absurd. It was spiritual. It was the inner quality of his life in which his divinity consisted. The two great protagonists for his divinity in the New Testament were John and Paul and neither directly nor indirectly did they ever allude to the virgin birth. No, the divinity of Jesus was a convinced and singing faith that God can come into human life because God had come into human life.

Take even the old creeds, the Nicene, for example, greatest of them all. We repeat no creeds in this church. We require no subscription to them. I would not use them as the natural phrasing of my faith. But all the more I am sometimes jealous that we should not misunderstand them. A modern liberal Christian hears the Nicene Creed calling Jesus "very God of very God," and says, I cannot believe that. I too should not naturally use the Nicene language, but yet see what the Creed was really trying to say! That Creed was formulated in a time when the contemporary philosophy had torn God and man completely asunder. On the one side was God, pure Being, utterly incapable of coming into contact with human life, and on the other side was man, sunk in the darkness of matter, utterly incapable of touching God. This was the prevalent philosophy. And this idea was so affecting Christian thought that even Christians were tempted to say that if Jesus were human he could not be divine and if divine he could not be human. So utterly diverse and separate were divinity and humanity that God himself could never come into human life. It was against this idea that the Nicene Creed rose magnificently up with its affirmation: God can come into human life; very God can come into human life; the divine and the human are not irreconcilable, like oil and water, which cannot be mixed. It never would occur to me to use the Nicene language as the natural expression of my faith, but what the Nicene Creed was driving at in the terms of its own day is my faith. Say it until it becomes real to your thought and living: God did not simply send Jesus; he was not simply with Jesus; he came in Jesus. God can come into human life because he has come into human life, and what the Fourth Gospel pictures the Master as saying is true: "He that hath seen me hath seen the Father."

Finally, the divinity of Jesus is an affirmation not only about God and about Jesus but about man. Have you ever seen a precious stone in the rough, carried out of the dark, where it seemed dull and dingy, into the light where the sunshine could break through it and in lustrous radiance reveal beauties no one could have guessed? So in Jesus human nature was carried out of the dark into the light, and from that day to this no one who has really known him has been able to think of human nature as necessarily dull and dingy. See, they have cried, what it can become when the Divine is released through it!

In this realm lies one of the common fallacies of those who refuse to see any meaning in Jesus' divinity. They say: Jesus is a good man, and simply because he is a good man he can be our ideal, for we can imitate him, but if he were divine we could not imitate him, for that would put him out of our class and spoil him as our ideal; let him be to us simply a good man!

I never heard an argument that seemed to me so to stand the truth upon its head. I should say in answer, Jesus is, indeed, an extraordinarily good man. His goodness was the only thing he had with which to make an impress on the world—no wealth, no prestige, no worldly learning, nothing but his goodness! And every year that goodness looms so much the higher that millions of us are sure its chief influence lies not behind but ahead. He was a marvelously good man. And now do you seriously mean that, being a good man like that, we can cheerfully and hopefully set out to imitate him? Upon the contrary, if Jesus is only a good man, he towers there, solitary and alone, an isolated phenomenon in human history.

If, however, that is not all the truth, if he is not simply a good man, if it was God in him who created his quality, and if the same God is seeking entrance to our lives, trying to live out in us, according to our capacity, the same spirit, then we may hope. Let us say it abruptly: It is not so much the humanity of Jesus that makes him imitable; it is his divinity. If he be only a good man, he is an isolated phenomenon like Shakespeare or Napoleon in other realms. How can I, pulling on my own bootstraps, set out to lift myself by imitation to the stature of such? But if Jesus is divine and if divinity is in each of us, like the vital forces which in winter wait in the frozen ground until the spring comes, that is a gospel! While the trees of the wood are still bare the crocuses bloom, but if they were only crocuses, that would be no good news. If, however, they reveal the vibrant life that runs through all the arteries of the waiting world, such news should make all the trees of the wood rejoice before the Lord; for he cometh in the springtime to redeem them all.

Such is the gospel of the New Testament about Jesus and his relationship with our lives. He is not an isolated phenomenon; he is "the firstborn among many brethren"; "till we all attain unto the unity of the faith, and of the knowledge of the Son of God, unto a fullgrown man, unto the measure of the stature of the fulness of Christ."

If one says that still his divinity in scope and compass far overarches ours, surely that is obvious. As Emerson says: "A drop of water has the properties of the sea, but cannot exhibit a storm." So we reveal God without the deeps and tides and currents which Jesus knew, without the relationships with the world's life which his influence has sustained. Yet the God who was in Jesus is the same God who is in us; you cannot have one God and two kinds of divinity. It was one of the supreme days in man's spiritual history when human nature in Jesus was carried out from the dark into the light and men saw as never before what could happen to it when the divine life was released through it.

Of all foolish things, I can think of nothing more foolish, when looking back over our race's history and discerning amid its tragedy and trouble this loveliest, strongest, spiritual life that has visited the earth, than to try to minimize him. Upon the contrary, exalt him! If you cannot discover the Divine in that life, then I do not see how you can vitally discover it anywhere. And if you do find the Divine in him, then that is indeed a great affirmation about God and about Christ himself. But last, and most practically of all, it is an affirmation about human nature that in these desperate days I need constantly to have refreshed—an assertion about the possibilities of human nature when the divine Life is released through man.

Jesus' Ethical Message Confronts the World

FOR some of us it is easier to believe in the Christian theology than in the Christian ethic. A generation ago many were saying: We cannot believe your Christian ideas of God, but the ethical principles of Jesus are the hope of the world. Today, however, it is the ethical principles of Jesus that are difficult. By the Christian ethic I mean no mere ordinary, humane decency, loving those who love us, but rather the radical, sometimes incredible, demands of Jesus that we love our enemies, that if smitten on one cheek we turn the other also or if compelled to go one mile we go two instead, that we do good to those who hate us and pray for those who despitefully use us and persecute us. There is the rub today.

The reason for this is the extraordinary vividness with which a powerful temptation assails us all, the temptation to resist evil with evil. When on the western prairies a conflagration starts, men fight fire with fire, burning a swath across which the advancing flames cannot leap. What is thus well done in the physical world we are continually tempted to do in the moral world. We fight evil with evil.

In war, if one side bombs open cities, the other side may at first be horrified, but in the end it too bombs open cities. It takes bombing to fight bombing. If one side uses conscription, which is of the essence of dictatorship, the other side, being a democracy, at first is shocked, but in the end copies the technique of the enemy. It takes conscription to fight conscription. In personal relationships we are habitually tempted to meet bad temper with bad temper, resentment with resentment, sometimes chicancery with chicancery, and in all this we are morally sustained because we think we are resisting evil—as, indeed, we are, but *with evil*. At that crucial point Jesus parts company with us. It is there that his revolutionary ethic begins.

Listen to him: "How can Satan cast out Satan?" Hidden away in the third chapter of Mark's Gospel that searching question stands, summing up, I think, the essential meaning of Jesus' way of life. "How can Satan cast out Satan?" How can evil be the cure of evil? How can two wrongs make a right? No question could be more pertinent to our modern world, where today violence rises on every side, ill will is rampant, aggressive iniquities must be resisted by good men, and the temptation to fight evil with evil is almost irresistible. Nevertheless, the question of Jesus haunts the Christian conscience and in quiet moments of insight reveals a strange, uncanny common sense—"How can Satan cast out Satan?"

In the first place, how can the vicious circle of evil answered by more evil, answered by more evil, answered by more evil still, ever be broken, unless somewhere, someone refuses to go on with it? Watch this vicious cycle of wrong answering wrong. Iniquity rises, demanding that we fight back. So, following the pattern of the natural ethic, against which Jesus took his revolutionary stand, we fight bitterness with bitterness, hatred with hatred, violence with violence, evil growing in a mounting crescendo as wrong answers wrong. This process is afoot everywhere, from international relationships, where they bomb our cities and kill our women and children and so we bomb their cities and kill them, to personal relationships, where we say, He has been unjust— I will show him; I will pay the devil in his own coin.

In this regard how like we human beings are to dogs! For one dog barks and the other barks back and the first barks more loudly and the second becomes more noisy still, in a mounting crescendo of hostility. So one man excused his terrier to the exasperated owner of another. "After all," he said, "the dog is only human."

From childhood, when we fell into angry name-calling, each trying to lay his tongue to some more stinging epithet, we all have faced this elemental problem, and now that, more mature, we are more dignified, our resentment taking a colder form but remaining still resentment quite unredeemed, who does not know that vicious circle of bitterness answered by bitterness, answered by bitterness again? It is the tragedy of the world!

Shakespeare dramatized this in *Romeo and Juliet,* which, far from being a drama of romantic love alone, is first of all a play about a feud—the house of Capulet against the house of Montague. The first and last words of the play concern the feud, one house against the other, hating each other, meeting violence with violence, evil growing by what it feeds upon and two wrongs never coming out right. Remember Mercutio, slain in the duel and in the insight of his dying moment crying: "A plague o' both your houses!" In the theater one sees people go out before the final scene as though, the love poetry being over, they thought the play was done. Shakespeare would have disliked that. It is the final scene, the climax of the play that he was driving at, where Capulet and Montague stand ashamed and penitent, their long and bitter feud stopped in midcourse by a love that broke the vicious circle of its hate. In that final moment of the play, when a Christian might kneel as before the mystery of the cross, Capulet says: "O brother Montague, give me thy hand."

So Shakespeare after his own fashion dramatized what the Christian ethic would say, that the world's feud can never end, and the vicious circle of wrong answering wrong come to a close, until somewhere, somebody refuses to go on with it. Jesus meant this by his homely saying that if a man is smitten on one cheek he should not smite back, starting thus an endless chain of retaliation. Let him try a new technique! Better, he would say, that one adventure on a revolutionary ethic and if two blows must be given take both rather than give one. Let him see if he cannot thus break the endless sequence of fighting evil with evil, whereby we always become the evil that we fight.

This, of course, is what the pacifists at their best are driving at with reference to war. The most dismaying aspect of our present international situation, I think, is the way we ape the enemies we hate. The dictatorships say, War! so we say, War! They build vast armaments, so we build vast armaments. Step by step, day by day, we become their yes-men. They say, Dictatorial control of the nation for the sake of war's efficiency! So we say the same. What apes we are! We copy those we hate. We fight evil with evil and become the evil that we fight. We will conquer them, we say, and so first of all we let them make us in their image. All this we do, thinking Jesus to be a visionary idealist. He is not. His ethic shows a more realistic insight into what is going on in this modern world than does our boasted hard-headedness. Despite their governments, the people of all the nations in their hearts and homes want peace. Somewhere, sometime, millions of men and women must stand up and cry, We're through! We will not go on forever with war causing more war, causing more war, causing more war still.

If someone says, But we may be compelled to go to war! I ask only that the meaning of that statement be realistically faced. For in the war you say America is compelled to enter, every cruelty that human beings, implemented with unprecedented instruments, can inflict on human beings will be inflicted. In that terrific wrestling bout no holds will be barred. The word "sacred" will be dropped from the human vocabulary, and neither child nor woman, home, church, school, honor, nor plighted faith will be respected. If we are the apes of our enemies in peace time, in wartime we will be apes indeed. Every cruelty they devise we will match. Every devastation they inflict on human beings we will equal. In the end no barbarity will be beneath us. The boys we bore in travail and reared in love in our homes, schools, and churches, will become the yes-men of the enemies we fight, in every dastardly deed they do. They will be compelled to. And when it is over, in a world where all agree that no one can really win a war, with civilization, it may be, wrecked, with a thousand new problems raised for every one solved, and countless hatreds engendered for every one satisfied, I can think of only one factor that still will stand quite unimpaired, namely: the strange man of Galilee whom many call a visionary idealist still asking with infinite sorrow, "How can Satan cast out Satan?"

Let us take a further step and note that whether or not this principle of Jesus that evil is not to be fought with evil appeals to us, depends primarily on what it is that most of all we want. Do we really want to cast out Satan? Do we most of all desire to get rid of the evil of the world? Multitudes of people want something else altogether—their own prestige, personal or national, their gain and profit, their vengeance even or their private conquest. Of course, to such Jesus' ethic is preposterous. We cannot see his meaning truly, any more than we can see the windows of a Gothic cathedral, until we go inside, and from within his life understand what most of all he wanted. Above all else he wanted to rid the world of its evil. Whatever it cost, whether it brought him to the cross or no, somehow to rid the world of its evil was his passionate desire. If *that* is what a man wants, then evil is not an instrument to use. It is only in the light of this supreme aim and motive of Jesus that one can see his ethical principles as reasonable. If one wants most of all to cast out Satan, then an alliance with Satan is no means to that end.

Translate this into personal life and its truth is clear. A man does a wrong to us; what do we want? It may be that our first impetuous desire turns to vindictiveness—an eye for an eye and a tooth for a tooth. So one man I know of had an

[165]

enemy. For years financially he laid for him until he got him, sold him out, lock, stock, and barrel, house and furniture, and, with a satisfaction which only the vindictive know, cried, "My God! but that's conquering!" If a man wants *that*, then Jesus' ethic is preposterous.

When, however, a man did Jesus a wrong, Jesus felt concern for the man. There are different ways in which one can intimate the presence of need and none more unmistakable than to be unfair, unjust, ungenerous. When a man does a wrong it is as though he flew unwittingly a flag of distress and uttered a cry for help. Evil-doing may be variously interpreted. It may cry to us, Revenge! It may say, Ignore me! It may say, S. O. S.; there is a need to be met, a deep want in this man's life, an evil that by goodwill, perchance, you may help to cure. So when the Samaritan villagers used Jesus despitefully, he was sorry for the villagers. When Judas betrayed him, he was heartbroken because he could not help Judas. It was the wrong-heartedness itself he wanted to get rid of, the unkindness and bitterness he wished to banish from the earth. When one takes the measure of this supreme motive, Jesus' ethic becomes not preposterous but inevitable. Satan cannot cast out Satan.

If someone says that this ethic is risky, that it is bound to cost sacrifice and when used on some people is sure to fail, I answer, Of course it is. During a blizzard, a woman living on a branch of the Ohio saw a poor dog drifting on the ice-floes, and, touched with pity, ran to the stream, with difficulty launched her boat, fought for two hours before she reached the dog and brought him safely back. Then he bit her and she died of rabies. There are human curs like that. Of all men in history, do you think Jesus did not know it? But he would say, I think, Take it any way you will, human life is risky; you cannot avoid risk in life, and the salvation of the world depends on men and women who will take *this* risk, to face ill will with goodwill, to try to break the vicious circle of evil's sequence, where wrong answers wrong, and when two blows must be given to take both rather than give one.

If we say, In certain personal relationships this ethic can be made to work and it was only of these individual relationships that Jesus was thinking, I suspect that statement shows how little we know about Jesus' world. He was not tucked off in a forgotten corner of the earth. He lived on one of the major highways of the Roman Empire. Every breath of news, I suspect, from the Thames to the Euphrates, soon or late came to Nazareth. He lived in a violent generation when force ruled the world and might made right as terribly as it does today. He lived in a nation seething with violent revolt. He dealt not only with Sadducees, compromising with Rome; not only with Pharisees, waiting for their supernatural Messiah to come from heaven and redeem them; but with Zealots, fiery, militant, revolutionary rebels, crying out for bloodshed to make right their heinous wrongs. This public situation, so dreadfully like ours, Jesus had in mind when he turned his back on revenge and bloodshed and based his ministry on undiscourageable goodwill.

It was this public situation he faced in the temptation at the beginning of his ministry, when the devil, as it were, showed him all the kingdoms of the earth and said: "All these things will I give thee, if thou wilt fall down and worship me." How perennial a temptation that is! How terribly it assails us all today! To join forces with the devil to beat the devil, to fight evil with evil—ah, Christ, how did you resist the pressure of it in your time and how in a world like this do you expect us to follow you?

Yet when in calmer moments one faces the facts, one wonders if he is not right. Satan cannot cast out Satan—all history is a running commentary on that. The means determine the end. We of all generations should understand that. Did we not fight a war to make the world safe for democracy? We were resisting evil. We prided ourselves on that. We were morally indignant against a real wrong and sacrificially devoted to a holy cause. We would make the world safe for democracy. Conscription to make the world safe for democracy! Poison gas, bombing of open cities, blockades that starved millions, to make the world safe for democracy! Dictatorial control of the whole nation's life—even of what we ate and wore—the very suspension of the Bill of Rights, to make the world safe for democracy! And in the end a treaty, the only kind of treaty modern war can issue in—vengeful, selfish, cruel—to make the world safe for democracy! So we woke up to find the world less safe for democracy than it had been in generations. We discovered that war, being essentially totalitarian and dictatorial, is ill-fitted to defend democracy, and that the means determine the end. Ah, Christ, you are not a visionary idealist; you are the sanest realist of us all. Satan cannot cast out Satan.

Let us take a further step and note the positive power of this ethic when it is put to work. For it is not weak, as the average man thinks, but very strong. Of all ridiculous beatitudes, some would say, the most incredible is the one where Jesus sums this ethic up and the faith on which it is built: "Blessed are the meek: for they shall inherit the earth." What nonsense! says the average man. Yet would you stake your credit upon the opposite? Blessed are the Hitlers for they shall inherit the earth! Would you? Grant him every temporary victory you think possible. Would you say that in the long run he will inherit the earth? I know no intelligent person who thinks that. All history rises up against that. Like children's sand houses built upon the shore, age after age the tides of destiny have risen and wiped out the empires built on force. Of all contrasts in history none could be more disproportionate than that between the Roman Empire on one side and Calvary's cross upon the other. Yet the Roman Empire has fallen and many another empire since, like children's blocks toppling in a row, but still that cross stands and haunts the conscience of the world. So I think Jesus sat many a day upon the hills above Nazareth and looked across the plain of Esdraelon, stretching mile after mile before his gaze. There the historic battles of the world had been fought. There the empires of the Euphrates and the Nile had clashed. Age after age violence had met violence and kings and pharaohs had fallen in futility, and Satan had never cast out Satan yet. It was from that vision, not first of an ideal but of the facts, that Jesus went out, I think, determined, though he died for it, to introduce into the world a new and revolutionary ethic —meet ill will with goodwill, dare to break the vicious circle of evil answering evil, never fight wrong with wrong. Satan cannot cast out Satan.

This does not mean that all use of force is satanic. Coercion has its proper place in life, always indicating a pathological condition but capable of salutary use in the interests of the whole community, as, for example, against the insane or the criminal. Even in such realms, however, the Christian ethic has been so far influential that not retaliation but cure and reformation have become the test and aim of intelligent procedure. Because one believes in municipal police one is not by any logic driven, as some seem to suppose, to believe in war. War is a highly specialized form of force, in its preparations, procedures, and results distinguishable from any other of force's exhibitions. One may believe in the police and think dueling wrong; one may grant the salutary nature of coercion communally applied for the good of all and still think gladiatorial shows are unmitigated and outmoded evil. So one may pray and work for an ultimate international community, in which the collective security of all is the aim of all, and the policing of the world is the joint affair of all, and may still see clearly that at the present moment no war will mean that, or anything aimed in that direction, but will be the old satanic, retaliatory process, motived by imperialistic ambitions and waged with sadistic savagery to an end catastrophically evil. War is satanic and only Satan has anything to gain from it.

However some may doubt the possibility of applying this principle to public affairs, however the titanic difficulties in its way may loom to dismaying proportions, how can one doubt its magisterial power in personal relationships? I would almost venture to say that any special fineness of spirit that anybody here possesses is his because sometime he has lived at the receiving end of this ethical principle. For there are three kinds of goodness in the world. First, coerced goodness, where someone is good to us because we can require it. That is not impressive. Then there is deserved goodness, where we have been good to someone and now, *quid pro quo,* so much for so much, he is good to us. That is not deeply impressive. Then there is undeserved goodness, where we have been unworthy, ungenerous, unkind, unjust, and lo! someone comes back at us with goodwill and friendliness. From the days at home when our parents so treated us, through all our lives, no force has reached so deep, laid hold so hard, lifted so powerfully, as that. Thank God not everybody has slapped back at us! Thank God some people did go the second mile with us! The salvation of the world depends on the multiplication of people who understand and practice that adventurous ethic.

Do not misunderstand me as saying that it is simple to apply this principle to the world's large affairs. It is desperately difficult. No one of us is wise enough to see around the next corner. Only this seems clear, that we Americans are at the fork of the road and that either we are going to throw the vast influence of this nation on the side of those constructive forces that make for international goodwill and conference instead of violence, or else we are in for an era dominated by our aping of our enemies. They make war! We make war! They build vast armaments! We build vast armaments! They use incendiary bombs! We use incendiary

bombs! They say, All restrictions off on the most brutal instincts of mankind! We say the same, until once more, fighting evil with evil until we are the evil that we fight, far from
conquering our enemies we let them make us after their own
image. So at long last, at the end of a ruinous era, we shall
be facing again the question—which God grant us grace to
face now before it is too late—"How can Satan cast out
Satan?"

God Talks to a Dictator

THIS is not the first time in history that the world has faced the military conquests of dictators. Long ago a Hebrew prophet lived through an era like ours, when his people were assailed by the Assyrians, but unlike most of us he achieved a standpoint from which to view the scene, that was distinctive of his religious prophethood—he heard God talking to the dictator.

Granted that in an absolute and literal sense no man can know what God would say to anyone! Yet this is one of man's distinctive attributes, that he can erect himself higher than himself and see the situations that confront him, not simply from a level stance but from above, as they might look to God. That is what a prophet is for—to help people see their contemporary world in wide perspective from a height, as God might see it. So Isaiah heard God talking to the dictator. "The Assyrian came down like the wolf on the fold," so that Judea lay under the thralldom of a conqueror, and in distress and confusion, as among us now, everyone was talking about him and to him. But history has thought it worth-while to record only what the prophet heard God say to him: "Ho Assyrian, the rod of mine anger, the staff in whose hand is mine indignation!"

The Jews hated that conqueror. He seemed altogether wild and lawless; he threatened their temple and their culture; his victory meant to them the downfall of their choicest values; he was to them anti-God, as though some volcanic evil, some demonic force, had escaped from God's control and was running amuck in the world. They felt about him as we feel about Hitler. Then Isaiah heard God talking to him, calling him, as Dr. Moffatt translates it, "my club in anger, the rod I wield in wrath." So that dictator was not merely wild and lawless; he had not escaped the sovereignty of God; he was a rod in God's hands; God had picked him up; God was using him; God could lay him down again. The dictator himself did not know this. Says Isaiah, "other plans has he, and other aims!" But even amid his devastations God talked to him as though to say, You are my instrument; I am using you; I took you up, and I can throw you down.

Like all typical religious language this is picturesque metaphor and simile. We may not interpret it to mean that God uses evil means to good ends. In two ways we deal with evil, sometimes choosing it as a method, as Jesus' enemies chose his crucifixion to secure a result they wanted, sometimes confronting it, as Jesus himself confronted the cross, not choosing it but forced to face it, and turning it to the purposes of man's salvation. The choice of evil for good ends is always wrong; the use of evil, when it is thrust upon us, to high purposes is one of the noblest forms of moral victory. It is in the second category, not the first, that we should place Isaiah's vision of God as he says to the Assyrian conqueror, You are my rod.

In the first place, Isaiah saw God using that conqueror as a just punishment on Judea for its sins. "Ho Assyrian, the rod of mine anger." That was a dreadful thing for the prophet to have to say to his own people, but he said it. He was like a faithful psychiatrist dealing with one of us when we blaze out with indignation against someone who, we think, is wronging us. For the psychiatrist says, Wait a moment; that was your own fault; you brought that on yourself. So Isaiah spoke to the people. They suffered their tragedy, he said, because they deserved it.

Unless we can see that truth about ourselves today, I am sure we have missed one of the major meanings of our catastrophe. We brought this disaster upon ourselves.

As a matter of historic fact, it was only by giving that

interpretation to the conquerors that the Jewish prophets achieved the monotheism they have bequeathed to us. For in those days the theory was that there were many gods, each nation having its own deities, and the theological question then was which nation's gods were most real and powerful. The answer to that polytheistic question was naturally made evident in war. If one nation conquered another, clearly the gods of the conquerors were real and strong, and the gods of the conquered weak. So when Assyria triumphed over Judea, the popular conclusion was swift and clear—the gods of Assyria must be real; the gods of Israel must be futile. Monotheism never could have come from that interpretation of the conqueror.

The great prophets gave us monotheism because they saw the conqueror from another point of view. They said not that he disproved the one true God, but that he represented the inevitable punishment of the one true God on his people's sin. The victory of Assyria was to the prophets not evidence of God's weakness or abdication, but of God's terrific reality as the impartial administrator of ethical cause and consequence. The one God of Israel, they cried, is still the God of all the world, but he is a God of moral law; not even a chosen people can escape his punishments! When, then, the Assyrian conquered Judea, and all the people were tempted to cry, That proves the gods of Assyria to be real! the prophet said, Rather that proves that we have sinned, and that the Eternal God of righteousness plays no favorites in this world, but brings down his judgment even on Judea when she rebels.

As a matter of historic fact that is the way we got monotheism—from prophets penitent enough to acknowledge that their catastrophe was the one God's just punishment on their own people's sin. And that is not ancient history. Some today say that Hitler and Mussolini prove that the gods of naziism and fascism are the true gods. Others say that these conquerors with their cruel devastations prove that there is no

God at all. The prophetic vision is needed afresh to see that what the dictators really prove is that we all have sinned, that this is a morally law-abiding world, that cause does bring consequence, that God cannot be mocked, that what we sow we reap, that our present tragedy is the inevitable result of our joint guilt.

There are many things in these troubled days that the church cannot do to help, but some things are the church's special business, and none, I think, more crucial and important than to keep penitence alive in this situation. Said a wise friend to me recently: "If all of us could go to the council table after this war is over in the spirit of penitence, there might be some hope." Well, without that there can be no hope at all.

Moreover, we of the democracies should be especially penitent. We won the last war. With utter and crushing completeness we won it. Never forget that. Endure, if you can, the reading of one paragraph from President Wilson's announcement of the Armistice to Congress in 1918: "We know that the object of the war is attained; the object upon which all free men had set their hearts; and attained with a sweeping completeness which even now we do not realize. Armed imperialism such as the men conceived who were but yesterday the masters of Germany is at an end, its illicit ambitions engulfed in black disaster. Who will now seek to revive it? The arbitrary power of the military caste of Germany which once could secretly and of its own single choice disturb the peace of the world is discredited and destroyed. And more than that—much more than that—has been accomplished." So completely did we, the democracies, win the war. We were in charge of the world. We could do what we would. As to what we did and did not do, the bill of particulars has been written again and again, and I know no judgment more unanimous than this—that we of the democracies are more responsible for the rise of the dictators than the plain people of the dictatorships themselves. Penitence becomes us well.

There are many angles from which one can look at Hitler and Mussolini today. I am not denying the truth in any of them, but they are partial and incomplete unless we humbly and penitently recognize that the dictators have come as an inevitable consequence of our joint sin, unless we hear, as it were, the moral order of this universe talking to them, saying: "Ho Assyrian, the rod of mine anger."

Now such penitence is not at home in wartime. In wartime pride is at home. Today pride rules our wills. In picking out sin and distributing blame we practice selective attention. We can easily see the iniquities of everyone except ourselves and our friends. We Christians should do better than that, as Lincoln did during the Civil War. I commend his spirit to you. "If God wills that . . . all the wealth piled by the bondman's two hundred and fifty years of unrequited toil shall be sunk, and . . . every drop of blood drawn with the lash shall be paid by another drawn with the sword; as was said three thousand years ago, so still it must be said, 'The judgments of the Lord are true and righteous altogether.' "

In the second place, however, this address of God to the dictator implies another meaning, namely, that God is employing the dictator to some good purpose of his own. When the populace upon the common levels saw the conqueror's victory, they cried, All is lost! But the prophets did not. God had picked up that rod of Assyria, they said; he would do something with it before he laid it down. They found, that is, not only humility and penitence, but courage and hope in the sovereignty of God.

There is a strange verse in one of the Psalms addressed to the Lord which says, "the wrath of man shall praise thee." How can that be true? It says that God can take man's evil and use it, that in his hands even man's wrath and iniquity are not a total loss. It says that God can use downright sin, as though a piece of grit that did not belong there, getting into an oyster shell, the oyster could make into a pearl after all. How can that be true about sin? Yet, where would we be in personal life if that were not true? When a man sins, need that be a total loss? No, not necessarily a total loss. It may seem dangerous for a preacher to give that answer, but it is the true one. Even downright wickedness need not be a total loss.

Did that Prodigal Son, for example, learn nothing in the far country that God could put to good use afterwards? He learned a lot that boys who stay at home never know. It was dreadful. Only a fool would go through what he went through for the sake of learning it. But when in after days some boy was tempted to seek the far country, who was it in that Jewish town that best could help him? That Prodigal. He knew. He could put his very sin to use for the sake of God and of that other boy now tempted. We are often told that we ought to capitalize our troubles, and transform them into sympathy, understanding, and increased usefulness. That is true also about our sin. Here it is, a great mistake, a wrong committed. It is a loss, but thank God it need not be a total loss. Capitalize it. There are some people we especially can help because of it. God can use it. He can make even the wrath of men praise him.

Even unredeemed sinners God uses. We constantly and rightly exalt the ways in which God has used Christ, his perfect instrument. Yes, but he has used Judas Iscariot too. Someone, I suppose, had to try that experiment of betraying Christ, and stand there, an example of the way such betrayal looks when seen in the retrospect of history. How many of us, then, in some pinch in our lives when we have been tempted to betray Christ, have thought of Judas, and have said, No! not that! I'll not do that! God can use even Judas.

I am pleading for what our fathers called an overruling Providence, as though man's wickedness, like a stream, could indeed go wild, break its banks, and let loose a torrential flood, but lo! there is a lie of the land that gets control in the end, a limit beyond which no stream's wildness can go, a contour to the landscape, a shape to the eternal hills, a declivity in the valleys, that at last bring even the wildest streams to terms and force them into channels that they did not choose. That fact about the world the great prophets saw. "Ho Assyrian!"

As a matter of history, this has been true in man's public affairs. The Roman Empire was a vast imperialism, cruel, selfish, bloody. Was it a total loss? Far from it! God used Rome for an overriding of racial and national boundaries, a unifying of the known world, a creative building of law and order, to which we still are incalculably indebted. The French Revolution was terrible, with tumbrils rolling down Parisian streets, and heads falling daily beneath the guillotine. Was it a total loss? Far from it! In the retrospect of history it left gains that cannot be measured. Hitler and Mussolini represent everything that most we fear and hate in public life. Will they be a total loss? Not unless history reverses itself. My friends, a radical change in the world order has been long overdue. Our military and economic imperialisms, our subjugation of native peoples, our insane tariff barriers, our unjust division of the world's resources, have long cried out for change. We the democracies might have done it peacefully, but alas! we failed. Now the dictators come. They are to me as terrible as they are to you, but be sure of this, in the retrospect of history they will not be a total loss. God is saying to them today: Ho Assyrian, my rod!

Indeed, has it not occurred to us that Hitler may turn out to be a powerful, even though unintentional, friend of democracy? For consider! We in the democracies were slipping. Indeed, we were! We were taking democracy for granted. Was it not a lovely way of living that our fathers had bequeathed to us? What we could get out of it, not what we should dedicate to it, was foremost in our thoughts. Our life in this country had become undisciplined, soft, indulgent, careless, and what we took so easily for granted we had forgotten deeply and sacrificially to value. But now democracy is in danger, and there has been in the United States more care about it, more study of what it means, more concern over its foundations, more sense of its value in the last year than in many a year before. Alas! we never value anything as we should until we face the peril of losing it. That is true even in the family, where some loved person who for years has been safely at our side, who has been assumed as part of the scenery of our life, falls ill, and we wake up to see how carelessly we have been taking for granted one whom we so easily might lose. So today we feel about democracy. It has become to us a very dear thing. We have faced the possibility of seeing democracy crushed, and we have said that democracy should not die as long as free spirits were left in the world. Who has wrought this change? Hitler. What then? Am I saying, Thank God for Hitler? Far from it, but thank God for God, who towers above Hitler, who can use him, despite himself, for causes that he has no mind to serve. Thank God for that lie of the land that no overflowing flood can ultimately escape, but that will turn the wildest currents to channels that not they but God chooses!

See what I am pleading for—faith in the God of history. Throughout my ministry two aspects of God have been predominant in my thought and preaching—the God of nature, and the God of inner personal experience. But in these days another aspect of deity grows imperative—the God of history. Not to be identified with any national policy, not even with our own, the God of history sitteth above the circle of the earth, and the nations are accounted as a drop in the bucket. And there he is today, and his word to the dictators has not lost its power: Ho Assyrian, my rod!

This leaves us a brief moment for the final truth involved

in the prophet's insight. When God picks up a rod, he can throw it down again. He always has. These rods of his, these conquerors that seem so strong, one by one have been thrown down. God picked them up. Well, then, "Shall the axe boast itself against him that heweth therewith? shall the saw magnify itself against him that wieldeth it?"

One of the great passages in Victor Hugo's *Les Misérables* is his description of the Battle of Waterloo. Recall how it ends: "Was it possible for Napoleon to win the battle? We answer in the negative. Why? On account of Wellington, on account of Blücher? No; on account of God. . . . When the earth is suffering from an excessive burden, there are mysterious groans from the shadow, which the abyss hears. Napoleon had been denounced in infinitude, and his fall was decided. He had angered God." Napoleon himself had an intimation of this fact, for he said once: "As long as I am necessary, no power in the world will be able to brush me aside. But the moment I become unnecessary, an atom will be enough to smash me."

I am not saying that in this grim crisis that confronts the world we can shoulder off on God all the responsibility of getting rid of the conquerors, as though he would settle everything. We have our tasks, many and imperative, to make these dictators unnecessary and impossible. But if we are to have strength for them, we need to see and hear more than the daily news brings to our eyes and ears. Not we humans alone, but God also is talking to the dictators, and in the broad perspective of history it is not too difficult to discover what he is saying: Ho Assyrian! the rod of mine indignation, the punishment of the world's sins—he is saying that. I am using you, and, far beyond your will, you will serve my purposes and not be a total loss—he is saying that. But he is saying also, When I am through with you, you are done! No wild stream, however madly it grows turbulent, can in the end escape the lie of my land.

Ah Christ! How utterly different you are from the dictators! How weak today you often seem in comparison with them! Yet the long perspectives of history suggest another judgment.

> I saw the conquerors riding by
>   With cruel lips and faces wan:
> Musing on kingdoms sacked and burned
>   There rode the Mongol Genghis Khan;
>
> And Alexander, like a god,
>   Who sought to weld the world in one;
> And Caesar with his laurel wreath;
>   And like a thing from Hell the Hun;
>
> And, leading like a star, the van,
>   Heedless of upstretched arm and groan,
> Inscrutable Napoleon went,
>   Dreaming of empire, and alone . . .
>
> Then all they perished from the earth,
>   As fleeting shadows from a glass,
> And, conquering down the centuries,
>   Came Christ the Swordless on an ass.

The Essential Elements in a Vital Christian Experience

THE worse the world is without, the deeper we all need to go within. The profound meanings of inward, personal, Christian experience become not less but more important in a turbulent and dismaying era. What, then, are the essential elements in a vital religious life, so basic that from Quaker to Roman Catholic all Christians at their best have shared them? Are they not a great need, a great salvation, a great gratitude, and a great compulsion?

Often the doom of Christianity has been announced. Many a time it has sinned against light and fallen on evil days. It has been used as a mere counter in a political game, as Napoleon used it and as more than one dictator would like to use it now. Often it has faced new world views and refused new knowledge. Time and again it has identified itself with some contemporary social *status quo* and has seemed to collapse with the downfall of the system it was tied to. How often the cry has risen which Voltaire voiced in the eighteenth century: "Ere the beginning of the nineteenth century Christianity will have disappeared from the earth"! But it has not disappeared. Its expressions change but at the heart of it are creative factors that everlastingly keep their hold: a great need, a great salvation, a great gratitude, and a great compulsion.

First, then, a great need. No one achieves a vital, personal, Christian experience without a profound sense of need. While many think of need as a sign of weakness, the fact is that there is no truer test of the status of any creature in the scale of existence than the size, amplitude, and quality of his needs. See this strange creature, man, that the materialists tell us is but an accidental bundle of atoms drifting toward oblivion. That estimate of man seems to some of us incredible if only because of what it takes to meet this creature's needs. If he wanted only food for his body, like some animals, then an animal he would be. But he has curiosity that must explore the farthest stars and build great telescopes to get at the stars he cannot see. That is an incredible thing for a mere bundle of atoms to need to do. The badge of man's dignity, the sign of his greatness, is this outreach of want without whose satisfaction he cannot be content. He needs music and books and art—not telephones and airplanes only, though that is mysterious enough, but ideals for himself and his society, a clear conscience, great purposes to live for, and high faiths to live by, if at his best he is to be content. Such need is incredible in a mere bundle of atoms. Need, first of all, is not a sign of weakness but the mark of a creature's status in the scale of existence. Consider, then, the fact that age after age millions of folk have sought a personal experience of Christ because they needed him.

To different people this need comes in different ways. With many it appears as a sense of inadequacy in meeting the demands of life. For the demands of life can be terrific. A father lately had to say farewell for the last time to his sixteen-year-old son. There on the hospital bed lay the boy, ill of an insidious disease but with no idea that he was going to die. And one evening the father, as though it were a matter of course, not at all revealing what he knew, had to say "Good night, son," and hear the boy say "Good night, Dad," knowing all the time that that was the final good-by and that before morning the boy would die. What demands life makes on us! Who can meet them? Not simply when they come suddenly but when they come slowly in the long drag of the years, putting burdens on us difficult to sustain, who can face life's demands, whether in youth or age, without a need of spiritual reinforcement to meet the strain?

To others this experience comes mainly through moral failure. For sin is a Trojan horse. We welcome it through a breach in our walls as the ancient city did, expectant of happiness, but it has inside it many hostile forces we never suspected, that in the night come creeping out! Habit, for example, so that we start free to sin and then wake up to discover that we are not free to stop. Guilt, for example, so that we begin with high anticipation of pleasure only to find that our sin passes from anticipation through committal into memory, and, changing its visage, becomes guilt and settles down to haunt us like a ghost. Explicit punishment, for example, for there is something terrific in this universe that finds out a man's mistakes and even at long last lays a heavy hand upon them. Perhaps, worst of all, we sin thinking only of ourselves and our pleasures and then discover that we have involved others and that the consequences of our evil blast the hopes and happiness of those for whom we really care. So, age after age, people facing moral failure and its tragic aftermath have sought a personal experience of Christ, his forgiveness and re-establishment, because they needed him.

To others this experience comes not so much from life's demands or even from moral failure, as from a positive vision of life's possibilities. When I was a boy I do not recall that I needed great music. I had little chance to hear any. Once, as a lad, I was taken to a symphony but I did not like it. Then one day some really great music broke through. That was a strange experience; to use Wordsworth's words, it disturbed "me with the joy of elevated thoughts." I awoke to a new need, something that ever afterward I must have to be content—a solace, comfort, incentive, and inspiration. That is a strange experience, to break into a new realm of need, where something you have not known before becomes necessary to you, and that experience is most often reduplicated through the awakening influence of great personalities. Remember Alcibiades saying to Socrates: "There is one experience I have in the presence of this man alone, such as no-body would expect in me; and that is, to be made to feel ashamed; he alone can make me feel it. For he brings home to me that I cannot disown the duty of doing what he bids me, but that as soon as I turn from his company I fall a victim to the favours of the crowd." Above all others, Christ has so disturbed people. They could not live beside him and still be what they were. They awoke to a new sense of need from a new vision of possibility.

Whatever way it comes to us, this is the first element in a vital Christian experience. If someone says he feels no such need, that is a pity. Some feel no need of music, or of books, or of the beauty of God's out-of-doors, and that fact is a revelation of their status in the scale of existence. What kind of person do you think he is who does not need interior re-sources of spiritual power to face life's strains, conquer its temptations, and fulfill its possibilities?

The second element in a vital Christian experience is a great salvation. To be sure, that word troubles me. Words can fall into bad company and be dragged down by their associates. When St. Paul's Cathedral in London was finished, the architect displayed it to the king on a state occasion and the king called it amusing, awful, and artificial. The architect was overjoyed at the royal compliment for in those days "amusing" meant "amazing," "awful" meant "awe-inspiring," and "artificial" meant "artistic." So words change their meaning, and "salvation" has often walked in undesirable intellectual company and gotten incredible connotations. I beg of you today to use the word, since there is no other to be used, in its finest and best sense.

If a man has ever been lost in the woods at night or on the sea in a fog in a small boat without a compass, and then help has come, he ought to know what it feels like to be saved. If a man has ever been unemployed and the long succession of days that were hard and nights that were terrible have worn him down, and then employment has come again, he ought to know what it means to be saved. If our family life was ever in peril and we had almost given up hope, and then a better spirit came and the rift in the lute was mended and what we cared more for than anything else in the world became lovely again, we ought to know what it means to be saved. And in the same realistic sense, if we have ever known a desperate need for help to stand life's strains, overcome its temptations, and fulfill its possibilities, and then victory has come through the revelation of power that Christ has brought, the word "salvation" ought to have a vivid place in our vocabulary. At any rate, across the ages millions of people have found a great need thus met by a great salvation.

This experience comes to most of us in two general ways. To many it is opportunity for a second chance. They have failed, messed up their lives, and have only the remnants left of their first opportunity. Then they face that amazing, unbelievable offer of a second chance. A friend of mine attended cooking school sometime since and the title of one of the announced lectures has fascinated my imagination ever since—"Putting the Lure into the Leftovers." That lesson is needed far outside a cooking school. Who has not needed *that?* The Prodigal in the far country with only the remnants of his first opportunity left needed something that would put the lure into those leftovers, and, all the ages since, men like Augustine—afterwards St. Augustine—who ran away from home and lived with his mistress, and even after he had felt Christ's attraction cried: "The worse that I knew so well had more power over me than the better that I knew not," have needed something or someone who could put the lure into the leftovers. Who of us here has not thus failed, made a mess of some first chance, stood with only the remnants left, and then faced that incredible miracle of forgiveness that reestablishes the old relationships as though we had not broken them, and offers a second chance?

Along with this first factor in a saving experience goes strength to make something of the second chance. For any kind of failure, moral failure in particular, is a Svengali to the soul. It hypnotizes us, and, casting upon us its horrid spell, towers over us, saying, You cannot; you have failed; you are whipped. Who has not experienced that? And who has not cried out for someone who could defeat that incantation, break that enchantment, and lift him up to answer back, as Paul answered even in a Roman prison, I can—"In Him who strengthens me, I am able for anything."

Sometimes I think we preachers, overawed by the formal dignity of the pulpit, talk too anonymously and impersonally. Here I am today, an older man talking to you about the secret of spiritual power in general, when all the time what I am really seeing in my imagination's eye is that young man I was years ago, shot all to pieces, done in and shattered in a nervous breakdown, foolishly undertaking too much work and doing it unwisely, all my hopes in ashes and life towering over me, saying, You are finished; you cannot; you are done for. People ask me why in young manhood I wrote *The Meaning of Prayer*. That came out of young manhood's struggle. I desperately needed a second chance and reinforcement to carry on with it. I was sunk unless I could find at least a little of what Paul had in mind when he said, I can— "In Him who strengthens me, I am able for anything."

That is salvation—forgiveness, a second chance, reinforcement, power, the voice of a friend out of the fog where all direction has been lost, saying, I am here, and, You can! Across the ages Christ has meant that to men—a great need met by a great salvation.

The third element in a personal experience of Christ is a great gratitude. One cannot understand the New Testament or the driving power of the Christian church at its best without taking the measure of the fact that a profound need met by a profound salvation has issued in a profound gratitude.

Mark this strange fact that the church is the only organization in the world that advertises itself as a company of sinners. That fact is worth walking around. In the second century Celsus the pagan jeered at the Christians because of this. To the heathen world it seemed a ridiculous, incredible thing that a great company of people should advertise themselves as sinners and to their fellowship welcome sinners. And still it is a unique phenomenon. Where else will you find people standing up to say that they have done those things they ought not to have done and have left undone those things they ought to have done and there is no health in them? And even when we do not use those words, how difficult it is to find a scripture or a hymn without the accent of penitence!

> When the worldling, sick at heart,
>   Lifts his soul above;
> When the prodigal looks back
>   To his Father's love;
> When the proud man, from his pride,
>   Stoops to seek thy face;
> When the burdened brings his guilt
>   To thy throne of grace.

Here is a unique phenomenon, the founding of a world-wide fellowship explicitly made up of sinners. One cannot understand what that means until one sees that a great need, met by a great salvation, has issued in a great gratitude.

That, of course, is the reason why the Lord's Supper, to a Christian who understands it, is the climax of Christian worship. The early Christians called it the Eucharist. What does Eucharist mean? It is the Greek word for "thank you." Just as in France we say *Merci*, or in Italy, *Gratia*, so in modern Greece we say *Eucharisto*, that is, Eucharist, thank you. The Lord's Supper is the church of Christ, knowing that it is made up of sinners, having faced a profound need, met with a profound salvation, going up before the cross of

[188]

Christ, the symbol of the price paid for our help, to express a great gratitude.

The ethical implications of such gratitude are immense. Gratitude, someone has said, is the mother of all virtues. That is a defensible proposition. Here is a man who has no spark of gratitude anywhere concealed about his person. He thinks life has been egregiously unjust to him. He is resentful and rebellious about life. You will get no great living out of him. Or here is another man who thinks life consists in getting what you have earned. It is *quid pro quo*, so much for so much, and he suspects he is breaking about even; he is getting what he earns and is earning what he gets. You will find no superior living in such a man. But here is a man who feels that no matter what he does he never can pay back the debt he owes. To be sure, there is injustice in his experience and *quid pro quo* too, but when life is taken as a whole, he feels that he has received what he never could deserve or earn. In all ages the finest living has come out of folk like that.

This is not simply a matter of religion. Consider, for example, the millions of us born in democratic nations, who have strolled into the privileges of democracy and nonchalantly have settled down there without a grateful thought. We have even been dominated by resentfulness over the failures of democracy or by nonchalance toward its liberties. But who can take the measure of these present days and not rise to another attitude? Freedom is precious in the world today. It was won for us, before we were born, by our fathers, who with thought, labor, and sacrifice built a democratic nation where the rights of individual souls and of minorities would be respected. We should be grateful. Our lives, our fortunes, our sacred honor are owed to democracy. There is something to be said for the idea that gratitude is the mother of all virtues. Certainly, there is no such thing as a vital Christian experience without it. Need of Christ, salvation in Christ, gratitude toward Christ—those three phrases are, as it were, the stethoscope where we can hear the very heartbeat of the gospel.

The fourth element in a creative experience of Christ is a great compulsion. For it stands to reason that if a man has known a deep want, met by a great redemption issuing in a profound thankfulness, then something has gotten hold of him. He is not his own. He has been taken possession of. He is under a powerful inner compulsion.

Now compulsion is a part of every man's life. One way or another, life coerces all of us and no one of us can escape the word "must." But how vast the difference between those mere creatures of circumstance, pushed and pulled by outward chance and fortune, on one side, and, on the other side, the elect spirits of the race whose compulsion is from within! The great musicians, the Beethovens, Tschaikowskys, Brahms, must write music. Why must they? No one makes them. But they know the need that only music can supply; they have had an experience of music bringing to them its saving satisfaction; they have a gratitude toward music that no words can express; and so they are under a compulsion strong as steel and ineluctable as destiny. They must give their lives to music. The elect spirits of the race know this compulsion from within.

So Paul said: "I must also see Rome." Why must he? No one made him undertake that risky adventure that ended with his beheading on the Appian Way. I must see Africa, said Livingstone. Why must he? No one coerced him from his Scottish home to die in his tent in Africa with his face fallen into the open pages of the Bible, a sacrifice to his high endeavor to paint the dark continent white. Here is the secret of man's greatness and his liberty, to have compulsion not from without but from within. And in quieter lives among our friends or in our families, who of us has not known such characters, who could have said: "O Love that wilt not let me go"?

No need of the modern world is so deep as the need for this kind of character. We could muddle along without much more scientific invention. We could get by with no more sky-scrapers and gadgets. But we cannot get by without more Christian character if by that we mean what we have been talking about. Theologies change; creeds alter; the world views of one generation are incredible to the next; the mental patterns that Paul, Augustine, Calvin used we cannot exactly copy. But when we range up into this experience of pro-found need met in Christ by a great salvation, that issues in a deep gratitude so that we are inwardly taken possession of by a high compulsion, we not only overpass the differences between our contemporary sects but the differences between the centuries. Paul would understand *that*, and St. Augustine and Luther and Phillips Brooks. In that experience is the real communion of the saints. When one pleads for that one is pleading for the basic structural material without which no decent society can be built. When one pleads for that one is pleading for a quality of character without which man at his best cannot be satisfied. If you lack it, seek it. If you have a little of it, deepen it—a great need, a great salvation, a great gratitude, a great compulsion.

When Great Events Make Common Tasks Seem Trivial

THIS terrific world situation affects us all in many ways, but one effect in particular every one of us must feel: it makes our ordinary daily tasks seem trivial. Here is a stupendous upheaval, threatening to shake civilization to pieces, the greatest world revolution, they tell us, since the downfall of the Roman Empire, and yet we go on, day after day, with our common duties, household tasks, personal relationships, office routine, professional service, getting on with people, helping a little here and there if we can—how trifling it all seems!

To be sure, this feeling of mediocrity and humdrum is one of the major curses of human life anyway, even in ordinary days. Because of this many people die long before they are really dead, their lives losing zest, and a dull, drab, gray fog of commonplaceness settling over them. One American humorist, after trying to make his diary sound important, says that at last he gave it up and began writing every day: "Got up, washed, and went to bed."

Many of us, however, who in calmer times did not surrender to this mood, are tempted to it now. We look at the world today with telescopic eyes—the events are far-flung and prodigious—and then when we turn those same eyes upon our day-by-day routine, we can hardly see it. It is, therefore, with a real situation in mind, affecting us all, that we turn our attention to a saying of Jesus: "He that is faithful in a very little is faithful also in much: and he that is unrighteous in a very little is unrighteous also in much."

This at least is clear, that to have our commonplace living elevated, dignified, and made meaningful, would be a redeeming experience. Why was Charles Dickens so popular? Because he did just that—he took ordinary people, limited, queer, commonplace, and he made their story more thrilling than the life of kings. They walked across his pages filled with interest, humor, gentleness, courage, and zest. Stefan Zweig is right in saying about Dickens: "He unveiled the poetry that was ambushed in the prosaic . . . he gave to simple things and unpretentious people a glory all their own. . . . To thousands, nay to millions, he revealed where to find the everlasting spark in their uneventful lives, where to look for the glow of quiet joy hidden beneath the ashes of the familiar."

Today we turn to a greater than Dickens, who says to us amid the stupendous events of our time: "He that is faithful in a very little is faithful also in much."

One element in our American temperament runs counter to the truth we are trying to get at. We Americans have been notoriously impressed by size. A big country, big buildings, big business, the biggest this or that—we are noted for our interest in large dimensions, and to say of anyone that he does things in a big way, is for all Americans a compliment. Someone has called this attitude "Jumboism." Unhappy the man today, however, who has no other view of life than that, for the big things are going wrong. Vast empires at war, whole races set against whole races, world-wide conflicts of economic imperialism, great nations outlawing religion and turning to atheism, one powerful land after another accepting communism, fascism, naziism—who can find light and hope in the way the big affairs of the world are going?

But now ask, Where are the sources of encouragement, so that we do keep going, sometimes with high heart, our joy in living refreshed, and even God made real? Surely the answer lies in little things. I know some homes that are a heaven on earth, some friends whose presence kindles all the best within, some characters making of small garden plots lovely places, some quiet souls carrying tasks and burdens with splendid courage, some spiritual lives that make one sure that God is there, and some groups of people, too, organizing goodwill to bring at least a little light in dark places.

This in general is a true picture of our world today, isn't it? The big things are going wrong, and the experiences that kindle faith and courage, dust us off and set us on our feet again, and sometimes even put a song upon our lips, come from sources characterized not by quantity but by quality—small, vital, quiet, deep, real, spiritual.. In a world like this we may not say, then, that it is unimportant how we handle our daily lives. That is where most of the world's light comes from today, that, as Portia said, shines like a candle in this naughty world. It comes from good people handling small affairs well. Let that light die out and the whole world would be dark indeed. What if Jesus, in a sense far profounder than we have commonly supposed, was right when he said: "He that is faithful in a very little is faithful also in much"?

Nevertheless, lest anyone should suppose that we are going to neglect the world's large affairs, let us organize our thought by asking, What are the great problems of the world today? What would you say they are?

Surely, for one thing, saving democracy. We all would say that. Let us start with that, then, and see how the truth of the Master's saying operates! It is a dangerous fallacy to suppose that democracy is mainly a matter of vast political overheads and constitutional arrangements, and to forget that democracy is the most spiritually demanding order of society ever proposed, its indispensable foundations in the character and attitude of plain people. One of the most interesting things in our time is to see the skeptics and cynics come over to join the preachers. I could name many who have done that. Mr. Walter Lippmann is typical. A few years ago we preachers were attacking Mr. Lippmann because of his frankly skeptical writings about religion, but now listen to him:

What is left of our civilization will not be maintained, what has been wrecked will not be restored, by imagining that some new political gadget can be invented, some new political formula improvised which will save it. Our civilization can be maintained and restored only by remembering and rediscovering the truths, and by re-establishing the virtuous habits on which it was founded. There is no use looking into the blank future for some new and fancy revelation of what man needs in order to live. The revelation has been made. By it man conquered the jungle about him and the barbarian within him. The elementary principles of work and sacrifice and duty—and the transcendent criteria of truth, justice and righteousness—and the grace of love and charity—are the things which have made men free. Men can keep their freedom and reconquer it only by these means. These are the terms stipulated in the nature of things for the salvation of men on this earth, and only in this profound, this stern, and this tested wisdom shall we find once more the light and the courage we need.

Well, that is preaching.

What has happened in one man after another to cause this change—not, it may be, in theoretical conviction, but in emphasis? Concern for democracy has caused it, and the perception that the huge political overheads of the democratic system will collapse like a house of cards save as democracy is sustained from underneath by the moral character and attitudes of millions of plain, ordinary people in the midst of their daily lives.

Many of us grew up in a generation when it was taken for granted that ever-increasing democracy around the world was the inevitable wave of the future. "Printing, which comes necessarily out of Writing," said Carlyle, "is equivalent to Democracy: invent Writing, Democracy is inevitable." But today we see one dictator after another seizing the printing press and using it to crush democracy. Invent the radio, and is democracy inevitable? But the radio can become one of dictatorship's most potent instruments. No, the taproot of democracy is not in any vast, large-scale thing whatsoever—not in mass printing, mass radio, or even mass politics. The taproot of democracy is deep in the daily life of the people. Democracy begins in homes where children are welcomed into the comradeship of a co-operative family life. It grows strong in schools where respect for personality is given expression and training, alike in its privileges and its obligations. It is disciplined in the running of small enterprises, neighborhoods, and communities, where men and women learn to do common things together. It is evidenced in daily business and social intercourse, where tolerance amid difference, and conference rather than violence are used to decide issues. Democracy is a way of daily living, and it gets its ultimate vitality in citizens whose consciences have been touched at least a little by the love of God, and who practice what Lord Moulton in his significant phrase called voluntary "Obedience to the Unenforceable."

Here in the thick of our daily, ordinary, commonplace living is where the fate of democracy will ultimately be decided, and yet we talk about the huge events of our time making our daily life seem trivial. That is getting life all out of focus. Ordinary daily living—homes, schools, churches, small enterprises, neighborhoods, communities, personal character— never mattered more in the world's history than it does today.

Suppose that the democracies should be outwardly defeated. I do not think they will be, but suppose they were, and the vast political overhead of democratic nations should collapse! Where would democracy find its resurrection day? You know! There are millions of us who have been brought up in democratic homes, democratic schools, democratic churches, who have had woven into us as part of the texture of our lives respect for personality, co-operation with others, the love of liberty. There, inside plain people in daily living, is the vitality that, though men should crucify democracy outwardly and bury it, would raise it from the dead again and roll the stone away.

So there are two ways of facing our generation: one is to say that its stupendous events make our commonplace, daily living seem mediocre, humdrum, and trivial; the other is to see that even in so critical a matter as maintaining the foundations of democracy Jesus is everlastingly right. "He that is faithful in a very little is faithful also in much."

Come further now and ask what another major problem of our generation is. Surely, getting on with people. There are many ways of describing war and its causes, but the gist of the matter is that people cannot get on with one another. I wonder if anybody wants this madness of modern war. Winston Churchill is marshaling a whole empire to desperate battle, but were one to ask him what he really thinks about war, he would say, what indeed he did say in 1936. War, Mr. Churchill said, used to be "cruel and magnificent"; now it is "cruel and squalid. . . . War has ceased to be a gentleman's game. To hell with it!" But despite all such revulsion against war, here it is, for a reason that carries the whole matter into the heart of our ordinary daily life: People find it hard to get on with one another.

Where, then, is the ground of our hope that sometime, even as great nations, we can get on with one another? That hope is grounded on the fact that in a thousand and one ordinary, day-by-day, little experiences, goodwill does work, friendship is effective, tolerance and mutual understanding do compose differences, co-operation displaces hostility, and we do get on with people. Do not say that these victories of friendliness and goodwill in daily personal relationships do not matter. They are the leaven in the lump.

Remember the motto of the American Friends' Service Committee: "It is better to light a candle than to curse the darkness." We are tempted today to spend much of our time cursing the darkness. Surely, it is dark. But all the more thank God for every candle of friendliness and goodwill, every victory of tolerance over bigotry, and co-operation over hostility, however small, assuring us that still light is in the world! "It is better to light a candle than to curse the darkness."

It is particularly interesting that of all people Jesus should have felt this. He too lived in a time of stupendous events. Take two phrases as typical of his era—"the Roman Empire"—that was the major fact of his generation and that was huge; "the Kingdom of God on earth"—that was his primary ideal, and that was all-inclusive. Yet listen to this strange man dealing with the Roman Empire as a fact and with the Kingdom of God on earth as an ideal! "Whosoever shall give to drink unto one of these little ones a cup of cold water, . . . he shall in no wise lose his reward." "Whoso shall receive one such little child in my name receiveth me." "Inasmuch as ye did it unto one of these my brethren, even these least, ye did it unto me." "If any man have a hundred sheep, and one of them be gone astray, doth he not leave the ninety and nine, and go unto the mountains, and seek that which goeth astray?" To the man with the one talent Jesus heard God saying, "Thou oughtest therefore to have put my money to the bankers." And of the woman who cast one farthing into the treasury, he said: "Verily I say unto you, This poor widow cast in more than all they." There is a glorification of the commonplace, unequaled, I think, in history, by one whose coming was to shake the world.

Moreover, when now across nearly 2000 years we remember him, we recall that he had an incidental conversation with a woman of Samaria at a well-side, that a man named Nicodemus one evening came to call upon him, that he visited Mary and Martha in their home, that Zacchaeus once invited him to dinner, that blind Bartimaeus called to him from the roadside, that he laid his hands on little children and took them in his arms! When one stops to think of it, what

[198]

we chiefly remember about Jesus is astounding—commonplace, ordinary, everyday living lifted up and made to illustrate the ideas, attitudes, and principles that alone can redeem the world. His whole life is a commentary on his own words: "He that is faithful in a very little is faithful also in much."

Consider another major problem of our time—liberating personality. That is the essence of our despair about the world today, this rise of oppressive regimes that imprison personality. One of you here this morning had lived all your life in Vienna, a scientist loving your work. Then the *Anschluss* took place and naziism moved in. Nobody outwardly disturbed you. Your daily life went on apparently as usual. You could have remained there untroubled. But something had happened. The air was stifling. You tell me that the climax came when one day you went out alone among the great mountains that from your boyhood you had loved. There you were amid the solitude of the mountains, but even the mountains were not the same. You could not endure them. Liberty was gone. So you are here today.

This, then, is one of the great problems of the world—setting personality free—but do we mean that this is a problem in the large only and not in the small? Does any one of us pass a single day without dealing with people, circumscribed, impeded, imprisoned, whom we can help to set free? During our Civil War Senator Charles Sumner, absorbed in his great plans for the abolition of slavery, was asked by Julia Ward Howe to meet some friends. He declined. "Really, Julia," he said in his top-lofty way, "I have lost all my interest in individuals." "Why, Charles!" she answered, "God hasn't got as far as that yet."

We are not saying that we can do nothing directly about the vast problems of the world. We can. We are citizens who should make our influence felt through every channel open to our impact. But for most of us the major part of every day must still be spent on common tasks. If, being common, they look also commonplace, it is because there is something the matter with our eyes. Some people make commonplaceness out of everything; some people in the humblest circumstances, say:

> Earth's crammed with heaven,
> And every common bush afire with God.

This is one of the most significant contrasts between people, and nowhere is this contrast more evident than in personal relationships. We thank God for America and her liberty, but for all that we could still have been imprisoned personalities had it not been for some people who thought that daily living was important, that making good homes, good schools, good churches, was important; people who tried to see what there was in us that could be released and brought out, who believed in it when we did not, and kept on believing in it when we were discouraged. The Africans have a proverb that any fool can tell how many apples there are on a tree, but that it takes a wise man to tell how many trees there are in an apple. Who of us here does not have reason to thank God for some people who in ordinary, daily relationships guessed what might be grown out of us? If liberating personality is one of the major problems of the world today, then he who is faithful in a very little is faithful also in much.

Finally, the preservation of Christianity is a major problem—and if that is not a personal matter of daily living, what is? In one great nation after another, institutional, organized Christianity is crippled or dead. In Russia it has gone. The Russian church has not a single seminary left in Europe for the training of its priests. In Germany the organized church is so limited, so watched and censored by the Gestapo that on any public issue it cannot even whisper. But even in Russia, they tell us, increasing numbers of peasant families are teaching their children about Christ. Christianity is still there and growing, not as an organization but as a movement among the people. And they tell us of the powerful drive of personal Christianity in Germany, underground, not institutionalized but private and individual. That is the way Christianity started in the first place in the Roman Empire; that is always the source of its ultimate dynamic and vitality. Hostile governments can smash its institutions, but so long as multitudes of plain people in ordinary, everyday living, cherish its truth, its resurrection day will come.

Indeed, think of the case even here in America where the church is free. What is the one argument for Christianity to which there is no answer? I do not know a single theological argument that cannot one way or another be answered. I do not know any great Christian organization that is not so faulty that a man, if he wants to, cannot one way or another justify staying out of it. But when one sees an honest-to-goodness Christian life, a person so humble, it may be, that he has no idea he is making any impression, but who in daily duty-doing and burden-bearing is a Christian, I do not know the answer to that.

These are days of prodigious events, but all the more and not the less important is our daily living. To be sure, it is not easy to handle little things as though they were significant. Life is full of humdrum and drudgery. Every great vocation, however thrilling as a whole, has long stretches in it of prosy and wearisome routine. George Herbert the poet sang:

> Who sweeps a room as for thy laws,
> Makes that, and the action, fine.

That is a noble sentiment, but after all George Herbert was a man and probably he never had to sweep a room; at least he did not have to do it day after day after day. To dignify drudgery is not easy. Yet it was an English servant girl—I wonder if she is in England today still carrying on—who wrote these lines:

Lord of all pots and pans and tins, I have no time to be
A saint by doing lovely things, by watching late with Thee,
Or praying in the dawnlight, or storming Heaven's gates.
Make me a saint by getting meals and washing up the plates.

Warm all the kitchen with Thy love, and fill it with Thy peace,
Forgive me all my worrying and make all grumbling cease.
Thou Who didst love to give men food, in room or by the sea,
Accept this service that I do—I do it unto Thee.

The Return to Discipline

OUR world today faces us with at least one elemental necessity—the need of discipline. Mankind can stand all sorts of evils, but it cannot long endure chaos, disorder, anarchy. When that reaches a certain point reaction sets in and some force rises to bring confusion under control and whip things into shape. The major movements of our time—communism, naziism, fascism, militarism, the growing elements of dictatorship in the democracies—are all endeavors to get some kind of order out of chaos, to put a bridle on this wild horse, to bring our nations and our world under disciplined control. Give the devil his due! The totalitarianism we fear today at home and abroad is an endeavor to get some social order out of the anarchic confusion of the world.

Willy nilly, therefore, we face a choice on which our personal lives and our social fortunes depend. Either we are going to have enough people who discipline themselves from within, or else we are going to have discipline imposed on us from without. From that dilemma there is no escape. In any population, large or small, let chaotic disorder reach too great proportions and the demand will rise, at all costs, for order. Though it take a dictator, that will seem a small price to pay for social order. The worst thing that mankind can face is anarchy.

Now there are two ways in which men achieve ordered societies: either they discipline themselves within, or else they have discipline imposed on them from without. The first gives leeway for liberty, and makes democracy possible; the second is the nucleus of dictatorship. This morning, then, we try to measure the importance of self-discipline, not only as one secret in great personal living but as one of the most towering social necessities of our time. For look at the world, and see! In so far as we do not discipline ourselves, someone else will impose discipline on us.

Self-control has not been characteristic of our generation. Have we in this country been a disciplined people? In our personal morals, in our respect for law, in our family life, in our subjugation of self-interest to the common welfare, in any regard that you can think of have we been a self-controlled people? We have had splendid virtues—energy, vigor, pioneering venturesomeness—explosive and aggressive virtues that could blast new roads through high mountains, and win for us what we call success. But winning that, how often has liberty turned to license, self-restraint been thrown to the winds, laxness rather than self-control characterized us! How often has our use of power, like a wayward stream at flood, burst its banks, and our personal lives been undedicated and uncontrolled! Well, America faces now one of the most fateful hours in its history, and no saying of Jesus, I think, is more pertinent to our need than this: "Wide is the gate, and broad is the way, that leadeth to destruction, and many are they that enter in thereby. For narrow is the gate, and straitened the way, that leadeth unto life, and few are they that find it." So! The loose life means ruin; only the disciplined life can be great.

Nevertheless, deep in human nature are moods and attitudes that resist this truth, so that we may well organize our thought this morning by listening as, one by one, these moods rise up in protest against it.

First of all, who does not feel within himself the mood that cries, I want a rich, free life; I resent restraint and control—that is not the end of existence; copious, plenteous, bountiful living is what I want? Confronting that mood is the fact that abundant life and how to get it was what Jesus was talking about. He said that a loose, sprawling, meandering course never reaches it, only the narrow gate and the straitened way of a disciplined and dedicated life.

The other day I heard Kreisler and the Philharmonic Orchestra play Beethoven's *Concerto in D Major*. It was glorious. He never arrived at that fullness of artistic power and life by traveling a broad, meandering course. He began playing the violin when he was a small boy, not too promising. When he was fourteen he toured the United States, only moderately successful, so that, returning to Vienna he could not get a position as a second violinist in the Philharmonic there. He dropped the violin, therefore, thinking he was a failure at it; tried medicine, did not like it; tried painting, was not contented with it; went into the army, was dissatisfied with it, and so came back to his first love again, the violin, and went to it. When he first made up his mind to that, he retired to solitude for eight solid weeks and did nothing except practice finger exercises, and from then till now he has daily gone through a narrow gate and down a straitened way of discipline. But it has been worth it.

What are the prerequisites of greatness in any realm? All of them, in Jesus' sense of the word, are narrow. *Attention* is narrow. When Gladstone was asked the secret of his success he replied in one word, "Concentration." The worthwhile mind can focus, but the inattentive mind sprawls every which way. *Decisiveness* is narrow. We cannot decide vaguely and in general; we must decide in particular. The decisive mind defines, excludes, wills this and not that, but the indecisive mind is a vagabond on a broad road. *Loyalty* is narrow. It binds me to a definite devotion. When I love my friend I am not loosely free; I do not wish to be loosely free; my limitation is my glory; I love my friend. But the unloyal man travels a broad road; he has no attachments; he is devoted to no friend; he is a man without a country—broad is the gate and wide is the way.

Here, as so often, Jesus is not so much a painter of beautiful ideals as a proclaimer of universal laws. Nothing left loose ever does anything creative. No horse gets anywhere until he is harnessed. No steam or gas ever drives anything until it is confined. No Niagara is ever turned into light and power until it is tunneled. No life ever grows great until it is focused, dedicated, disciplined.

One of the widest gaps in human experience is the gap between what we say we want to be and our willingness to discipline ourselves to get there. From the homeliest aspects of life—people who say they want to reduce ten pounds, but who will not discipline themselves to do it—to the greatest aspects of life—people who say they want to be Christians, but who will not leave their meandering course of inattentive, indecisive, undevoted living to achieve it—how wide the chasm is between our professed ideals and our willingness to pay the cost! And the cost in every realm is always self-discipline.

Today we confront a world that presses this matter home. One nation has shaken the earth to its foundations, and at the source of its power to do that one hears that nation's leaders commanding the people, Give up butter for guns. We all pray that such discipline may not be necessary here, but it is preposterous to suppose that we in America can preserve our democracy by living in a fool's paradise, with loose morals, disintegrated family life, self-interest taking precedence over public welfare, and a general attitude of loose and easy-going living. Broad is that gate and wide is that way, but it leadeth to destruction. And the very pith and marrow of the matter are here: Nothing worth having in this world, least of all democracy, can be achieved save as the cost of it is paid in self-discipline.

Nevertheless, a second mood within us rises in protest against this truth: I resent restraint and repression, it says; I want to do what I please, follow my whims, fancies, and passions; I want to let myself go. To which the answer seems plain to anyone who knows modern psychology at all. Which self do you want to let go? Do not tell us that you have only one self! You have a lot of selves. No one escapes the elemental problem that James M. Barrie's character, Sentimental Tommy, so well describes when he struggles to make up his mind: "It's easy to you that has just one mind, but if you had as many minds as I have—!" Self-discipline, therefore, begins of necessity at home within our own lives. Not all our selves can have gangway, or if we try to give it to them our inner life will be a mess that even the psychiatrists cannot put to rights. Some chosen self, out of all these many selves, must assume the regency within, must arrange the hierarchy of our loves and interests, establishing some government in the soul so that what we wish on top shall be on top and what we wish subdued shall be obedient. Self-dedication is a basic psychological necessity.

In the chapel at Harvard University is a tablet in memory of old Dr. Peabody, and the end of the inscription runs thus:

His Precept was Glorified by His Example
While for Thirty-Three Years
He moved among the Teachers and Students of Harvard College
And Wist not that His Face Shone.

Facing that kind of life, what does one mean by letting oneself go? Such a man as that inscription celebrates, among all the selves that thronged his life, chose which self should lead, and which should follow after. Unless one's life within is to be a mere mob, it must, one way or another, be organized, integrated, made into hierarchy with supreme values ascendant. All modern psychology at its best underlines the ancient saying: "He that ruleth his spirit is better than he that taketh a city."

It is a strange thing that so many people should talk of doing what they please in a world where modern science has come. No scientist in his special realm thinks he can do what he pleases. Tackle any new problem in the laboratory, strive after any new discovery, and there are countless ways of missing the mark, finding nothing, coming out nowhere. Broad is the gate and wide the way that leads to no discovery. But only one way leads to that particular truth you seek; there is only one way of so fulfilling the law-abiding conditions that you will get what you are after. Narrow is that gate.

I do not know why God so made the world that the wrong way is broad and the right way is narrow, but this is the way he made it, and in view of that I stand in fear of a sentimental kind of religion which forgets that. It was when Ophelia went crazy that she began distributing flowers indiscriminately to everybody. Some persons want a religion like that, and come to church, I fear, hoping that the preacher will imitate Ophelia and promiscuously distribute sweet messages—"Pansies, that's for thoughts." Jesus was not at all like that. Go through his teaching and his life from beginning to end and see if you can find anything sentimental; lovely, yes! beautiful, yes! but through it all a realistic facing of facts and a realistic statement of universal spiritual laws. There are as many ways of messing life up as there are ways of missing truth in a scientific laboratory, but if we wish a life not messed up, then there is only one way and the gate is narrow—dedication, interior organization, integration, discipline, self-control.

Recall that great phrase of Ignatius Loyola about the man who puts on spurs, but no bridle, to ride a fiery horse. Too many of us have been doing that with ourselves in this country—spurs, but no bridle, to ride a fiery horse—and now we face a world where a dilemma confronts us. Either we are going to discipline ourselves for our own sake, the nation's sake, and the world's, or else discipline will be imposed on us from without.

Nevertheless, still another mood, native to us all, rises in

protest against this truth. I hate coercion, it says; I resent
repression; I want to be my own master and not the slave of
the codes and prescriptions of society; I want to be free.

That is what Jesus wanted. "Ye shall know the truth, and
the truth shall make you free." Throughout the New Testament the note of freedom everywhere resounds: "Where the
Spirit of the Lord is, there is liberty." Moreover, at the
center of Jesus' ministry and of Paul's Epistles is a revolt
against the small, enslaving scrupulosities of the ancient legal
codes. Ask the Pharisees about Jesus, and they would have
said that he himself was a rebel, refusing obedience to the
prescriptions of the law, and traveling a dangerously broad
road in a perilously loose and undisciplined manner. A friend
of mine on a train trip sat behind a mother and her small son.
She began saying "Don't" as soon as she came in, and my
friend counted. Fifty-nine times in one hour and a half she
said "Don't" to that boy. No one wants to live under such
restriction, and least of all is Jesus' ethic like that.

At the start, therefore, we may expect his sympathy when
we protest against repression and want freedom. Not all our
so-called American looseness has been bad. Many trivial
scrupulosities have masqueraded under the disguise of discipline. A woman of my generation can remember the Dean
of Vassar College saying to the students: "Young ladies, I
hope that I may never see the day when you will so far forget
your dignity and delicacy as to appear upon the campus without gloves." All the way from that to endless rules and regulations in the moral realm, caricatures of discipline have clut-
tered up the field. No man is worth his salt who does not
sometimes rise in rebellion, smash through some nonsensical
repression, and claim his freedom.

When, however, we are through with that, we still face an
inescapable fact—there are some things we can never be free
from. Free thinking is not freedom from the laws of thought.
Free living is not freedom from the laws of life. All scientific

creativity goes back to obedience to scientific law. All artistic creativeness depends upon obedience to the laws of beauty. No one is free until he is mastered.

> Make me a captive, Lord,
> And then I shall be free;
> Force me to render up my sword,
> And I shall conq'ror be.

That is not poetry alone, but basic psychological fact.

Mark Twain, for example, lost his fortune. The accumulations of his brilliant life work tumbled into an abyss of debt. According to the public law he could have escaped all responsibility in bankruptcy. Why did he not travel that broad and easy way? Why did he voluntarily assume the burden of those debts, circumnavigating the globe, even, although on the threshold of old age, tirelessly speaking and writing until he paid the last penny? He told us why in one brief sentence: "Honor is a harder master than the law." Something inside himself he had to live up to. In Tennyson's phrase, he was "loyal to the royal" in himself. Narrow was that gate, and straitened that way, but it led to life. That kind of disciplined character is not a matter of small scrupulosities.

Today we may well celebrate the men and women in high or humble places who thus have within themselves something fine that they must live up to. They are the prerequisite of democracy. The storms of life beat on them, as they beat on all of us today, but they have a compass, something within them that they are true to and steer by. Over against that kind of life put the loose, lax, immoralism of our generation, where many voices have cried, like the witches in *Macbeth*, "Fair is foul, and foul is fair." We preachers are tempted to think of such loose living solely in ethical terms. We call it sin. But it is more than that. It is psychological and emotional disintegration. Such a life never gets itself together around any center, never is dedicated and disciplined to any end. Such a man has to say, like a character in one of H. G. Wells' novels, "I'm not a man but a mob." Only one who has been mastered by something worth being mastered by ever can be a real person.

Wherever you find a real person in any realm, Toscanini in music, for example, one thing is present—a devotion that it is his pride, joy, and freedom to live up to and discipline himself for. That is different from letting yourself go. That is not the same thing as subservience to conventional codes. That is having something within you, stimulating, empowering, controlling, around which your life grows integral and unified, so that your joy and liberation are in living up to it and out from it.

Until religion means that to a man it is an ineffective conventionality. When in Shakespeare's drama the Earl of Kent went out to King Lear in his exile to offer his allegiance, he gave this as his explanation: "You have that in your countenance which I would fain call master." When a man says that to Christ in earnest, until within himself Christ's spirit and way of life become an organizing center, an inner criterion, then he is a Christian.

America today desperately needs people who thus within themselves have something that they must live up to. See how we sit in comfort here! Destitution will not mark our dinner tables when we go home; fear will not haunt our night with sirens warning us that the bombing planes are coming. What right have we to this ease? I am not saying, Give up butter for guns. May that kind of coercion be spared us! But in a day when all the world on both sides of the battle line—often with a courage and self-sacrifice that make us salute the grandeur of human nature even while we are appalled at what human nature does—is displaying magnificent self-dedication and self-control, by what exemption have we a right to live a lax, loose, unbuttoned life?

If America should ever fail, if after the promise of its

start, and the unexampled marvel of its opportunity, it should come from a fair springtime to a barren autumn, what would be the reason? Not lack of laws, not lack of outward regulation, not lack of dictatorship even, for we would try that before we fell, but lack of people who so disciplined themselves from within that they were self-propelled, having liberty because they deserved it, keeping democracy because they helped create it, running themselves so well from the inside that they did not need to be run from the outside. And that profound and inner matter is, at its deepest, a great religion's gift. For the roots of a self-disciplined character are profoundly spiritual—faith that there are values worth being dedicated to, faith that there are ends worth being self-disciplined for, faith that beyond the torture of these years, by God's grace, there is a possible world, decent, fraternal, peaceable, that self-disciplined men and nations can build. When such faith is lost, it is all up with democracy. And the place for this kind of living to begin is within each of us. Whatever else we can or cannot do for the world, at least we can give it one more life that proves Tennyson's words true:

> Self-reverence, self-knowledge, self-control,
> These three alone lead life to sovereign power.

How Believe in a Good God in a World Like This?

WE FACE an old question this morning: How can we believe in a good God in a world like this? Job confronted it ages ago, and Sophocles wondered how the gods could look complacently down on so much suffering and pain. Our generation feels afresh what Keats called "the giant agony of the world." How shall we reconcile an all-good and all-powerful God with earthquakes and cyclones, cholera and cancer, the long ruthlessness of the evolutionary process, ills like insanity that fall on individuals even at their birth, and all the welter of lust, poverty, and war, that human life involves? We come to church to sing the praises of the all-great and all-good God, but in how many hearts the question rises, How can he be all-good and all-great if he made a world like this?

Our difficulty in dealing with this problem is accentuated by the fact that the higher our concept of God, the more perplexity we face. If we could be polytheists, believing in many gods, then we could blame life's good and evil on the various deities. If we could be Zoroastrians and believe in two gods, one of light and one of darkness, one all benevolence and one all malice, then we could blame life's evil on the evil god. When, however, we believe in one God, our Father, all-powerful and all-good, we face perplexity. Arson is a crime among men, but the Creator habitually looses lightning and volcanoes that burn up men's habitations. Murder is a crime among men, but the Creator habitually looses earthquakes that slay multitudes. Poisoning is a crime among men, but the Creator makes the cobra and viper. As has often been noted, the Creator habitually does on a vast scale things for which men are sent to prison or executed. The first effect of Christian faith in a God of love is not to solve this problem but to state it in its most difficult form. To believe in one God, all-good and all-powerful, makes the cruelty of life hard to understand.

No easy escape from this problem is possible by blaming the evil on man's sin. Man's sin is responsible for many evils, and if man could be redeemed to decency this world would be a far happier place; but man is not responsible for the long ruthlessness of the evolutionary process, or for lightning, volcanoes, earthquakes, or for disease germs, or for the planetary setting of human life with the inevitable struggle that it involves. The Creator must bear his heavy share of responsibility. Why, then, do we believe in a good God?

Of course, one reason is that when we decide not to believe in a good God because of the world's evil, we discover that far from solving any problem we have merely jumped from the frying pan into the fire. It is difficult to explain the presence of evil in the world of a good God, but to some of us it is impossible to explain the goodness in the world on the basis of no God. One, for example, looking at Calvary, may center his attention on the cross alone, saying, There can be no good God in a world where such unjust cruelty befalls; or he may center his attention on Christ upon the cross, saying, There must be a good God in a world that produces him. There is more than the mystery of evil here to explain—there is the mystery of good.

Once I decided that I could not believe in the goodness of God in the presence of the world's evil, and then discovered that I had run headlong into another and even more difficult problem: What to do about all the world's goodness on the basis of no God? Sunsets and symphonies, mothers, music, and the laughter of children at play, great books, great art, great science, great personalities, victories of goodness over evil, the long, hard-won ascent from the Stone Age up, and all the friendly spirits that are to other souls a "cup of strength in some great agony"—how can we, thinking of these on the basis of no God, explain them as the casual, accidental by-products of physical forces going it blind? I think it cannot be done. The mystery of evil is very great upon the basis of a good God, but the mystery of goodness is impossible upon the basis of no God.

Most of us have seen the Great Stone Face on the New Hampshire mountain, that Nathaniel Hawthorne made famous, carved by cosmic weathering. That face came as the accidental by-product of physical forces going it blind. But we have known other faces—in our families, and among our friends, and others still—that, like the Christ, have revealed to us divinity itself, and for which that explanation is inadequate. To say that those faces came from casual cosmic weathering, that they are the accidental by-products of aimless atoms, presents us with a sheer absurdity in comparison with which the problem of evil pales.

Our ultimate decision in this matter depends largely on where we center our emphasis. Blindness and deafness fall upon a little child, and we instinctively cry, No good God would allow a thing like that! But then we shift our emphasis to Helen Keller herself, upon whom the blindness and the deafness fell, her spirit, her faith, her courage, her victory, standing a few years ago in the University of Glasgow to receive an honorary degree, and saying of the honor: "It is a sign that darkness and silence need not bar the progress of the immortal spirit." Some people center their attention on the physical affliction, and say, There can be no good God! Some of us cannot lose sight of Helen Keller herself, and say, There must be a good God! Moreover, when you ask Helen Keller—as so often happens when you think not of sympathetic spectators who look on trouble, but of those who bear it—that is what she says too.

This, then, is the first reason why some of us believe in the good God. The problem of evil is very difficult when we believe in a good God, but the problem of goodness seems to us impossible when we do not.

Another reason encourages us to believe in the good God, namely, that as we have grown older, we have come to take mystery for granted, not to resent it as much as we used to, and not to expect to crowd the explanation of an infinite universe within the confines of a limited mind. Listen to this from a contemporary scientist: "At the present day the scientific universe is more mysterious than it has ever been before in the history of thought." To be sure it is! And if that is true of the physical cosmos, how much more true of this realm where our thought is moving.

If a man lays it down as a precondition of his believing in the good God that he must get an explanation that will answer all questions and solve all problems, he might as well stop where he is, for there is no such explanation, theistic or atheistic.

I can remember in my early years bitterly resenting this mystery of evil, this weird, uncanny, cruel incidence of unexplained suffering. It still troubles me. I have no formula that solves it all. My father used to say that the chief reason why he wanted to go to heaven was that he might get God off in a corner and ask him some questions. I agree! Still, I do not resent the mystery as I once did. Any way you take it, this is a mysterious universe. Always it presents itself to us in terms of a strange dualism—light and darkness, right and wrong, good and evil, happiness and pain, life and death. Everything comes in opposites. All the great religions have so pictured life in terms of conflict. Hinduism called it a conflict between reality and illusion; Zoroastrianism a conflict between light and darkness; Platonism a conflict between spirit and matter; traditional Judaism and Christianity a conflict between God and Satan. Behind this dualism we believe that somehow there is monism, that this is a *uni*verse, springing from one power; but in actual experience it presents itself as a dualism.

If, in that dualism, a man starts by believing that the basic and creative element is evil, how does he explain good? How did such goodness as we know ever come to pass in a world where the basic element is evil? But if a man starts with the conviction that the basic and creative element is good, then, while he faces the mystery of evil, it still may be true that good can yet surmount it, rise above it, transmute its lead into gold—yes, more than that, use it until as from some travail shall come a birth worth all that it has cost. This is what faith in the good God means. Cried Paul: "The whole creation groaneth and travaileth in pain together until now." Paul knew *that* as well as any evolutionary scientist. Creation is travail, he said, but it is waiting for a birth, the "revealing of the sons of God." Faith in the good God means this daring confidence. It is no neat, slick, varnished creed, as it sometimes seems to be when it is repeated in a church. It is a great venture of faith in a universe deeply mysterious, whose basic element is not evil but good.

For still another reason some of us are encouraged to believe in the good God, namely, that what we call evil, pain, tragedy, plays a positive role in life. There may be more sense in it than at first we think. When we complain against the tragedy of life, what are we asking for? A world that shall be all ease, pleasure, and happiness? There are hours when we would welcome that. We are fed up with trouble. We have seen too many tragedies that crush the lives and souls of men with no conceivable good consequence. Yet if even in such indignant and rebellious hours I were offered a chance to go to the traditional heaven, all pearly gates and golden streets, endless idleness and singing, nothing hard to undertake or difficult to do, I should shrink back. I should be dead sick of that within a week. Everybody knows that strange factor in human nature that made MacMillan, the explorer, say after a terrific twelvemonth with Peary in the Arctic: "This has been the grandest year of my life." Everything most worth-while in our living has come out of a background of struggle against obstacles.

Look again, then, at this tragic world about which we complain. All the suffering we bear comes from four factors. Out of four factors, singly or conjointly working, comes every ill that falls on human life.

First, the law-abidingness of the universe. How much trouble comes from that! If we break the law of gravitation, we suffer. No cosmic law ever slips its leash.

Second, the evolutionary nature of the world. Life always starts us in a low and ill estate, and makes us fight our way up toward a better. We are introduced into an unfinished world, and called on painfully to help complete it. We are started with animal nature, ignorance, superstition, poverty, war, and with faith and valor have to struggle out toward something better. How much suffering comes from that!

Third, the power of moral choice. It is not unlimited, but it is real. We are not mere automata. We can choose. And that power of initiative can be misused. How much trouble comes from that!

Fourth, the intermeshed relationships of human life. We are not set like bottles in the rain in solitary endurance of our fate. We are interrelated. We flow into one another. We are members one of another, and as individuals and nations our woes, problems, and tragedies spill over from one into the other's life. We are intermeshed in an unescapable mutuality. How much of human tragedy comes from that!

Every suffering that falls on man comes from the single or conjoint operation of those four factors. The law-abiding universe, the progressiveness of human society, the individual power of choice, the intermeshed mutuality of living—there is no tragedy that does not spring from them. Yet if you had omnipotence for an hour, would you eliminate from the universe a single one of them? Would you make this universe whimsical and capricious and not law-abiding? Would you make it static, like Aladdin's palace, made by magic for lazy occupancy, and not progressive? Would you make human beings mechanical automata with no power to choose? Would you tear us apart from our relationships and leave us like bottles in the rain, freed from those ties that make life beautiful? Everything worth-while in life also comes from these same four factors whence its tragedies spring.

We are not pretending that this is a complete theoretical explanation of the problem of evil. There is no such explanation that we can grasp. But considering that if we were granted omnipotence, we would not dare abstract from the structure of the universe a single one of the major factors from which human tragedy comes, we may well look with fresh eyes of hope and courage on this strange, mysterious scene. Maybe it is travail for a birth, vaster in significance than we think—the whole creation groaning and travailing in pain together until now, but with a consequence that shall be worthy of the struggle.

Once more some of us believe in a good God because we long since have given up early childish, naïve ideas of God that once we held. An almighty carpenter, making this world just as he wants it, an omnipotent monarch, sitting on a throne and ruling this world just as he pleases—those are childish pictures of God. If God is an omnipotent monarch who can do anything he pleases, he has no business to please to do some things he does, and permit some things that he allows.

I could not believe in the good God unless I had another way of conceiving him. Deep at the heart of this universe there is a constructive, creative Spirit not ourselves. He has made a cosmos here vast and orderly, whose laws never slip, so unified that they say that even if one lifts one's finger the very stars feel the impulse, so simple that it is all made up

[219]

of less than a hundred elements, and so intelligible that it fits into mind, and mind fits into it. A constructive, creative power is here, not so much like matter as like mind.

Moreover, that creative power comes to spiritual conse-quence. He makes not stars alone but souls, not rocks alone but minds. Man is not self-created, but with his spiritual life he too came up out of the source of all things. Einstein's in-tellect, Shakespeare's genius, Beethoven's beauty, Christ's character—they too are the overflow and consequence of the creative power, and they reveal his quality.

Moreover, this constructive and creative power works out to moral victories. Across the long ages he swings up a spiral, so that for all our low estate one would be a fool who would choose to go back to live in the Stone Age. Again and again in history great evils have won great triumphs, only in the end to find themselves undone and made fools of. Pilate sat in judgment on Jesus, but now Jesus sits in judgment on Pilate. Such strange reversals are the commonplace of his-tory. Countless incidents illustrate Lowell's lines:

Though the cause of Evil prosper, yet 't is Truth alone is strong,
. . . .
Truth forever on the scaffold, Wrong forever on the throne,—
Yet that scaffold sways the future, and, behind the dim unknown,
Standeth God within the shadow, keeping watch above his own.

Moreover, in this vast, creative process, pain is not an accident. It is indispensable. Ever as one moves up in the scale of life, sensitivity increases. No creativity without sen-sitivity! No music, no art, no sympathy, no character, no social hope, without increased sensitivity. But all increase of sensitivity means increase of capacity for pain. Pain, there-fore, is not an intruder in the universe; it is part of the warp and woof of life. No pains, no gains.

When I believe in the good God I believe in that creative, constructive Spirit not ourselves, who makes for righteous-ness. He is not omnipotent in any popular sense of that word.

He cannot make a triangle, the sum of whose angles is not equal to two right angles. He cannot make wrong right, or truth false. He cannot even do with us what he wants to do, if we inwardly and stubbornly resist him. God too has a fight on his hands. He is up against something. We may not phrase his antagonist in terms of the traditional devil, but God is still up against something, in the universe and in ourselves. He has a struggle on his hands. And to believe in him is no neat and finished creed. It is betting one's life on the constructive forces of goodness in this universe against all the evils that sometimes seem to win the victory.

This, then, is the conclusion of the matter. The contribution of Christian faith to the problem of evil has lain not so much in supplying a theory to explain it as in furnishing power to surmount it. Our English friend Maude Royden even says: "I never try to explain evil. If anybody asks me to explain suffering, I say I can't. I say I have a power that can surmount it." Jesus himself never said, I have explained the world, but he did say, I have overcome it.

Early Christianity certainly did not dodge trouble. It started with tragedy in its darkest form. It began with a cross, and a man hanging on it, saying, "My God, my God, why—why hast thou forsaken me?" There never has been an adequate answer to that question. But one thing the cross made plain—that in this world now, and in ourselves if we will have it so, there is a power that can surmount such evil, rise above its tragedy, carry off a victory in the face of it, use it, transmute the symbol of the cruelest punishment the ancient world knew into the symbol of salvation, until the miracle happens of multitudes singing:

> In the cross of Christ I glory,
> Towering o'er the wrecks of time.

The Decisive Babies of the World*

FROM our youth up we have heard about the decisive battles of history. One of the earliest books some of us remember is Creasy's famous volume on *The Fifteen Decisive Battles of the World*. But now Christmas comes again, engaging the thought and warming the heart of multitudes around the globe, and it concerns not a decisive battle but a decisive baby. "Unto us a child is born, unto us a son is given."

Even today, when all the world is obsessed with the clash of arms, Christmas suggests how much more decisive a baby can be than a battle. We moderns have lost faith in miracles, and if by miracles we mean occurrences involving the breaking of nature's laws, we are right, for nature's laws are God's and are never broken. But even so, the word "miracle" does not drop from our vocabulary, for some things are so unforeseeable, in advance of their happening so incredible, that they are to us miraculous. When Jesus was born in Bethlehem, what were the decisive elements in the world's life? Surely, Cæsar Augustus upon his throne, the Roman Empire's vast extent and power, and legions tramping every road—any realistic mind would have pointed to such potent factors as the determining elements in mankind's life. As for a baby, born of a lowly mother in obscure Bethlehem upon the far fringes of the Empire, it would have been madness then to have supposed that two millennia afterwards millions of us would be singing of that event:

> Yet in thy dark streets shineth
>   The everlasting Light;
> The hopes and fears of all the years
>   Are met in thee tonight.

* A Christmas Sermon.

[222]

The Decisive Babies of the World

This is the miracle of Christmas—that a baby can be so decisive.

Babies are decisive. Long ago in Egypt a slave girl held in her arms a newborn infant for whom there seemed no hope, so that she framed for him a floating cradle, and pushed him out upon the waters of the Nile to survive or perish. But now, in retrospect, see what immense issues in the world's life went floating down the river in that slender craft! For Moses was one of the decisive babies of the world.

In our own country the forces of disunion were threatening; already the premonitions of disruptive strife were ominous, when out of a camp meeting in Kentucky a young frontiersman and his bride went to build a rough cabin on Nolan's Creek, and there a babe was born. Who can imagine what America's history would have been without Lincoln? He was one of the decisive babies of the world.

Today in the midst of war, pressed upon as we are by huge, impersonal forces that often seem irresistible, let us look at some of those deep needs in our lives to which this special message of Christ's birthday is pertinent!

In the first place, when we center our attention on the decisive babies of the world, a mood of expectancy and hope arises. If babies are among the main determinants of history, then we never can tell what may happen. Around the corner in a crib may be the tiny hand that will yet push open the door of a new era.

We habitually think of babies as small and weak, for whom we must care. True! But look at history in the large and see how often, when the world seemed hopeless, when the limits of man's achievements seemed reached, when the forces ranged against man's progress seemed irresistible, a babe was born who became the pioneer of a new era. Who, in the fifteenth century, thought that anything important had happened when in Genoa that child was born, unadvertised, unheralded, who was to open the door of the most amazing geographical expansion in history? Always when the world least expects it some Columbus is being born to introduce a new era. So long as there are babies, you never can tell!

The year 1809, for example, was one of the most discouraging in Europe's history. Napoleon was dominant, as Hitler is now. His battles and victories were the absorbing news, and, evil as our times are, I suspect that to those who lived then, 1809 seemed as bad or worse. But think of what was going on in 1809 that was not in the news at all. In that year Charles Darwin was born. In that year Lincoln was born. In that year Gladstone was born, and Tennyson, and Edgar Allan Poe, and Oliver Wendell Holmes, and Cyrus McCormick, the inventor of the harvester, and Mendelssohn. At the very least, one must say that the world was not as hopeless as it looked.

Indeed, how transient for the most part are the effects of the decisive battles, and how permanent, often, are the effects of the decisive babies! Concerning the wars of 1809, history in the main writes, "futility," but concerning the babies of 1809, history will be thinking seriously for ages yet. In 1814, when Napoleon had been defeated, Russian and Austrian armies invaded Italy and took their vengeance by massacring many of the inhabitants of Piacenza. In one village the women fled to the church for safety, but the soldiers followed them even there, and slew them before the altar. One mother, however, with an infant at her breast, hid in the belfry and saved her child. That infant was Verdi, the composer. And now most of us could not tell a single thing about those decisive battles—not one—but we are listening still to *Rigoletto*, *Aïda*, *La Traviata*, *Il Trovatore*.

So Cæsar Augustus perishes—overpassed, futile, and damned in history—and the Roman Empire itself crumbles and falls, but 2000 years afterwards multitudes still sing, as though of a contemporary event:

O holy Child of Bethlehem,
Descend to us, we pray;

[224]

Cast out our sin, and enter in;
Be born in us today.

Indeed, take this truth not only literally but figuratively. All great ideas are born small, like babies. Why cannot great ideas come into the world full armored, like Minerva from the head of Jove? They never do. All saving ideas are born small. As Jesus said, they are like leaven, a little thing in the beginning, or like mustard seed, the smallest of all the seeds in the ground. In every generation, therefore, if we are to believe in the creative forces to which the future belongs, we must believe in something inconspicuous, newborn, just growing. Who of us does not need to see that truth today? If we believe in the noisy and ostentatious violence of the world, as though that alone were the real and determining factor in our time, what hope is there? But the wise men believed in a baby. That is the essence of the Christmas message to me this year—the wise men believed in a baby. Wise men? we are tempted to say; rather, fools and sentimentalists to do that, to follow a Star to a young child's manger, and worship where a newborn life was at its small beginning! But what the wise men did is a parable of mankind's best wisdom in every realm. They did not believe in Augustus, in Herod, in Cæsar's legions, in the imperial power that loomed so large and seemed so permanent. They did not believe in the noisy, the obvious, the ostentatious. They believed in a newborn thing.

Always, in every realm, that is the mark of wise men. The idea that the earth goes around the sun was once a newborn thought in the mind of Pythagoras, a tiny intimation long neglected that like a stray waif was picked up centuries afterward, tended, nursed, and cared for by Copernicus. Once more it was the wise men who believed in a baby. So William James of Harvard put it: "As for me, my bed is made: I am against bigness and greatness in all their forms, and with the invisible molecular moral forces that work from individual to individual, stealing in through the crannies of the world like so many soft rootlets, or like the capillary oozing of water, and yet rending the hardest monuments of man's pride, if you give them time."

If today we are to believe in anything worth-while at all, the possibilities of peace, for example, in a decent and fraternal world, organized at last for brotherhood and not for war, we must believe in it so. Peace is not a large and ostentatious matter now. But the idea of it, the hope of it, faith in it, the first tentative plans for it have been born. Such ideas are decisive in the end, and the hope of the world is in wise men who, even while Cæsar Augustus reigns in Rome, believe in them. The vulgar mob always follows the obvious, the blatant, the ostentatious, but all the wise men of the world, in every realm, have followed a star until it stood over a place where something newborn lay.

Let us go further now to see that this message speaks not only to our need of hope in days of discouragement, but to our sense of personal helplessness in the face of the world's catastrophe. Who does not feel at times this sense of helplessness, as though, in this wild disaster that has broken on the world, he were facing some titanic eruption of nature's forces, a hurricane or an earthquake? What can he do to stop it? But listen to the Christmas gospel. Personality counts, it says. Again and again the world seems to have reached an impasse; it is stymied; it lands in a dead end street, and, lo! a child is born, and a new way opens to unsuspected hopes. Personality counts. Who can watch what the decisive babies have meant in history and not see that?

Today one fears not so much that someone here will deny the abstract truth of this as that someone will deny its application to himself. This sermon, someone may be thinking, is not about me at all. I was not a decisive baby. I am no messiah for whose birth the world was waiting. I am plain, ordinary, everyday, commonplace John Smith. If the hope of the world lies in some messiah to be born who will open the door to a new era, that lets me out.

To such a one, I answer, My friend, consider what it is that makes a baby decisive. It is not the baby alone. What made Charles Darwin decisive? Countless people puzzling over the problem of how all these different species of animals came to be. For generations people had puzzled over that, and more than once the query had arisen: Did these species suddenly appear, or was it by a long process of developmental change? The air was full of guesses, wonderings, intimations, prophetic insights. Read even Tennyson's *In Memoriam*, written before Darwin had published anything at all, and you will find evolution foreshadowed there. Then, and only then, that unsuspecting babe was born who was to draw all this together and focus it. That is what a decisive life does—he focuses into a burning flame what had been there already, everywhere dispersed and unco-ordinated. Darwin could not have been Darwin without all that preparation. Multitudes of people helped to make his life decisive.

Of all decisive lives this is true—they are concentration points where multitudes of hopes, thoughts, faiths, and aspirations of common men and women are drawn together and focused. This is the meaning of Paul's saying about our Lord in his Letter to the Galatians: "When the fulness of the time came, God sent forth his Son." So even Christ could be born and be Christ only when the fullness of the time had come. If he had come a few centuries before, he could not have been himself. Multitudes of plain people had to come first to prepare the way of the Lord, and make straight in the desert a highway for our God. Prophetic spirits, catching glimpses of his coming truth, hungry souls wanting it, intimations and foreshadowings of a gospel greater than the world had known, hopes of a new birth of spiritual life, faith in a new era of God's power—all these were in the air when Jesus came in the "fulness of the time," and he precipitated them. Multitudes of people helped to make him decisive.

Indeed, this truth has its dreadful as well as its inspiring side. What has made Hitler decisive? Hitler is more than Hitler. He is a burning glass that has gathered into a consuming flame the humiliations, the bitterness, the sense of gross injustice, the desire for vengeance, the compensatory dream of a master race, that the last war and its aftermath left everywhere among his people. For good or ill, it is we, the plain folk, who always make the messiahs possible. It is we who supply the heat that they focus into flame.

So everyday, ordinary, commonplace people do count. Indeed, I venture a prediction, buttressed I think by history. Some day, I predict, a man will rise by whose hands a federation of the world will be so effected, and wars so stopped thereby, that his name will go down across the centuries associated with that great achievement, as Copernicus' name is with the new astronomy, or Lincoln's with the preservation of our union. That man will come. Some day he will arise. For all we know he may be lying this morning in some unknown village in his crib. But when he comes, what will it take to make him decisive? Multitudes of us who have gone before, who have believed in peace when belief was difficult, prophetic spirits undaunted by man's brutality, hungry souls wanting peace, wise souls seeing war's futility, courageous souls with faith in brotherhood's possibility—a multitude of plain people must prepare the way before the decisive messiah can come with peace in his hands. All of us do matter; personality even in us does count.

So far we have said that this truth about the decisive babies of the world brings to us a two-fold encouragement—hope in our hopelessness, and a sense of importance and responsibility in our seeming weakness. But it does more than that. It brings rebuke as well, a stern and chastening rebuke, for what we in this brutal world do to the newborn children.

Even in the Christmas story, despite our popular sentimentalizing of it, there are brutal elements. Herod nearly killed the infant Jesus. He tried his hardest. He slew all the little ones of Bethlehem, so runs the story, to stop if he could this decisive babe from growing up. What if he had succeeded? How incalculable the difference to the world! Well, that is what war does all the time, and poverty, and slums, and all our social cruelties. They kill decisive babies.

In 1805 Napoleon bombarded Vienna. The bombardment was terrific for those days. The shells burst everywhere, and one of them struck the Jesuit Grammar School, falling in the stone-flagged corridor, and blasting walls and windows. One of the students, an eight-year-old boy, was in his room practicing on the piano, and in terror he fell to the floor and hid his face. Then in a moment came the voice of one of the schoolmasters, calling through the ruined corridor: "Schubert, Franz Schubert, are you all right?" So nearly did war take its toll of a decisive child.

Has someone here been tempted to think that this talk about decisive babies is sentimental? No, in the light of the scientific doctrine of evolution it is not. What is one of the most decisive factors in the whole story of evolution? Ask the scientists and they will tell you that it is the development of the human child. For the human child has a prolonged infancy; he cannot take care of himself; he must be taken care of. So, say the scientists, the whole ethical life of man grew up around the child. The first human altruism was for him. The first self-sacrifice was for him. The first co-operative loyalty was the family's united support and sustenance of him. The child in the evolutionary process was the creator of every impulse of unselfishness and goodwill that mankind knows. When Jesus put a child in the midst of his disciples, he did in his way what the scientists have done in theirs. And now, in this so-called modern world, we have reversed the process, turned back the course of evolution, and we decide our national disputes and settle the issues of our so-called statesmanship by starving children, bombing children, murdering children. How many a father or mother, do you suppose, after the havoc of some fearful raid, has called out for some boy or girl who might have been decisive to the world: "Schubert, Franz Schubert, are you all right?" only to receive no answer?

I say this not to play upon your feelings, but for an ethical reason. We all are tempted in these days to become hard, callous, so used to brutal things that we do not care much any more. I plead with myself and with you against this hardening of our hearts. Never get used to the idea of war—never! And when tempted to that, remember what war does to children, all children that it touches, decisive children that could have been the hope of the world. Listen to this—I will give you two guesses as to who said it: "War is one of the first necessities of civilization. War in a righteous cause lifts men above the sordid and selfish things of life, and discloses in them those Divine attributes which the Maker gave when He created man in His own image." Who said that? Hitler or one of his minions? No! Mussolini, or one of his minions? No! That was said by one of our own American Major Generals. That way of thinking is here in America today, growing in power, casting its spell upon millions of our people. Surely it is right that on the festival of Christ's birthday the church should cry out against that dreadful blasphemy, that ultimate profanation of the name of God, that blots from the skies of human faith and hope the song of peace and exalts the way of war, applauds Herod, slayer of the children, as the revelation of the Divine nature. Never get used to the idea of war! Never think of it without hearing the cry that every war has caused innumerable times: "Schubert, Franz Schubert, are you all right?"

One step further, however, we must go, to reach the personal conclusion of this matter. We have spoken of Jesus as though he were one of the decisive babies of the world, but to us, as Christians, he is more than that. He is *the* decisive baby of the world. So Christendom acclaims him this Christmas-tide. But, I ask you, how decisive has he been in your life and mine? That is not a general question, but a particular and individual inquiry that each one for himself must answer.

Say, as we will, that in the realm of music Johann Sebastian Bach was decisive, yet there are many people of whom it is true that so far as they are concerned Johann Sebastian Bach might just as well never have been born. Whether or not anybody is decisive for us depends on us. So when one thinks of all the outward show of Christmas, its endless pageantry and singing, even its lovely commemoration in our homes and churches, the question still rises about many of us carried along in this stream of public festivity: How decisive now, is Christ in your life and mine?

> Though Christ a thousand times
> In Bethlehem be born,
> If He's not born in thee
> Thy soul is still forlorn.

The Christmas story represents the very angels in heaven as knowing how conclusive his coming was, but to how many he was not important in the least! To those people at the inn who crowded him out, so that he was laid in a manger, he did not mean a thing. And one knows well that here today we cannot take it for granted that Christ has been in any serious sense a decisive influence in our lives. Rather, our affirmation that he is decisive changes now to a question and a challenge. Is he really that to us? How differently do we live because he came? How deeply are our attitudes toward life, toward war, toward human need and personal character affected by his coming?

This is no year to be content with the frills of Christmas. This is no year for its sweetness alone to fill our thoughts. For the world is dark, and out of its black background come such cries of suffering and need as human ears have not often heard before. Far from being less significant because of this, Christ seems to me amid this darkness to hold in the substance of his teaching and the quality of his spirit, that guidance for men and nations to which in the long run we must come back again if there is to be any hope. It is true: They that sat in darkness have seen a great light. His coming was decisive. He has it in him to be decisive. He waits for the hour when his determining influence can be made decisive. But all that comes back to each individual's doorsill. When Christ has become decisive for enough people, one by one, he will become indeed the most decisive baby in the world.

The Cross, an Amazing Paradox*

IT IS one thing to preach a Christmas sermon about the radiant stories that light up the birth of Jesus; it is another to preach a Palm Sunday sermon about the tragic events that culminated in the cross. John Milton celebrated the birth of Jesus in his glorious ode, "On The Morning of Christ's Nativity," but when he tried to write a companion piece on Jesus' death he gave it up. In his published works one finds the uncompleted beginning, with a note appended saying: "This subject the Author finding to be above the years he had when he wrote it, and nothing satisfied with what was begun, left it unfinished." What preacher, trying to speak about the cross, does not share Milton's despair and his desire to surrender the endeavor? Quite apart from any recondite theology, the cross confronts us with some of the most perplexing paradoxes we can face.

One of the simplest of them is that the cross, with its associated events, presents an ancient historic spectacle on a grand and panoramic scale and yet it is an intimate, personal matter that involves us, everyone. Many spectacular events loom large in history such as the campaigns of Alexander and the fall of Rome, before which we stand as before some Niagara, some Grand Canyon of the Colorado—huge phenomena. Among them one of the most impressive is the last week of Jesus' earthly life. The characters of that drama are momentous. Rome was there with her imperial power; one of the world's great religions was there in an hour of critical decision; the most moving figure in man's spiritual record was there; and the total tragedy, as it worked itself out, was intensely dramatic and incalculably influential. Yet this historic

* A Palm Sunday Sermon.

[233]

spectacle in the grand manner, now nearly 2000 years old and in a far distant land, personally includes you and me.

Recall that moving Negro spiritual, "When they crucified my Lord, were you there?" Even to ask that question is strange. Suppose it concerned the slaying of Julius Cæsar. That, too, was a momentous tragedy yet who ever thought of asking whether we were there? But this other question is asked and has been asked in manifold ways times without number across the centuries: "When they crucified my Lord, were you there?" Well, we were there; in a deep sense we are there. All the major factors in that tragedy involve you and me. The blindness of religious leaders who cannot see a new and larger truth, the selfishness of a business community that does not want the profitable traffic in the temple courts disturbed, the disloyalty of Judas, who cares more for himself than for Christ, the political shrewdness of Pilate, who does his best to free Jesus, but, finding it costs too much, washes his hands of it, the emotionalism of the crowd, stirred by effective propaganda to cry for they know not what, the fearfulness of disciples who run away—who of us was not there?

Not one unusual sin was involved in the crucifixion of Jesus. Say, as we will, that the tragic result was the towering crime of history, doing to a shameful death the "young Prince of Glory," still it was our small, familiar, day-by-day sins that did it. I have walked the streets of Jerusalem and recapitulated in detail the events of that last week, and alas, how easy for one to imagine oneself sharing in it all! When they crucified our Lord, we were there.

Consider, for example, the crowd's choice of Barabbas rather than of Jesus. Barabbas was no common criminal. He was, says Matthew's Gospel, "a notable prisoner." His name means "son of a rabbi." He was a patriot, an outstanding nationalist, tired of subjection to Roman rule, calling for violent insurrection. He himself had dared murder, trying to foment rebellion. He appealed to the admiration of the crowd; they wanted him released. But this Jesus, this idealist, this believer in spiritual forces, who even told them to love their enemies, "Away with him, crucify him!" That is not ancient history. That is the contemporary world in all its ruinous barbarity, its trust in force. Listen in the public places of the world, and it is as though echoes came from a far-off time, crying, "Release unto us Barabbas."

Every factor that sent Jesus to the cross involves our familiar, day-by-day iniquities. Recall how at the Last Supper Jesus said to the disciples, "One of you shall betray me," and they all asked, we read, Peter, James, John, and all the rest, "Is it I?" So one walks in imagination through the streets of Jerusalem that last week and at every step one has to say, "Is it I?"

A still deeper paradox follows. The crucifixion of Jesus was so cruel and unjust a crime that no worse thing, I think, can be said about man than that man is capable of doing *that*; yet the cross of Christ, more than any other influence in history, has elevated and dignified man's sense of his essential worth and possibility. That is a paradox.

Look at the cross in its stark horror. What happened there has been called "the loneliest death in all history." Jesus' nation had rejected him as a traitor; his church had rejected him as a heretic. He was alone. The Roman soldiers had spit upon him; Pilate had washed his hands of him; the crowd jeered at him; his friends forsook him. He was alone. The Fourth Gospel says, to be sure, that Jesus' mother was there, but the Fourth Gospel was not written before 100 A.D., and the first three Gospels, written earlier, say nothing of Jesus' mother at Calvary. I am afraid we will have to stand by the first three Gospels. I am afraid he really was alone, until his heart broke in the most desolate of all cries: "My God, my God, why hast thou forsaken me?" It was the loneliest death in all history.

[235]

Man did that. That is what man is capable of doing to the choicest soul that ever visited the earth. There the full measure of man's sin stands revealed, the abyss of baseness man can fall to. What a beast and devil man can be! How full of such barbarity his history is! How can one believe in man, hope anything from man, when one sees the cross as the exhibition of his stupidity, and his pitiless cruelty wreaked through all his history upon the innocent?

Well, here is the paradox. The cross of Christ, supremely in history, has elevated and dignified man's sense of his essential worth and possibility. Man, cries the New Testament, is the "brother for whose sake Christ died." So the same cross that revealed man at his worst made man believe in himself at his best. That is a strange paradox.

The humanist scholar, Muretus, in the seventeenth century, a fugitive from France, fell ill in Lombardy, and looking like a vagabond in rags asked aid of the doctors. The physicians discussed his case in Latin, not thinking that this bedraggled pauper could understand the learned tongue. *Faciamus experimentum in anima vili,* they said, "Let us try an experiment with this worthless creature." And to their amazement the "worthless creature" spoke to them in Latin: *Vilem animam appellas pro qua Christus non dedignatus est mori?*— "Will you call worthless one for whom Christ did not disdain to die?"

The influence of that idea has been incalculable. When a king stoops to pick up something it must have value. When Christ dies for someone there must be something in him worth dying for. Christ died for every man, says the New Testament. Let that idea once get really started and something is bound to happen to the estimate of man. Christianity has failed miserably in many ways but at its best it has reached out to those whom the world has commonly treated as worthless creatures—the wicked, the neglected, the insane, the blind, the prisoners; it has believed in the value of personality even in its bedraggled forms, and the story of its sacrificial philanthropy toward the lowly and the lost, its Elizabeth Fry, John Howard, David Livingstone, Sir Wilfred Grenfell, and all the rest, constitutes the noblest element, I think, in human history. And at the fountainhead of this stream of faith in man has been the cross with its insistent appeal: "Will you call worthless one for whom Christ did not disdain to die?"

The cross, where man is at his worst, has, more than any other influence, made man believe in his best. As Paul said: "Where sin abounded, grace did much more abound." That is a strange paradox. Surely there must be something real, potent, saving, victorious, at the heart of the spiritual world to achieve a consequence like that. When I so see the cross I believe afresh in God.

This, however, only leads to another paradoxical fact about Calvary: It was the most terrible thing that could have happened to Jesus and yet it was the best thing that happened to him. That is strange. The harrowing fact that it was the most dreadful thing that could have befallen him we need not expand upon. Suffice it to say that Jesus himself must have seen crucifixions. When he was a boy at Nazareth, the Jews broke out in insurrection in Sepphoris, barely five miles away, and Josephus tells us that two thousand were crucified by the Romans along the roadside. It is incredible that Jesus should not have seen many a crucified man hanging on a cross. He knew what the barbarity meant. No wonder he prayed in an agony: "If it be possible, let this cup pass away from me."

Yet this calamity, so much the worst thing that could happen to anyone in the Roman world, was the best thing that could have happened to Jesus. The New Testament says that. "It became him," says the Epistle to the Hebrews, "in bringing many sons unto glory, to make the author of their salvation perfect through sufferings." Ah Christ, it is easy enough for someone after the event, in retrospect, to see that, but the marvel is that you saw it yourself. It is no sufficient statement of the case to say that your enemies put you to death; you put yourself to death; you walked straight into it with your eyes open; that is what you said: "I lay down my life. . . . No one taketh it away from me, but I lay it down of myself." You set your face steadfastly to go to Jerusalem. You dared the cupidity of the temple ring and overturned their money tables. You prayed it out in Gethsemane when you might have run away. You put yourself on that cross. You knew—but how did you know—that this, the most appalling thing that could happen to you, was the best thing that could happen to you, your supreme chance to get at the heart of the world. How could anyone have known that 2000 years afterwards millions would be singing: "In the cross of Christ I glory"? Yet you did know that this, the worst that could befall you, was the best.

This mystery in the cross lights up many of our lesser mysteries. Browning has a phrase in one of his poems: "The worst turns the best to the brave." How often that happens, even in our lesser lives! Whistler failed at West Point. He was deeply humiliated, but it is the best thing that could have happened to him. Otherwise he never would have been an artist. Oliver Goldsmith failed an examination as hospital mate and he could get no clientele as a physician. He was grievously disappointed, but if he had not failed he might never have written *The Vicar of Wakefield*. Daniel Defoe failed in business at the price of humiliation and suffering, for which we may all be thankful, for otherwise he would never have written *Robinson Crusoe*. Often the worst turns the best to the brave. In the light of the cross it is clear that trouble, hardship, disappointment, tragedy, are not accidents and intruders in life but part and parcel of it and that no one is prepared to live at all who is not prepared to welcome them, walk up to them, take them in, sometimes in the service of a sacrificial cause deliberately seek them and transmute them into good.

In one of O. Henry's stories a shop girl keeps a picture of Lord Kitchener upon her bureau. She does not know much about him but she keeps his picture there and at times when her life is in danger of going weakly to pieces that stern face challenges and rallies her. Say as we will that Jesus was gentle, tender-hearted and friendly, be sure that he too had a stern face. He could confront the most dreadful thing that could happen, knowing that it was the best that could befall him.

We say we adore and love Christ. That is not the whole story. He is like the sea. I love it, but at times it is fearful. Then one stands in awe of it and wishes to see it only from a distance. So is Christ. Who that sees him clearly can help being drawn to him, but who that sees him clearly can help shrinking from him when with his stern face he says that some difficult and sacrificial thing we fear to do or suffer is the best thing that can befall us. He bought the right to say that in a hard market. He lived out that paradox himself. In a world where that can happen, there must be something like God.

This, however, leads us to a deeper paradox. The cross was a crushing defeat of righteousness and yet it was one of the greatest victories that righteousness ever won.

Here in this church today and throughout Christendom a mystery is present: Nearly 2000 years after the event, we are celebrating this week one of the most colossal failures of history. On Palm Sunday Jesus swung round the brow of Olivet amid the hosannas of the crowd but by Friday the crowd was crying, "Crucify him!" He had failed. In the sacred city of his faith he appealed for a reform of religion and the leaders of the people answered in Pilate's court, "Away with him." He had failed. He trusted his disciples to be the nucleus of the coming Kingdom of God, but one betrayed him, another denied him, and they all fled. He opposed violent revolt against Rome, differed not only from the Pharisees and Sadducees, but from the Zealots, those vehement nationalists and militarists of their day, and lo! he was accused of trying to make himself a king against Cæsar, and Rome crucified him. It was a complete, sardonic, and colossal failure. That Friday night Pilate and the leaders of the people and all Jerusalem, and the disciples too, thought that Jesus was done for.

What can we make of the enigma that the future belongs to that failure? Of course, in understanding that enigma one cannot leave the Easter message out, the exultant reassurance of the disciples as the conviction dawned upon them, however it arose, that Jesus was not dead, but alive. Along with that, however, is a companion fact that ever since has made not merely Easter morning but the cross itself a source of Christian triumph. Here is the mystery: the most potent and impressive factor in the moral experience of man is vicarious self-sacrifice. The cross itself has in it a paradoxical duality: on the one side it is failure complete and awful; on the other it is power, the most impressive and moving power in man's ethical experience, the potency of a life that gets at the heart of the world by caring enough about the world to die for it. So one of the most colossal defeats of righteousness in history became one of the greatest triumphs righteousness ever won.

See how the ancient situation is now reversed! Did Pilate sit in judgment on Jesus? Does not the whole world know that Pilate sat in judgment on himself? Did Judas betray his Lord? Does not the whole world know that Judas betrayed himself? When the people in the Praetorium, clamoring for his death, cried: "His blood be on us, and on our children," what merciful soul with any pity in him would not cry out to them, as it were, across the centuries, Unsay that! Unsay that before it is too late! There is an old legend that after

Pilate died his body was cast into Lake Lucerne in Switzerland, under the shadow of Mt. Pilatus, and that every Good Friday his spirit is dragged by demons out of the waters and enthroned, while he still unavailingly washes his hands. So all who shared in Jesus' crucifixion, could they return, would, if they might, wash their hands of it. For the future belonged to the failure.

In days like these we may well be grateful for this paradox at the heart of the gospel. If the future belonged to the things that seem to succeed, then were all our hopes undone today, whether of democracy, or Christianity, or decent human brotherhood. But there is something in the world deeper and stronger than the things that succeed, namely, the things that fail, the things that are everlastingly right and that honorably and sacrificially fail. They are the strongest elements in the world. George Tyrrell, a brave soul fighting a hard battle for his truth against many enemies, wrote once: "Again and again I have been tempted to give up the struggle, but always the figure of that strange Man hanging on the cross sends me back to my task again." So! That "strange Man" hanging on the cross, that colossal failure, whose pierced hands still hold the future in their grasp!

To be sure, now long after the event, the principle on which all this is based has percolated into human thinking and the seers have voiced it. Says Ruskin: "It is better to prefer honorable defeat to a mean victory." Says George Eliot: "Failure after long perseverance is much grander than never to have a striving good enough to be called a failure." Says Browning:

> For thence,—a paradox
> Which comforts while it mocks,—
> Shall life succeed in that it seems to fail.

But ah, Christ, how did you know that to fail *as you did* would be the surest way to succeed? For you said: "Except a grain of wheat fall into the earth and die, it abideth by itself alone; but if it die, it beareth much fruit." So they killed you on Calvary but you had in your possession a power they did not reckon with, the potency of a life that gets into the heart of the world by caring enough for the world to die for it.

This, then, is the conclusion of the matter, the crowning paradox of all. The cross was a denial of God, a blatant, cruel denial of God, and yet it was supremely the revelation of God. Why across the centuries, through changing world views and theologies, has the cross of Christ so held the fascinated attention of mankind? This, I suspect, is the main reason: Our life itself is an enigma, and it takes an enigma to meet its need. What good would Christianity be to us today if it were centered and confined in the lovely stories of Bethlehem, with adoring wise men and shepherds and singing angels? That is no adequate representation of what life confronts us with. Life is a mysterious, baffling, often tragic enigma, and the cross, which is an enigma too, talks to our true estate—a huge, historic tragedy that yet takes in you and me, a revelation of man at his worst that yet awakens faith in man at his best, the worst that can happen that yet turns the best to the brave, a crushing defeat of righteousness that yet is one of the greatest victories righteousness ever won, and so a supreme denial of God that yet has supremely revealed him. Thus the enigma of human life is matched and illumined by the enigma of Calvary:

> When I survey the wondrous cross
> On which the Prince of glory died.

A Great Year for Easter

WE MAY not pretend this Easter morning that amid the tremendous events of our days we have been thinking much lately about a future world. We have been thinking about this world, and here today we shall continue thinking about this world. George Bernard Shaw once remarked that "if the other planets are inhabited the earth is their lunatic asylum." Yet insane and barbarous as this earth seems today, it is here we live and not somewhere else, and we may not escape dealing with this world by dreaming of a future heaven. One thing, however, this Easter morning we can sincerely do—ask ourselves what life on this earth ultimately means. Easter is not simply the celebration of a past event or of a future hope; it is the celebration of a whole philosophy of living, a triumphant and challenging idea of what life here and now and everywhere and forever means.

Who does not need in these days such a sustaining philosophy? Most people live by their feelings. They have moods about life. But moods are like the weather—now clear, now foggy, now fair, now tempestuous—and in these days a man's moods can be stormy and black. A great philosophy, however, concerning life's meaning, is like a compass. It points true in all weathers. It is not at the mercy of the changing winds. It sustains relationships with factors in the universe above the fog and unaffected by the temporary storms. Who does not need such a steadying philosophy today?

Military victory and defeat are not the church's business, but spiritual victory and defeat are, and there is plenty of spiritual defeat today. Discouragement, disillusionment, cynicism, skepticism, futility—they thrive in days like ours. Go through this congregation now, looking beneath the panoply of our Easter worship and the triumphant sound of our Easter hymns and anthems, and in how many of us there is another mood altogether! This is a strange and often terrific world. The more we know about it, the stranger it gets. The longer we live in it, the harder it is to understand. What does it mean? Indeed, does it ultimately mean anything?

Now Easter is the celebration of a great message that puts meaning into life. Remember Paul's familiar words, as Dr. Goodspeed translates them: "I never lose heart," he writes, and then, as one reads on to see how that can be, he adds, "because I keep my eyes not on what is seen but what is unseen. For what is seen is transitory, but what is unseen is eternal." So Paul kept a good heart about life because he had something to rest his eyes on steadier than the world's vicissitudes. No one can accuse Paul of not dealing with this present world. He dealt with it powerfully. No one can say that he lived in an easy time. His age was terrific too, and his personal career was packed with hardship and climaxed by martyrdom. But he could write "I never lose heart," because at the center of his thinking here and now there was something steady and abiding he could keep his eyes upon.

Today, then, let us rehearse together some elements in this challenging philosophy. In the first place, it is an affirmation concerning the universe that something worth-while is coming of it. If materialism were true, nothing would triumph in the end except death. Cosmos would end in chaos. A frozen planet and a burned-out sun would be the futile finale.

The difficulty with that view is not simply that it runs against our wishes, but that it runs against so many of our facts. For the fact is that up to date the more we have found out about this universe, the more incredibly marvelous it has turned out to be. Go back only a few millennia when men thought they lived on a flat earth set amid neighborly stars and planets, and who then could have imagined even the little that we now know about the universe? The earth looked flat but it was not. It looked stationary but it was traveling 600,000,000 miles a year around the sun. As for the new astronomy, Einstein's relativity, quantum physics—our whole experience even with the physical aspects of the universe has been like that of children in a palace, every door we have opened revealing more doors to open, and every new door unclosed revealing marvels hitherto incredible. Can it be that such a universe has no meaning and is coming to nothing?

Moreover, we are faced not only with the deepening marvel of the universe but with its creativity. It is forever producing something new. Millions of years ago the great sharks ruled the sea, ferocious beasts to whom the world of life seemed to belong. One looking on them would have said, They are the last word. But in the mud and scum along the shore little creatures one would not have noticed were trying an experiment, essaying what it would be like to live not only in the water but in the air, adventuring into a brand new element where no life had ever been before, and naturalizing themselves in that higher environment. No one then could have guessed what would come of that. That era, however, is overpassed in marvel by the next, in which souls appeared, experimenting with a still higher element than air, the world of spirit, adventuring into the realm of goodness, truth, beauty, to see what it would be like to live in such an atmosphere. And although this newest era has barely begun on earth, some souls have become fully naturalized citizens of that spiritual world—some even that we have loved long since and lost awhile, and one above all others, whom we call Master. A creative universe like this is not easily conceived as coming out nowhere. One suspects that it has barely started. "Cosmos cannot have chaos for its crown." So H. G. Wells, who is no sentimentalist, said: "All this world is heavy with the promise of greater things."

There is deep grounding, therefore, for our invincible surmise that amid this cosmic scene, so much of which is transitory and fugitive, like a scaffolding, something abiding is being built. To be sure, all things visible, from suns and stars to our bodies, perish, but already we are now inhabitants of another world, unseen. No one ever saw an idea, but an idea can be the most creative force in life. No one ever saw a purpose, but a purpose can direct and drive living to great issues. No one ever saw love, but as we love we are. And we ourselves who harbor ideas, are mastered by purposes, and live by love, are invisible too. Only the outer shell and phys- ical integument of us is visible, but the real self, its thoughts, memories, hopes, its moral quality, its commanding purposes, are as invisible as God. If in this universe there is anything that lasts, carries through, and gives meaning to it all, it must be here in the realm of abiding spirit.

There are only two basic philosophies about this—Easter and anti-Easter. Anti-Easter says that nothing in the universe lasts, not even Christ, that all is fugitive, transitory, discon- tinuous, beginning nowhere and coming out nowhere, the whole cosmos, as one writer put it, a "gigantic accident con- sequent upon an infinite succession of happy flukes." Some of us cannot believe that. We have tried, but we cannot. It is too great a strain on credulity. We turn to Easter, for Easter says that this universe has meaning, and that involves the conviction that something here abides, carries through, and comes out somewhere, and that eternal element must be in the spiritual life we know in persons. All investments made there are made in a bank that will not break. That is a great philosophy to come home to at night and start out with in the morning. "I never lose heart," said Paul; "what is seen is transitory, but what is unseen is eternal."

Come further now and see that this Easter message is an affirmation about God—that he cannot be the God of unfin- ished business. Easter of course involves faith in God. If one's philosophy is materialistic, then obviously death ends all for you and me, and all our offspring, and the last word will be a dead sun and a frozen planet and everything as though it had never been at all. But just as soon as one believes in God even a little, in almost any kind of God worth believing in at all, another conviction rises—God cannot be the God of unfinished business.

What in your thinking is the real mystery about Christ? To many people today it will be his survival, the faith that death had no dominion over him. I am not thinking now of physical resurrection. Deal as you will with the stories of his resuscitated body—believe them, doubt them, disbelieve them, put them aside as an insoluble problem—as you will. The central message of Easter is the survival of his spirit, the faith that when they drove nails into his hands and a spear into his side, there was in him an eternal element they could not reach, that the cross did not stop him. What a mystery, many think, such survival is! But to me the first and greatest mystery is not Christ's survival but his arrival. That such a soul should come to earth at all is the miracle. That a spirit like his should arrive in the first place—the incontestable fact of his arrival is the great mystery. If a life like that can arrive, why shouldn't it survive? *That* is not so strange. If God starts anything like that, will he leave it unfinished business?

Even within our experience of earthly history God is always running into obstacles that seem to end what he had begun. He began a great spiritual development in Israel, and the exile in Babylon seemed to finish it, but it didn't. He opened a new era in Christ, and that fatal Friday night everybody in Jerusalem—Caiaphas and Pilate, and even the frightened disciples—thought that the cross had stopped it, but it hadn't. Again and again tyranny has triumphed over liberty, and the ruthless dominion of the strong has seemed to bring to an end the hopes of freedom. But always freedom has had its resurrection day. "Truth crushed to earth will rise again" —behind that saying is a great mass of historic fact. If naziism should win now and plunge us into one of the most discouraging epochs in human history, do you really think that a regime founded on such principles has in it the basis of permanence? All history bears witness against that. This recurrent aspect of human affairs cannot be an accident. Repeatedly, wrong is victorious, and the discouraged and cynical cry, Nothing succeeds like success. But then history later records the outcome, writing, Nothing recedes like success, and behind all this the Easter faith perceives more than the haphazard collocation of atoms going it blind. It sees the sovereign activity of God, who, despite the sin and folly of man, forever refuses to be the God of unfinished business. What God once made alive will not finally stay buried.

In days like these that is a great philosophy to live by, and I see no reason why it does not apply to death. That is an obstacle that seems to stop some lovely spirits God began. Schubert dying at thirty-one and leaving his *Unfinished Symphony* is a parable of human life. Even if we do not die at thirty-one, but live to be as old as the psalmist's span, still there is an unfinished symphony. Corot, the artist, when he was seventy-seven years old, said: "If the Lord lets me live two years longer I think I can paint something beautiful." Here, indeed, is the deep mystery of human life—that while our bodies are the natural prey of death, our minds and spirits already have started on a road that has no visible terminus. The more truth we learn, the more truth we see to learn. The more goodness we achieve, the more goodness we see there is to achieve. Such realms are essentially eternal. Death has no relevance to them. The farther we go in them, the farther there is to go. William James, of Harvard, said once that his interest in personal immortality was not of the keenest order, but that as he grew older his belief in it grew stronger, and when asked why, he answered: "Because I am just getting fit to live."

This basic fact about life plainly involves God. We Americans blame ourselves because we have wasted the natural and human resources of our continent, but if death ends all, then of all wasters of human resources God is the worst. He forever produces spirits and throws them away half finished. He creates capacities he never uses, possibilities he never fulfills. He makes the most valuable thing we know—personality—and leaves it unfinished business. He launches ships he does not sail; he blows soap bubbles and watches them burst. I do not believe it. I know all the difficulties that confront faith in immortality. It is a great mystery. I do not think that any picture we have of it can possibly be true. What eye hath not seen, what ear hath not heard, and what hath not entered into the heart of man, that has God prepared—Paul is right about that. But Paul is right about another thing: What is seen in us is transitory, and what is unseen is eternal. "So," said Paul, "I never lose heart."

Come further now and see that the Easter message is an affirmation not only about the universe and about God, but about our own spiritual lives. It says that they really belong in this world. To me the most dreadful thing about materialism is its necessary declaration that the best elements in us, our finest ethical qualities, are misfits in this universe, strange accidents that do not belong here and do not correspond with the real facts. One of our neighbors in the University, one of the most forthright atheists of our time, puts it frankly: "It grows more and more likely that [man] must remain an ethical animal in a universe which contains no ethical element." Get that picture! It is the inevitable corollary of the materialistic philosophy—man an ethical animal in a universe that contains no ethical element. Yes, man an intellectual animal in a universe that contains no intellectual element; man a purposeful animal in a universe that contains no purposeful element; man a loving animal in a universe that contains not the slightest shred of goodwill; all our best ethical life a chance intruder, a misfit, as Bertrand Russell calls it, "a curious accident in a backwater"; that is the philosophy of anti-Easter.

I am grateful these days that I do not have to live on that philosophy, but what troubles me most about it is not simply its emotional undesirability but its intellectual high-handedness in dealing with the facts. For spiritual life is a fact—the most notable and amazing fact we know. What made Plato, Plato, and Christ, Christ, and Mozart, Mozart, and my mother, my mother—these are facts, and to call such facts accidental intruders and misfits, incongruous interlopers that do not belong, is too easy and supercilious a way of disposing of them. Why should a physical atom be a fact on which I must build a whole philosophy of the cosmos, but Christ's life and character be a fact which I must brush aside as a strange example of an ethical animal in a universe with no ethical element in it? It will not do. Intellectually it will not do. And it will not do to live on.

Here, then, is a philosophy to strike one's roots into—that spiritual life does belong in this universe, not a misfit nor an accident but a revelation of what eternally is so; that Christ, the representative of that spiritual life which is man's glory, was not a chance interloper on this scene; that he came from the Eternal, revealed the quality of the Eternal, and lives still in the Eternal; that, as Emerson cried,

> . . . What is excellent,
> As God lives, is permanent!

That is the philosophy of Easter, and it meets our deep need when we ask what life really means.

Some people suppose we Christians want to believe in immortality because we want to go to heaven when we die and be rewarded for being good. Nonsense! That is not the issue. Who wants to go to any traditional heaven he ever heard about? Who wants a future life that he may be rewarded for being good? The issue involved in the Easter faith is present

[250]

and profound. Here in people we know and love now is goodness, beauty, nobility of character, integrity of soul—in such living lies all the hope and all the desirable significance of existence on this planet. Tell us that such living is "a curious accident in a backwater," and that colors our whole thought of life's meaning. Tell us that such living is a revelation of the Eternal and that death has no dominion over it, and that completely changes the color.

I know that this is doctrine, and that doctrine is supposed to be unpopular, but the world today is fighting about doctrine. Communism is a doctrine; naziism is a doctrine; the whole philosophy of secularism and materialism is a doctrine, and we Christians desperately need a new hold on our great philosophy of life, which Easter celebrates, if we are to stand our ground in a world full of such anti-Christian dogmas.

Finally, come close home to our individual selves, for this Easter message is an affirmation not simply about the universe and God and the meaning of man's spiritual life, but about every one of us. It says to each man that death is not the end of him. To some people this assertion of personal immortality seems colossal egotism. Why should I think my existence of such importance to the universe, they say, that I expect my individual continuance? Would not a decent humility lead a man to be more modest, and not charge the cosmos with failure because his life does not go on?

The matter, however, is not so simple as that, for if when I die that is the end of me, then when you die that is the end of you. In this regard we are all tied up in one bundle. If I die and that is the finale, death is the finale of every person. Then all our forefathers are dead and gone forever; we shall all be dead and gone forever; our children and their children will all be dead and gone forever, until at last, when the planet, once uninhabitable, becomes uninhabitable again, all personalities will be dead and gone forever, and everything will be as though nothing had ever been at all. Do not say that to care about that is egotistical. To care about that is to care about the whole philosophy of life. As Professor Hocking, of Harvard, put it: "There are no eternal values unless there are eternal valuers."

Indeed, at this point we run into one of the commonest misapprehensions about this whole question. Faith in immortality, some think, is an emotional comfort for weak souls. Feeble people, who cannot make the grade here, dream of heaven as a compensatory consolation. I suppose they do. Compensatory consolations are always being sought by those who need them, and there are many worse ones, I suspect, in this congregation now, than faith in a future heaven. But do not mix up the caricature with the genuine article! The supreme creators of, and believers in, the reality of the unseen world and the persistence of personality, have been not the weak souls but the strong. Read Plato's *Phaedo*—was Socrates weak? Read the Gospels—was Jesus weak? Read Paul's letters—was Paul weak? Indeed, how many of us would have to say that in our weak hours we do not care much one way or another about immortality? We may be, as another said, only "snowflakes upon a river," but what of it? Who of us when he is done in, tired out, fed up with life, would not be glad enough to lie down and go to sleep and have that the end of it?

> From too much love of living,
>   From hope and fear set free,
> We thank with brief thanksgiving
>   Whatever gods may be
> That no life lives for ever;
> That dead men rise up never;
> That even the weariest river
>   Winds somewhere safe to sea.

That is a natural expression of a subnormal and debilitated mood. But there are other hours when the thought of a creative universe engaged in big business, of a God who eternally carries through what he begins, of a spiritual world of endless possibilities, and of personality as the vehicle of the Eternal purpose, challenges us. That is a great and difficult philosophy for men to face in their strong hours and try to live up to. Who of us does not need it? For, that being so, even in dark days like these, we may say, "I never lose heart," and on an Easter shadowed by a world at war, we may even cry, "Hallelujah! The Lord God Omnipotent reigneth!"